PRENTICE HALL

WORLD
HISTORY
THE MODERN ERA

Reading
and Note Taking
Study Guide

ADAPTED VERSION

PEARSON

Upper Saddle River, New Jersey • Boston, Massachusetts • Chandler, Arizona • Glenview, Illinois

13-digit ISBN: 978-0-13-372429-5
10-digit ISBN: 0-13-372429-8

2 3 4 5 6 7 8 9 10   V084   13 12 11

Contents

How to Use This Book

The **Reading and Note Taking Study Guide** will help you better understand the content of *Prentice Hall World History*. This book will also develop your reading, vocabulary, and note taking skills.

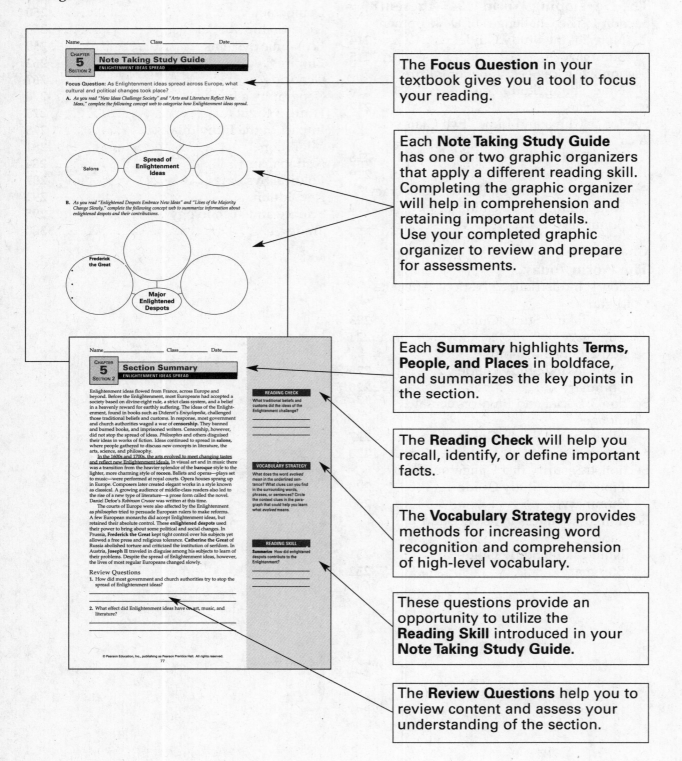

The **Focus Question** in your textbook gives you a tool to focus your reading.

Each **Note Taking Study Guide** has one or two graphic organizers that apply a different reading skill. Completing the graphic organizer will help in comprehension and retaining important details. Use your completed graphic organizer to review and prepare for assessments.

Each **Summary** highlights **Terms, People, and Places** in boldface, and summarizes the key points in the section.

The **Reading Check** will help you recall, identify, or define important facts.

The **Vocabulary Strategy** provides methods for increasing word recognition and comprehension of high-level vocabulary.

These questions provide an opportunity to utilize the **Reading Skill** introduced in your **Note Taking Study Guide**.

The **Review Questions** help you to review content and assess your understanding of the section.

The **Concept Connector Journal** supports the **Concept Connector** features and the **Concept Connector Essential Question Review** found in each chapter of your text, as well as the **Concept Connector Handbook** found at the end of your textbook. These journal sheets will help you to compare key concepts and events and to see patterns and make connections across time.

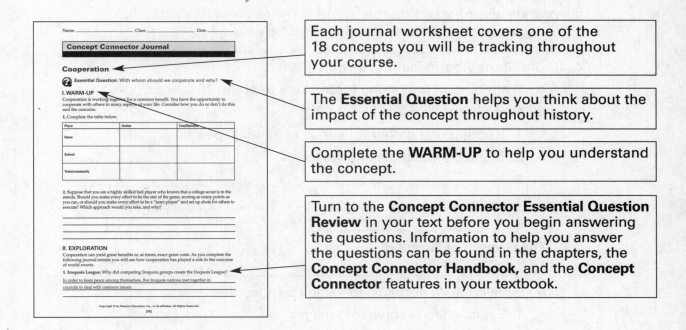

Each journal worksheet covers one of the 18 concepts you will be tracking throughout your course.

The **Essential Question** helps you think about the impact of the concept throughout history.

Complete the **WARM-UP** to help you understand the concept.

Turn to the **Concept Connector Essential Question Review** in your text before you begin answering the questions. Information to help you answer the questions can be found in the chapters, the **Concept Connector Handbook,** and the **Concept Connector** features in your textbook.

The WebQuest is an important part of building understanding of the Essential Question. Go online at **PHSchool.com** and input the Web Code to find the directions for completing a WebQuest on each Concept Connector topic. In your journal, write a brief explanation of how the WebQuest affected your response to the Essential Question.

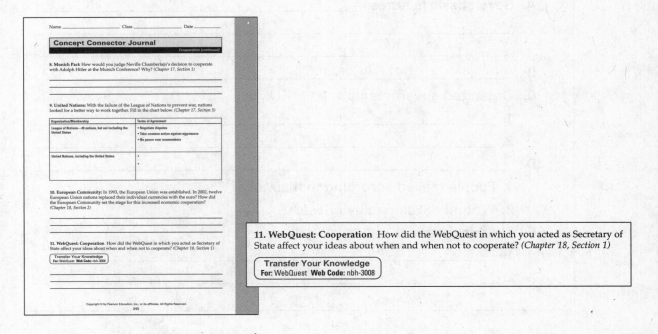

11. WebQuest: Cooperation How did the WebQuest in which you acted as Secretary of State affect your ideas about when and when not to cooperate? *(Chapter 18, Section 1)*

Transfer Your Knowledge
For: WebQuest **Web Code:** nbh-3008

PART 1.1 Note Taking Study Guide
TOWARD CIVILIZATION

As you read this section in the textbook, complete the outline below to summarize information about the periods of early human history and the development of civilizations. Some items have been completed for you.

I. Old Stone Age/Paleolithic Period

    A. From time of first stone toolmakers to about 10,000 B.C.

    B. Nomadic way of life

        1. Hunting and gathering bands of 20 to 30 people

        2. Made simple tools and weapons

        3. _____

        4. _____

        5. _____

II. The Growth of Farming

    A. _____

    B. Evolved from nomadic to settled farming life

        1. Established permanent villages

        2. _____

        3. _____

        4. _____

III. Beginnings of Civilization

    A. Seven basic features: _____

        _____

        _____

    B. _____

    C. Organized governments

        1. _____

        2. _____

    D. _____

        1. People ranked according to their jobs

        2. Writing developed by priests

    E. The first empires

        1. _____

        2. _____

Section Summary
TOWARD CIVILIZATION

The period from the making of the first stone tools to about 10,000 B.C. is known as the **Old Stone Age,** or the Paleolithic Period. Paleolithic people were **nomads.** They moved from place to place to hunt for animals and plants to eat. They made simple tools and weapons and clothing from animal skins. They developed spoken language and learned to build fires.

About 10,000 years ago, nomads learned to farm. This allowed them to remain in one place. This was the beginning of the **New Stone Age,** or Neolithic age. Neolithic people settled in permanent villages. They also learned to tame animals. Village life changed the roles of men and women. <u>Success in battle allowed some men to gain status as warriors. This gave them power over both women and other men.</u> The status of women declined.

About 5,000 years ago, the advances made in farming villages led to the rise of civilizations. Historians list seven basic features of most early civilizations: well-organized central governments, complex religions, job specialization, social classes, arts and architecture, public works, and writing.

Food surpluses in the river valleys of Africa and Asia helped populations grow. Some villages grew into cities. The need to control flooding and channel waters to fields caused city governments to develop. Large projects required well-organized governments. Over time, government **bureaucracies** grew. Social organization also grew more complex. People were ranked according to their jobs. Priests and nobles were usually at the top, followed by merchants and **artisans,** or skilled craftworkers. Below them were the peasant farmers. Slaves were at the very bottom. Priests developed writing to record information. Early writing was made up of **pictographs,** or simple drawings that represented ideas.

Ancient rulers gained more power and conquered territories beyond their cities. Some created empires. An **empire** is a group of states, territories, and peoples ruled by one person.

Review Questions

1. What are the seven basic features of most early civilizations?

_____

_____

2. What was early writing like?

_____

_____

9

READING CHECK

What is the term for people who move from place to place?

_____

_____

_____

VOCABULARY STRATEGY

Find the word *status* in the first underlined sentence. What do you think it means? Note that men who had "*status* as warriors" had "power over women and other men." Also note that as men gained *status* as warriors, the *status* of women declined. Use these context clues to help you understand the meaning of *status*.

READING SKILL

Identify Causes and Effects
Complete the flowchart below to show how the development of farming led to the growth of cities in river valleys.

Nomads learned to farm.

↓

↓

↓

Some villages grew into cities.

Name_____ Class_____ Date_____

PART 1.2

Note Taking Study Guide
FIRST CIVILIZATIONS: AFRICA AND ASIA

As you read this section in your textbook, complete the outline below to summarize information about the first civilizations in North Africa and the Middle East. Some items have been completed for you.

I. Ancient Kingdoms of the Nile
   A. Villages in Nile River valley joined into two kingdoms.
   B. _____
   C. Old Kingdom (about 2575–2130 B.C.)
   D. _____
   E. _____

II. Egyptian Civilization
   A. _____
   B. _____

III. _____
   A. Started along Tigris and Euphrates rivers
   B. Floods and irrigation
      1. _____
      2. _____
      3. _____
   C. Advances in learning
      1. _____
      2. _____

IV. _____
   A. Sargon of Akkad conquered Sumerian city-states to create first empire, about 2300 B.C.
   B. _____
   C. _____
   D. _____

V. Roots of Judaism
   A. _____
   B. _____
   C. _____
   D. _____
   E. _____

PART 1.2	**Section Summary**
	FIRST CIVILIZATIONS: AFRICA AND ASIA

The first civilizations grew in river valleys and developed complex ways of life. In the **Nile River** valley in Egypt, villages joined together into two kingdoms. They were later united under King Menes. The history of ancient Egypt after King Menes is divided into three periods, the Old, Middle, and New Kingdoms. During the Old Kingdom, Egyptian rulers, called **pharaohs,** built a strong government. They also built pyramids as tombs. During the Middle and New Kingdoms, Egypt came into contact with other civilizations through trade and war. This led to **cultural diffusion.** Egyptians worshiped many gods and goddesses. Their society was organized into classes, with the pharaoh at the top.

Another civilization, the **city-states** of Sumer, developed along the Tigris and Euphrates rivers in **Mesopotamia.** Mesopotamia was a part of the **Fertile Crescent,** an arc of rich land northeast of the Nile. The Sumerian city-states often fought for control of land and water. War leaders eventually became rulers, and a social **hierarchy** developed. The Sumerians built **ziggurats,** or pyramid-temples. They also invented the earliest form of writing, called **cuneiform. Scribes** learned to read and write and kept records.

About 2300 B.C., Sargon, the ruler of Akkad, conquered the Sumerian city-states. He built the world's first empire. About 1790 B.C., Hammurabi, king of Babylon, conquered much of Mesopotamia. His law code was the first major collection of laws in history.

About 2000 B.C., the **Hebrews** came from Mesopotamia to Canaan. They developed Judaism. Judaism is a **monotheistic** religion based on the belief in one God. **Prophets** preached a strong code of **ethics** and urged the Hebrews to obey God's law. The Hebrews set up a kingdom, called Israel. Later, invading armies captured the Hebrews, who became known as Jews. About 2,000 years ago, many Jews were forced to leave their homeland. This scattering of the Jews is known as the **diaspora.**

Review Questions

1. Who was Hammurabi?

_____

_____

2. What is a monotheistic religion?

_____

_____

READING CHECK

What were Egyptian rulers called?

_____

_____

_____

VOCABULARY STRATEGY

What does the word *complex* mean in the underlined sentence? *Complex* is similar in meaning to the word *complicated.* Both come from Latin roots meaning "to weave together." Both are used to describe things that have many interwoven or interrelated parts. Which of the following words means the opposite of *complex*?

1. involved

2. simple

READING SKILL

Compare and Contrast Compare and contrast the geography of the Egyptian and Sumerian civilizations. In what ways were their locations similar? In what ways were they different?

_____

_____

_____

Name_____ Class_____ Date_____

As you read this section in your textbook, complete the outline below to summarize information about early civilizations in India and China. Some items have been completed for you.

I. Cities of the Indus Valley

  A. India's first civilization arose in Indus River valley about 2600 B.C.

  B. _____

  C. _____

II. Kingdoms of the Ganges

  A. Origins

    1. _____

    2. _____

  B. Society

    1. _____

    2. _____

  C. _____

    1. Beliefs in many gods (polytheistic)

    2. _____

    3. _____

III. Early Civilizations in China

  A. _____

    1. Physical barriers separated China from rest of the world.

    2. _____

  B. Shang and Zhou dynasties

    1. _____

    2. _____

  C. Religion

    1. _____

    2. _____

    3. _____

  D. _____

    1. Planets and eclipses studied; calendar created.

    2. _____

    3. _____

PART 1.3 Section Summary
EARLY CIVILIZATIONS IN INDIA AND CHINA

India's first civilization developed in the Indus River valley about 2500 B.C. It was the largest civilization of ancient times. Its two main cities, **Mohenjo-Daro** and Harappa, had plumbing and sewers. By 1700 B.C., though, most of these cities were abandoned, maybe because of floods or earthquakes.

Meanwhile, herders from Central Asia moved into northern India and intermarried with its people. Their descendants, called **Aryans,** built a new civilization in the Ganges Valley. Most of what we know about the Aryans comes from the **Vedas,** their religious teachings. The Aryans divided people into a system of **castes.** These are groups based on occupation that people are born into and cannot leave. The Aryans were **polytheistic,** or believed in many gods. They eventually came to believe in a single spiritual power, called **brahman.** Some Aryans became **mystics** and devoted their lives to seeking truth.

<u>Physical barriers, such as mountains and deserts, separated China from the rest of the world.</u> This led the Chinese to believe that China was the center of Earth and the source of civilization. Chinese history began in the Huang He valley. About 1650 B.C., the Shang people came to power in northern China. In 1027 B.C., the **Zhou** people overthrew the Shang. The Zhou **dynasty,** or ruling family, lasted until 256 B.C. They used the idea of the Mandate of Heaven to justify their rule. This idea was later used to explain the **dynastic cycle,** or the rise and fall of dynasties.

The Chinese prayed to many gods and nature spirits. Over time, they began to call on the spirits of their ancestors. The Chinese also believed in a balance between two forces, yin and yang. They studied the planets and created an accurate calendar. They also developed bronzemaking and silkmaking and made the first books.

Review Questions

1. What were the two main cities of the Indus River valley civilization?

_____

_____

2. Where did Chinese history begin?

_____

_____

READING CHECK

What is the term for belief in many gods?

_____

_____

_____

VOCABULARY STRATEGY

Find the word *barriers* in the underlined sentence. What does it mean? Note that the *barriers* "separated China from the rest of the world." Use these clues to help you understand the meaning of the word *barriers*.

READING SKILL

Identify Main Ideas List four main ideas about the Aryans from the second paragraph of the Summary. Your list should answer the following questions: Who were the Aryans? Where did they build a new civilization? What was their society like? What kind of religious beliefs did they have?

_____

_____

_____

_____

Name_____ Class_____ Date_____

As you read this section in your textbook, complete the outline below to summarize information about the religions and empires of India and China. Some items have been completed for you.

I. Hinduism and Buddhism

    A. Both developed in ancient India.

    B. Hinduism

        1. _____

        2. _____

    C. _____

        1. Founded by Siddhartha Gautama/the Buddha

        2. _____

II. Powerful Empires of India

    A. Maurya dynasty

        1. _____

        2. _____

    B. _____

    C. Pillars of Indian life

        1. _____

        2. _____

III. _____

    A. Confucianism

        1. _____

        2. _____

    B. _____

        1. Teachings of Chinese philosopher Hanfeizi

        2. _____

    C. _____

        1. _____

        2. _____

IV. _____

    A. _____

    B. Han dynasty lasted from 206 B.C. to A.D. 220

        1. _____

        2. _____

PART 2.1	**Section Summary**
	EMPIRES OF INDIA AND CHINA

Hinduism and Buddhism both began in ancient India. Hinduism has no single founder or sacred text. Hindus believe that everything is part of the spiritual force called brahman. Reincarnation allows people to work toward the goal of union with brahman. **Reincarnation** is the rebirth of the soul in another body

Unlike Hinduism, Buddhism had a single founder, **Siddhartha Gautama.** He is known as the Buddha. Buddhists seek enlightenment through meditation, not through the priests, rituals, and gods of Hinduism. The goal of Buddhism is **nirvana,** or union with the universe and an end to the cycle of rebirth.

In 321 B.C., Chandragupta Maurya founded the first great Indian empire. The Maurya dynasty conquered much of India. Then the great Maurya emperor Asoka converted to Buddhism. His policies brought peace and wealth. However, after his death, rivals battled for power. About 500 years after the Mauryas, the Gupta dynasty reunited much of India. Under the Guptas, India enjoyed a golden age of peace and achievement. Most Indians were peasants. The village and the family maintained order. Caste rules controlled every part of life.

Ancient China's most important philosopher, **Confucius,** was born in 551 B.C. He was concerned with social order and good government. He put **filial piety,** or respect for parents, above all other duties. Another Chinese philosopher, Hanfeizi, insisted that strict laws and punishments were needed to keep order. Hanfeizi's teachings came to be known as Legalism. A third philosophy, Daoism, arose around the same time. Daoists tried to live in harmony with nature. They thought government was unnatural.

After the Zhou dynasty weakened, a new ruler, **Shi Huangdi,** unified China. He built a strong government and the Great Wall. After his death, the **Han** dynasty was founded. Under the Han, the Chinese made huge advances in trade, government, technology, and the arts. At this time, the Silk Road linked China to the Fertile Crescent.

Review Questions

1. Where did both Hinduism and Buddhism begin?

_____

_____

2. Who was China's most important philosopher?

_____

_____

READING CHECK

What is reincarnation?

_____

_____

_____

VOCABULARY STRATEGY

Find the word *converted* in the underlined sentence. What does it mean? *Converted* is the past tense of a verb. It comes from the Latin verb *vertere*, which means "to turn." What did Asoka *convert* to? If a person "turns" to a new religion, what does that mean? Use these clues to help you understand the meaning of *converted*.

READING SKILL

Contrast Contrast the following features of Hinduism and Buddhism: (1) founder; (2) way to enlightenment; (3) goal.

_____

_____

_____

PART 2.2

Note Taking Study Guide

ANCIENT GREECE

As you read this section in your textbook, complete the outline below to summarize information about ancient Greece. Some items have been entered for you.

I. Early People of the Aegean

  A. Minoans

    1. Traders on the island of Crete

    2. _____

  B. _____

    1. Sea traders who flourished between 1400 and 1200 B.C.

    2. _____

II. _____

  A. _____

  B. Began to build many small city-states

    1. _____

    2. _____

  C. Governing the city-states

    1. _____

    2. _____

    3. _____

  D. _____

    1. _____

    2. _____

  E. Victory and defeat in the Greek world

    1. _____

    2. _____

III. The Glory That Was Greece

  A. _____

  B. _____

  C. _____

IV. _____

  A. King Philip of Macedonia built a superb army.

  B. _____

PART 2.2 Section Summary
ANCIENT GREECE

The Minoans created the first civilization in the Aegean region. They were traders from Crete. By about 1400 B.C., the Minoan civilization had disappeared. The Mycenaeans soon dominated Crete and the Greek mainland. They are best remembered for their part in the Trojan War. This war was described by **Homer** in the *Iliad* and the *Odyssey*.

After Mycenaean civilization declined, the Greeks lived in small farming villages. They later built many small city-states. They often fought among themselves, but they shared a common culture. The Greeks created a unique version of the city-state, called the **polis.** Their cities often had two levels. They built temples on the **acropolis,** or high city, above the main city. At first, the ruler of each polis was a king. This type of government is called a **monarchy**. Power slowly shifted to a group of noble landowners, or **aristocracy.** Wealthy merchants, farmers, and artisans came to rule some city-states. They formed an **oligarchy,** or rule by a small, powerful elite.

Two of the most important Greek city-states were Sparta and Athens. Sparta was a warrior society. Athens was a **democracy**, or government by the people. Sparta, Athens, and other Greek city-states joined together to defend themselves against the Persians. After the Persian Wars, Athens thrived. Under **Pericles,** culture flourished, and Athens developed a **direct democracy.** In this system, many citizens took part in day-to-day government. Philosophers like Socrates, Plato, and Aristotle developed new ideas about truth, reason, and government. They used observation and reason to find causes for events. Greeks also developed new styles of art, architecture, poetry, and drama.

Greece was eventually controlled by King Philip of Macedonia. After his death, his son **Alexander** the Great conquered a vast area beyond Greece. In this area, Greek culture blended with other cultures to create the Hellenistic civilization.

Review Questions

1. What was the first civilization in the Aegean region?

_____

_____

2. Name three Greek philosophers who developed new ideas about truth, reason, and government.

_____

_____

READING CHECK

What unique version of the city-state did the Greeks create?

_____

_____

_____

VOCABULARY STRATEGY

Find the word *thrived* in the underlined sentence. What does it mean? The sentence that follows the underlined sentence contains a word that means the same as the word *thrived.* What is that word?

1. flourished

2. developed

READING SKILL

Categorize The Greek city-states had four types of government: monarchy, aristocracy, oligarchy, and democracy. Into which category does Athenian government under Pericles belong?

_____

PART 2.3

Note Taking Study Guide
ANCIENT ROME AND THE RISE OF CHRISTIANITY

As you read this section in your textbook, complete the outline below to summarize information about ancient Rome and the rise of Christianity. Some items have been completed for you.

I. The Roman World Takes Shape

   A. Rome began as a small city-state in Italy.

   B. Romans overthrew Etruscan king and set up a republic.

      1. At first, patricians controlled the government.

      2. _____

   C. _____

II. From Republic to Empire

   A. _____

   B. Roman general Octavian restored order.

      1. _____

      2. _____

      3. _____

III. _____

   A. Spread Greco-Roman civilization to distant lands

   B. _____

   C. _____

IV. _____

   A. Jesus was born about 4 B.C. in Bethlehem.

      1. _____

      2. _____

      3. _____

   B. First Christians

      1. _____

      2. _____

      3. _____

V. The Long Decline

   A. _____

   B. Empire split into two parts—east and west.

      1. _____

      2. _____

      3. _____

Section Summary
ANCIENT ROME AND THE RISE OF CHRISTIANITY

Rome began as a small city-state in Italy. The Romans over-threw the Etruscans who ruled them and set up a **republic.** In this type of government, officials are chosen by the people. At first, **patricians,** or members of the upper class, controlled the government. Eventually, **plebeians,** or commoners, also served in the Roman senate. Meanwhile, Rome's armies helped spread Roman rule from Spain to Egypt.

Rome became very wealthy, but this wealth led to corruption. Many civil wars followed. Eventually, a Roman general named Octavian restored order. He took the name **Augustus.** <u>Augustus exercised absolute power, and he changed Rome from a republic to an empire.</u> Roman emperors brought peace and order to the lands they controlled. As a result, the 200 years from Augustus to Marcus Aurelius are known as the *Pax Romana,* or "Roman Peace."

The Romans borrowed many Greek ideas. They spread their blended, Greco-Roman civilization to distant lands. They also built roads, bridges, and aqueducts. However, their greatest legacy is probably their ideas about law and justice.

During the *Pax Romana,* Christianity began in the Middle East. A Jew named **Jesus** was born about 4 B.C. He called himself the Son of God. He taught that his mission was to bring salvation and eternal life. Jesus was put to death, but his disciples believed he rose from the dead. Some Jews believed that Jesus was the **messiah,** or savior sent by God. They became the first Christians. For a while, Christianity was a **sect** within Judaism. Then Paul spread Christianity to non-Jews. At first, Rome persecuted Christians, but it later accepted Christian beliefs.

The Roman empire eventually split into two parts, east and west. In the west, the empire declined because of corruption, poverty, and declining moral values. Germanic invaders finally conquered Rome in 476. However, the eastern empire prospered. It became known as the Byzantine empire.

Review Questions

1. What is a republic?

_____

_____

2. What religion began in the Middle East during the *Pax Romana?*

_____

_____

READING CHECK

Who conquered Rome in 476 A.D.?

_____

_____

_____

VOCABULARY STRATEGY

Find the word *exercised* in the underlined sentence. The word *exercise* often refers to physical activity, but it has a different meaning here. Note that Augustus *exercised* "absolute power," and his rule changed Rome from a republic to an empire. Complete the sentence below, using the word that means the same as *exercised.*

Augustus did not just have absolute power, he also _____ it.

1. used

2. wasted

READING SKILL

Recognize Multiple Causes
Besides corruption, what are two reasons why the western Roman empire declined?

_____

_____

_____

Name_____ Class_____ Date_____

As you read this section in your textbook, complete the outline below to summarize information about the early civilizations in the Americas. Some items have been completed for you.

I. Olmecs, the First American Civilization

   A. _____

   B. _____

II. Civilizations of Middle America

   A. First settlers were nomadic hunters.

      1. _____

      2. _____

   B. The Maya

      1. _____

      2. _____

   C. _____

      1. _____

      2. _____

III. _____

   A. Came down from Andes of Peru in the 1400s

   B. _____

   C. Inca government

      1. _____

      2. _____

   D. _____

      1. _____

      2. _____

IV. _____

   A. The Ancestral Puebloans—in the desert southwest

      1. _____

      2. _____

   B. _____

      1. _____

      2. _____

   C. Inuits—in the far north

   D. _____

PART 2.4 Section Summary
CIVILIZATIONS OF THE AMERICAS

The first settlers in the Americas were nomads. They probably came across a land bridge from Siberia to Alaska. The first American civilization, the **Olmec,** began along the Mexican Gulf Coast. Later, other civilizations developed in Central and South America. The **Maya,** for example, built city-states in Central America. They created pyramid temples, a writing system, and a calendar. Each city-state had its own ruling chief. Another civilization was the **Aztec.** They conquered most of Mexico. The Aztec empire grew wealthy from **tribute,** or payment from conquered people. The Aztecs also developed a complex social structure with a single emperor at the top.

In the 1400s, the **Inca** came down from the Andes mountains of Peru. Led by Pachacuti, they conquered a huge empire. The Inca emperors claimed to be divine and had absolute power. Government officials kept records on quipus, or collections of knotted colored strings. The Inca united their empire by imposing their language and religion on conquered people. They also created a great road system.

Before 1500, many different culture groups lived in North America. In the desert southwest, the **Ancestral Puebloans** built large villages, or pueblos, of stone and adobe brick. Later, they built cliff dwellings. At the center of their village life was the **kiva.** This was a large underground chamber used for religious rituals. In the Midwest, farming cultures emerged. The Hopewell people left behind giant earthen mounds. <u>Objects found in the mounds suggest that trade networks stretched from the Gulf of Mexico to the Great Lakes.</u> The Hopewell culture was replaced by the **Mississippians.** They built large towns and ceremonial centers.

Differences in climate and resources led to the development of different cultures in other parts of North America. In the far north, for example, the Inuits adapted to a frozen climate. In the Northeast, Iroquois tribes, known as the Five Nations, formed the Iroquois League.

Review Questions

1. How did the Aztec empire get its wealth?

_____

_____

2. What were the villages of the Ancestral Puebloans like?

_____

_____

READING CHECK

What was the first civilization in the Americas?

_____

_____

_____

VOCABULARY STRATEGY

Find the word *networks* in the underlined sentence. What does it mean? The word *network* contains the word *net.* A net has many parts or strands that are woven or connected together. What parts do you think would be connected in a "trade *network*"? Use these clues to help you understand the meaning of *networks* in this sentence.

READING SKILL

Compare and Contrast Compare and contrast the governments of the Maya, Aztec, and Inca. What form of government did each civilization develop? What type of rulers did each have?

_____

_____

_____

_____

_____

Name_____ Class_____ Date_____

As you read this section in the textbook, complete the outline below to summarize information about Europe during the Middle Ages. Some items have been completed for you.

I. Germanic Civilization

    A. _____

    B. _____

II. The Early Middle Ages

    A. Charlemagne reunited much of Western Europe.

        1. _____

        2. _____

    B. _____

    C. _____

    D. _____

III. _____

    A. Feudalism

        1. _____

        2. _____

        3. _____

    B. Manor was the heart of medieval economy.

        1. _____

        2. Most peasants on manors were serfs.

            a. _____

            b. _____

IV. _____

    A. _____

    B. Western church became Roman Catholic Church.

        1. _____

        2. _____

V. Economic Expansion and Change

    A. _____

    B. Advances made in commerce led to increased wealth.

        1. _____

        2. _____

Section Summary
THE RISE OF EUROPE

Germanic peoples ended Roman rule in the West. They divided Europe into many small kingdoms. Their culture was very different from Roman culture. They had no cities and no written laws. Instead, they lived in small communities ruled by elected kings.

In the 800s, **Charlemagne** reunited much of Europe. He revived learning and spread Christian civilization into northern Europe. He also set up a strong, efficient government. After Charlemagne's death, his grandsons divided his empire into three regions. Muslims, Magyars, and Vikings attacked these regions. People needed protection from the invaders. As a result, a new system, called **feudalism,** developed.

Under feudalism, powerful lords gave land, or **fiefs,** to lesser lords, called **vassals.** In exchange for land and protection, vassals promised service and loyalty to the greater lord. Many nobles trained as **knights.** They adopted a code of conduct called **chivalry.** This code said that knights should be brave, loyal, and true to their word.

The **manor,** or lord's estate, was the center of the medieval economy. Most of the peasants on a manor were **serfs.** They could not be sold like enslaved people, but they spent their lives working on the manor. In return, the lord gave them protection and the right to farm some land for themselves.

After the fall of Rome, the Christian Church split into an eastern and a western church. The western church became known as the **Roman Catholic Church.** It grew stronger and wealthier. It became the most powerful **secular,** or worldly, force in medieval Europe. The Church also had absolute power in religious matters because it controlled the sacraments.

By the 1000s, improvements in agriculture and commerce caused the economy in Europe to revive. New iron plows and the three-field system improved farming. New trade routes and goods increased wealth. Merchant **guilds,** or associations, began to dominate life in medieval towns.

Review Questions

1. Who reunited much of Europe in the 800s?

_____

_____

2. How were serfs different from enslaved people?

_____

_____

READING CHECK

After the Christian Church split, what was the western church called?

_____

_____

_____

VOCABULARY STRATEGY

Find the word *efficient* in the underlined sentence. What does it mean? *Efficient* comes from the Latin word *efficere,* which means "to bring to pass" or "accomplish." Which of the words below is similar in meaning to *efficient*?

1. effective

2. useless

READING SKILL

Identify Supporting Details
What three sentences in the Summary support the following idea: By the 1000s, improvements in agriculture and commerce caused the economy in Europe to revive.

_____

_____

_____

PART 3.2

Note Taking Study Guide

THE HIGH AND LATE MIDDLE AGES

As you read this section in the textbook, complete the outline below to summarize information about the High and Late Middle Ages. Some items have been completed for you.

I. **Growth of Royal Power in England**

   A. _____

   B. _____

   C. Evolving traditions

     1. Kings had conflicts with nobles and the Church.

     2. _____

   D. _____

     1. _____

     2. _____

II. _____

   A. _____

   B. _____

   C. Popes clashed with Holy Roman emperors.

     1. _____

     2. _____

III. _____

   A. The Crusades begin

     1. _____

     2. _____

     3. _____

   B. _____

     1. _____

     2. _____

IV. _____

   A. Schools sprang up around cathedrals, eventually becoming universities.

   B. _____

   C. _____

V. _____

   A. Bubonic plague, called the Black Death, spread.

   B. Famine and war added to the turmoil of the period.

PART 3.2 Section Summary
THE HIGH AND LATE MIDDLE AGES

William the Conqueror took the throne of England in 1066. He helped unify England and strengthen the monarchy. Other kings developed the basis for English **common law.** This is law that is the same for all people. A jury system also developed. A **jury** was a group of men sworn to speak the truth. In the early 1200s, a group of nobles forced England's King John to sign the **Magna Carta,** or Great Charter. The Magna Carta had two main ideas. First, it said that nobles had certain rights. Second, it made clear that the king must also obey the law.

The **Holy Roman Empire** arose out of the many Germanic kingdoms that formed after the death of Charlemagne. When a ruler united these kingdoms, the pope crowned him "emperor." Later rulers began to use the title "Holy Roman emperor." Popes soon had conflicts with the Holy Roman emperors. Refusing to obey the Church could result in **excommunication.** This meant that someone could not receive the **sacraments,** or sacred rituals of the Church.

In the 1050s, Muslim Turks invaded the Byzantine empire. The Byzantine emperor asked the pope for help. Thousands of Christian knights went to the Holy Land to fight **crusades,** or holy wars. The Crusades had several effects. They caused religious hatred. They also increased European trade, the power of the pope, and the power of monarchs.

In the High Middle Ages, schools sprang up around cathedrals. These schools eventually became the first universities. The works of Muslim scholars reintroduced ideas from ancient Greece. New writings began to be produced in the **vernacular,** or everyday language of ordinary people.

In the late Middle Ages, bubonic plague spread through Europe. The plague was also called the **Black Death.** One in three people died. The plague brought social and economic turmoil. Famine and war added to the chaos.

Review Questions

1. What two main ideas are found in the Magna Carta?

_____

_____

2. Out of what kingdoms did the Holy Roman Empire arise?

_____

_____

READING CHECK

What disease was called the Black Death?

_____

_____

_____

VOCABULARY STRATEGY

Find the word *unify* in the underlined sentence. What does it mean? *Unify* has two parts, *uni-* and *–fy*. *Uni-* means "one," and *-fy* means "make" or "cause to become." Put these two meanings together to figure out the meaning of *unify*.

READING SKILL

Understand Effects Besides religious hatred, what were three other effects of the Crusades?

_____

_____

_____

PART 3.3

Note Taking Study Guide
THE BYZANTINE EMPIRE AND RUSSIA

As you read this section in the textbook, complete the outline below to summarize information about the Byzantine empire, Russia, and Eastern Europe. Some items have been completed for you.

I. The Byzantine Empire

   A. Roman emperor Constantine rebuilt Byzantium and renamed it Constantinople.

      1. Eastern Roman empire became known as Byzantine empire.

      2. _____

   B. Justinian's Code

      1. _____

      2. _____

   C. _____

      1. Emperor controlled Church affairs.

      2. _____

   D. Byzantine heritage

      1. _____

      2. _____

II. _____

   A. Slavs lived in Ukraine during Roman times.

   B. _____

   C. _____

   D. _____

   E. The Mongol conquest cut Russia off from Western Europe.

   F. _____

      1. Princes of Moscow gained power and defeated Mongols.

      2. _____

      3. _____

III. _____

   A. Many ethnic groups settled in Eastern Europe.

   B. _____

PART 3.3 Section Summary
THE BYZANTINE EMPIRE AND RUSSIA

By 330 A.D. the Roman emperor Constantine had rebuilt the Greek city of Byzantium. He made it his capital and renamed it **Constantinople**. Constantinople grew wealthy from trade. The eastern Roman empire eventually became known as the Byzantine empire. The emperor **Justinian** had the laws of ancient Rome organized into a collection. This collection became known as Justinian's Code. <u>This code preserved and spread the heritage of Roman law.</u>

In the Byzantine empire, the emperor controlled Church affairs. He did not accept the pope's authority. By 1054, disagreements caused a **schism,** or permanent split in the Christian Church. This resulted in two separate churches, Eastern (Greek) Orthodox and Roman Catholic.

During Roman times, a people called the Slavs lived in present-day Ukraine. In the 700s and 800s, Vikings began to trade with the Slavs. The city of **Kiev** became a trade center and the center of the first Russian state. From Constantinople, missionaries brought Christianity to Russia. They also developed an alphabet for the Slavic languages. In the early 1200s, the Mongols overran Russia. The absolute power of the Mongols became a model for later Russian rulers. Eventually, the princes of Moscow defeated the Mongols. Between 1462 and 1505, **Ivan III,** or Ivan the Great, controlled much of northern Russia. He took the title **tsar.** This is the Russian word for *Caesar*. His grandson, Ivan the Terrible, ruled with absolute power.

Many ethnic groups settled in Eastern Europe. An **ethnic group** is large group of people who share the same language and cultural heritage. These groups included Slavs and Asian and Germanic peoples. Byzantine missionaries brought Eastern Orthodox Christianity to the Balkans. German knights and missionaries spread Roman Catholic Christianity to the area. Jewish settlers came to Eastern Europe to escape persecution. Many kingdoms developed in Eastern Europe, including Poland, Hungary, and Serbia.

Review Questions

1. How did the Mongols influence later Russian rulers?

_____

_____

2. Why did Jewish settlers come to Eastern Europe?

_____

_____

READING CHECK

What two churches resulted from the schism in Christianity?

_____

_____

_____

VOCABULARY STRATEGY

Find the word *preserved* in the underlined sentence. What does it mean? *Preserved* means the opposite of *destroyed*. Which of the words below is similar in meaning to *preserved*?

1. saved

2. ruined

READING SKILL

Recognize Sequence Number the following events from Russian history to show the correct sequence. The first event should be "Slavs live in Ukraine" and the last event should be "Reign of Ivan the Terrible."

_____ Kiev becomes the center of the first Russian state.

_____ Mongols overrun Russia.

_____ Slavs live in Ukraine.

_____ Ivan the Great takes the title of tsar.

_____ Princes of Moscow defeat the Mongols.

_____ Ivan the Terrible reigns.

_____ Vikings begin to trade with Slavs.

PART 3.4

Note Taking Study Guide
MUSLIM CIVILIZATIONS

As you read this section in the textbook, complete the outline below to summarize information about the rise of Islam and Muslim civilizations. Some items have been completed for you.

I. Rise of Islam
  A. Muhammad
    1. Born in Mecca in western Arabia about 570
    2. Muslims believe he is God's messenger.
    3. Spent much of his life spreading Islam
  B. Muslim beliefs
    1. _____
    2. _____
    3. _____

II. _____
  A. Abu Bakr—successor to Muhammad
  B. _____
  C. _____

III. Golden Age of Muslim Civilization
  A. _____
  B. _____
  C. _____
  D. _____

IV. _____
  A. In the late 1100s, a Muslim sultan defeated Hindus.
  B. _____
  C. Muslims and Hindus
    1. _____
    2. _____
  D. Mughal India
    1. _____
    2. _____

V. _____
  A. The Ottoman empire
    1. _____
    2. _____
  B. _____
    1. _____
    2. _____

PART 3.4 Section Summary
MUSLIM CIVILIZATIONS

Muhammad was born in Arabia about 570. According to Muslim belief, he was called in a vision to become God's messenger. He spent the rest of his life spreading Islam. Like Judaism and Christianity, Islam is a monotheistic religion. All Muslims accept five basic duties, known as the Five Pillars of Islam. These include belief in one God, daily prayer, charity to the poor, fasting, and the hajj. The **hajj** is a pilgrimage to Mecca. Muslims believe that the Quran is the word of God and the final authority on all matters.

When Muhammad died, Abu Bakr was elected the first **caliph,** or successor to Muhammad. He was the first of many rulers who spread Islam through military conquests. Muslim merchants also spread Islam through trade. Eventually, the Abbasid dynasty made **Baghdad** the capital of Islam. Baghdad became a great center of learning. Muslims made advances in many fields, including algebra and medicine. Islamic architects created beautiful domed **mosques,** or houses of worship.

In the late 1100s, a **sultan,** or Muslim ruler, defeated Hindu armies in India. His successors founded the Delhi sultanate. Muslim rule brought changes to India. Buddhism declined as a major religion. Many Hindus were killed. In 1526, Turkish and Mongol invaders poured into India. They were led by Babur. He ended the Delhi sultanate and set up the **Mughal dynasty.**

In 1453, the Ottomans captured Constantinople. They renamed it Istanbul. The **Ottoman empire** eventually reached from Hungary to Arabia and across North Africa. Under Suleiman, the Ottoman empire had its golden age. <u>Ottoman poets adapted Persian and Arab models to produce works in the Turkish language.</u>

Another Muslim dynasty, the Safavid, created a strong empire in present-day Iran. Shah Abbas the Great ruled from 1588 to 1629. He brought back the glory of ancient Persia.

Review Questions

1. What are the Five Pillars of Islam?

_____

_____

2. What name did the Ottomans give to Constantinople?

_____

_____

READING CHECK

What is the term for a Muslim house of worship?

_____

_____

VOCABULARY STRATEGY

Find the word *adapted* in the underlined sentence. What does it mean? *Adapt* comes from the Latin word *adaptare*, which means "to fit to." When you make something "fit," what do you often have to do to it? Which of the words below is similar in meaning to *adapted*?

1. copied

2. changed

READING SKILL

Identify Supporting Details Two sentences in the Summary support the idea "Muslim rule brought changes to India." One of those sentences is "Many Hindus were killed." What is the other sentence?

_____

_____

_____

Name_____ Class_____ Date_____

PART
3.5

Note Taking Study Guide

KINGDOMS AND TRADING STATES OF AFRICA

As you read this section in the textbook, complete the outline below to summarize information about the kingdoms and trading states of Africa. Some items have been completed for you.

I. Bantu Migrations

II. Early Civilizations of Africa

   A. The Kingdom of Nubia

      1. _____

      2. _____

      3. _____

   B. _____

      1. Ruled for a time by Greeks and then Romans

      2. _____

      3. _____

III. _____

   A. Camel caravans created trade across the Sahara.

   B. _____

   C. The Kingdom of Ghana

      1. _____

      2. _____

      3. _____

   D. _____

      1. _____

      2. _____

   E. _____

      1. _____

      2. _____

IV. Trade Routes of East Africa

   A. _____

   B. _____

V. _____

   A. Nuclear family was typical in some societies.

   B. _____

   C. _____

   D. _____

PART 3.5 Section Summary
KINGDOMS AND TRADING STATES OF AFRICA

Two important civilizations developed along the Nile River in Africa. One was Egypt. The other was **Nubia,** or Kush. Powerful kings ruled Nubia for thousands of years. Nubians adopted many Egyptian traditions. About A.D. 350, armies from the kingdom of Axum overran Nubia.

Egypt and North Africa were ruled, for a time, by the Greeks and then the Romans. <u>Linked to a global trade network, North African ports prospered.</u> Camels from Asia revolutionized trade across the Sahara. Gold and salt were the main trade items. North Africans wanted gold to buy European goods. West Africans traded gold to North Africans in exchange for salt.

By A.D. 800, the kingdom of **Ghana** had been formed in West Africa. The king controlled the gold-salt trade routes. Muslim merchants brought Islam to Ghana. Ghana was eventually overtaken by the kingdom of Mali. Mali controlled both the gold-mining regions and the salt supplies of the Sahara. The greatest emperor of Mali was **Mansa Musa.** As Mali weakened in the 1400s, a new West African kingdom arose. This kingdom was Songhai. It was the largest state that had ever existed in West Africa. The kingdom controlled trade routes and cities like Timbuktu.

Axum was an important trading center long before it conquered Nubia. It linked trade routes from Africa, India, and the Mediterranean world. As Axum declined, other trading centers rose along the East African coast. By 1000, East African port cities were thriving because of trade across the Indian Ocean.

African societies were diverse. In some societies, the **nuclear family** was typical. In other communities, the family included several generations. Religious beliefs were also varied. Some Africans followed traditional beliefs. Others followed Christianity or Islam. **Griots,** or professional storytellers, preserved African values and history. Migrations, such as the **Bantu migrations**, also helped make cultures in southern Africa more diverse.

Review Questions

1. From what civilization did Nubians adopt many traditions?

_____

_____

2. What did West Africans trade to North Africans for salt?

_____

_____

READING CHECK

Who are griots?

_____

_____

_____

VOCABULARY STRATEGY

Find the word *global* in the underlined sentence. What does it mean? *Global* comes from the word *globe*. If something is *global*, what do you think it is like? Which word below means the same as *global*?

1. local

2. worldwide

READING SKILL

Identify Causes What caused East African port cities to thrive? When identifying causes, look for phrases like "because of," "resulted from," or "led to."

_____

_____

_____

Name_____ Class_____ Date_____

Note Taking Study Guide
SPREAD OF CIVILIZATIONS IN EAST ASIA

As you read this section in the textbook, complete the outline below to summarize information about the civilizations in East Asia. Some items have been completed for you.

I. Sui Dynasty

    A. _____

    B. _____

II. Two Golden Ages of China

    A. Tang dynasty (618–907)

        1. _____

        2. _____

    B. _____

        1. Golden age of wealth and culture

        2. _____

    C. Government and society

        1. _____

        2. _____

    D. _____

        1. _____

        2. _____

III. The Mongol and Ming Empires

    A. Mongols invaded China and toppled Song dynasty in 1279.

    B. _____

    C. Exploration

        1. _____

        2. _____

IV. _____

    A. _____

    B. _____

V. The Emergence of Japan

    A. _____

    B. _____

VI. _____

    A. _____

    B. _____

    C. Tokugawa shogunate ruled from 1603 to 1868.

PART 3.6 Section Summary
SPREAD OF CIVILIZATIONS IN EAST ASIA

In the 500s, the Sui dynasty reunited China. Then, a Sui general and his son set up their own dynasty, the **Tang.** Tang armies forced neighboring lands to become **tributary states.** Tang emperors restored the bureaucracy and redistributed land to the peasants.

The Tang dynasty collapsed in 907. The **Song** dynasty soon rose to take its place. The Song period was a golden age of wealth and culture. Under both the Tang and Song, China was a well-ordered society. The two main classes were the gentry and the peasantry. The gentry were wealthy landowners. Most scholar-officials came from this class.

In the 1200s, the **Mongols** invaded China and ended the weakened Song dynasty. They established peace and order. Trade flourished along the Silk Road. In 1368, a rebel army drove the Mongols out of China. A new dynasty, the **Ming,** worked to make China great again. Under the Ming, Zheng He led a series of sea voyages as far as East Africa.

China influenced other peoples. Korea, for example, absorbed many Chinese traditions. However, it also improved on Chinese inventions, including book printing and an alphabet. Japan also felt China's influence, but the seas protected and isolated it. This allowed Japan to maintain its own distinct culture. However, in the early 600s, Japan's Yamato rulers sent young nobles to study in China. They brought back Chinese ideas that influenced Japanese society.

Japan eventually evolved into a feudal society. In theory, the emperor was at the head. <u>In fact, he was a powerless, though revered, figurehead.</u> The **shogun,** or supreme military commander, had the real power. He gave land to warrior lords who agreed to support him with their armies. These lords were called **daimyo.** They, in turn, gave land to lesser warriors called **samurai.** In 1603, Tokugawa Ieyasu founded the **Tokugawa** shogunate. The Tokugawas brought peace and stability to Japan.

Review Questions

1. What were the two main classes in Tang and Song China?

_____

_____

2. How did geography affect Japanese culture?

_____

_____

READING CHECK

Who led expeditions as far as East Africa during the Ming dynasty?

_____

_____

_____

VOCABULARY STRATEGY

Find the word *revered* in the underlined sentence. What does it mean? *Revered* comes from the Latin word *revereri*, which means "to feel awe." Based on this word-origins clue, which of the words below is closest in meaning to *revered*?

1. honored

2. hated

READING SKILL

Recognize Sequence A partial list of dynasties from the Summary is given below. Fill in the missing dynasties, in the correct chronological order.

Sui

_____

_____

Mongol

_____

Note Taking Study Guide

CHAPTER 1 SECTION 1

THE RENAISSANCE IN ITALY

Focus Question: What were the ideals of the Renaissance, and how did Italian artists and writers reflect these ideals?

As you read this section in your textbook, complete the following outline to identify main ideas and supporting details about the Italian Renaissance. Some items have been completed for you.

I. What was the Renaissance?
    A. A changing worldview
        1. Reawakened interest in classical Greece and Rome
        2. New emphasis on human experience and individual achievement
    B. A spirit of adventure
        1. Looked at universe in new ways
        2. _____
    C. The growth of humanism
        1. Study of classical Greece and Rome to understand their own times
        2. _____

II. Italy: Cradle of the Renaissance
    A. Italy's history and geography
        1. _____
        2. _____
        3. _____
    B. _____
        1. _____
        2. _____

III. Renaissance art and artists flower
    A. _____
        1. _____
        2. _____
    B. _____
        1. _____
        2. _____

(Outline continues on the next page.)

CHAPTER 1 SECTION 1

Note Taking Study Guide

THE RENAISSANCE IN ITALY

(Continued from page 34)

C. _____
  1. _____
  2. _____
D. _____
  1. _____
  2. _____
E. _____
  1. _____
  2. _____
F. _____
  1. _____
  2. _____
IV. _____
  A. _____
    1. _____
    2. _____
  B. _____
    1. _____
    2. _____

Name_____ Class_____ Date_____

A new age began in Italy in the 1300s and eventually spread throughout Europe. It was called the Renaissance, meaning "rebirth." It marked the change from medieval times to the early modern world. During medieval times, people focused on religion. In contrast, Renaissance thinkers explored human experience. There was a new emphasis on individual achievement. At the heart of this age was an intellectual movement called **humanism.** Humanists studied the classical culture of Greece and Rome. <u>They used that study to comprehend, or understand, their own times.</u> They emphasized the **humanities**—subjects including rhetoric, poetry, and history. Poet Francesco **Petrarch** was an important Renaissance humanist.

Italy was the birthplace of the Renaissance for many reasons. Italy had been the center of the Roman empire. Rome was also the seat of the Roman Catholic Church. The Church was an important **patron,** or supporter, of the arts. Italy's location encouraged trade. Trade provided the wealth that fueled Italy's Renaissance. In Italy's city-states, many merchant families had become rich through trade. One was the Medici family of **Florence.** They were important patrons of the arts.

Renaissance art reflected the ideas of humanism. Painters returned to the realism of classical times. They developed new techniques for representing humans and landscapes. The discovery of **perspective** allowed artists to create realistic art and paint scenes that looked three-dimensional. The greatest of the Renaissance artists were **Leonardo** da Vinci, **Michelangelo,** and **Raphael.**

Some Italian writers wrote guidebooks to help ambitious men and women rise in the Renaissance world. The most widely read of these was *The Book of the Courtier,* by **Baldassare Castiglione.** His ideal courtier was a well-educated, well-mannered aristocrat who mastered many fields. **Niccoló Machiavelli** wrote a guide for rulers on how to gain and maintain power. It was titled *The Prince.*

Review Questions

1. What intellectual movement was key to the Renaissance?

_____

_____

2. What is one reason why the Renaissance began in Italy?

_____

_____

READING CHECK

What does *Renaissance* mean?

_____

_____

_____

VOCABULARY STRATEGY

Find the word *comprehend* in the underlined sentence. What clues to its meaning can you find in the surrounding text? In this case, there is a synonym, or word that means the same as *comprehend,* in the same sentence. Circle the word in the sentence that could help you figure out what *comprehend* means.

READING SKILL

Identify Main Ideas What were two main features of the Renaissance?

_____

_____

_____

Name_____ Class_____ Date_____

CHAPTER 1 SECTION 2

Note Taking Study Guide

THE RENAISSANCE IN THE NORTH

Focus Question: How did the Renaissance develop in northern Europe?

As you read this section in your textbook, complete the following chart to record the main ideas about the Renaissance in the North. Some items have been completed for you.

Renaissance in the North

Humanists

- Humanists stress education and classical learning to bring religious and moral reform.
- Erasmus spreads humanism to a wider audience and calls for a translation of the Bible into the vernacular.

Artists and Writers

- Flemish painter Jan van Eyck portrays townspeople and religious scenes in realistic detail.
- Flemish painter Pieter Bruegel uses vibrant colors to portray scenes of peasant life.

Printing Revolution

- In 1455, Johann Gutenberg produces the first complete Bible using a printing press.
- Printed books are cheaper and easier to produce.

CHAPTER 1 SECTION 2 — Section Summary
THE RENAISSANCE IN THE NORTH

By the 1400s, northern Europe enjoyed enough economic growth to start its own Renaissance. An astounding invention—the printing press—helped spread Renaissance ideas. In about 1455, **Johann Gutenberg** produced the first complete Bible using a printing press. The printing press caused a printing revolution. Before, books were copied by hand. They were rare and expensive. Printed books were cheaper and easier to produce. Now more books were available, so more people learned to read. Printed books exposed Europeans to new ideas and new places.

The northern Renaissance began in the prosperous region of **Flanders.** It was a rich and thriving trade center. Flemish painters were known for their use of realism. Among the most important Flemish painters were Jan van Eyck, Pieter Bruegel, and Peter Paul Rubens. Painter **Albrecht Dürer** traveled to Italy to study the techniques of the Italian masters. Dürer applied the painting techniques he learned in Italy to **engraving,** a printmaking technique. Many of his engravings and paintings portray the theme of religious upheaval. He brought back Renaissance ideas to northern Europe.

VOCABULARY STRATEGY

Find the word *prosperous* in the first underlined sentence. Read the second underlined sentence of the Summary. What does it tell you about the region? Use that information to help you figure out what *prosperous* means.

Northern European humanist writers also helped spread Renaissance ideas. The Dutch priest and humanist Desiderius **Erasmus** wanted the Bible translated into the **vernacular,** or everyday language. Then many more people would be able to read it. The English humanist **Sir Thomas More** called for social reform in the shape of a **utopian** society. He pictured a society where people lived together in peace and harmony. The major figure of Renaissance literature, however, was the English poet and playwright William **Shakespeare.** His plays explore universal themes, such as the complexity of the individual. He set his plays in everyday, realistic settings. Shakespeare's love of words also enriched the English language. He alone added 1,700 new words to the language.

READING SKILL

Identify Main Ideas What is the goal of a utopian society?

_____

_____

_____

Review Questions
1. Identify one major change caused by the invention of the printing press.

   _____

   _____

2. What theme did Dürer explore in many of his works?

   _____

   _____

Name_____ Class_____ Date_____

Focus Question: How did revolts against the Roman Catholic Church affect northern European society?

As you read this section in your textbook, complete the following concept web to identify main ideas about the Protestant Reformation. Some items have been completed for you.

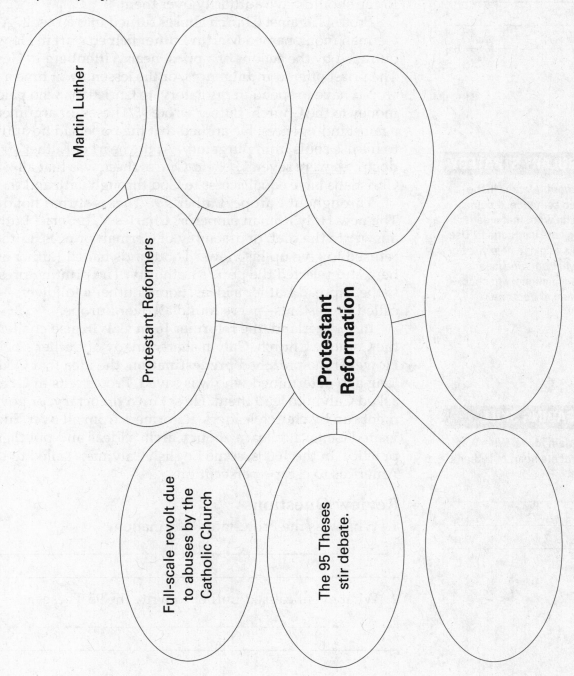

- Martin Luther
- Protestant Reformers
- Protestant Reformation
- Full-scale revolt due to abuses by the Catholic Church
- The 95 Theses stir debate.

Name_____ Class_____ Date_____

CHAPTER 1 SECTION 3	**Section Summary**
	THE PROTESTANT REFORMATION

READING CHECK

Which reformer in Switzerland also challenged the Catholic Church?

_____

_____

_____

VOCABULARY STRATEGY

Find the word *doctrine* in the underlined sentence. It comes from a Latin word that means "teaching" or "instruction." Use the word's origin to help you figure out what *doctrine* means. Then use a dictionary to check the meaning of *doctrine*.

READING SKILL

Identify Main Ideas What was one idea at the heart of Luther's teachings?

_____

_____

_____

In the 1500s, the Renaissance in northern Europe sparked a religious upheaval. It was known as the Protestant Reformation. Many Christians began to protest some practices in the Catholic Church. Popes, for example, led lavish lives. Many Christians also began to question why the Church in distant Rome should have authority over them.

Protests against Church abuses turned into a revolt. A German monk named **Martin Luther** helped start it. He was outraged by the actions of a priest near **Wittenberg** in Germany. The priest offered **indulgences,** or the lessening of time a soul would have to spend in purgatory, to Christians who paid money to the Church. Luther wrote 95 Theses, or arguments, against indulgences. He argued that the pope had no authority to release souls from purgatory. <u>At the heart of Luther's doctrines were several beliefs.</u> One of these was that all Christians have equal access to God through faith and the Bible.

Throughout Europe, Luther's 95 Theses stirred hot debate. The new Holy Roman emperor, **Charles V,** ordered Luther to answer to the **diet,** or assembly of German princes. Luther refused to give up his views. Thousands hailed Luther as a hero and rejected the pope's authority. The printing press helped spread Luther's ideas. Soon, Luther's followers—now called Protestants—were found all over Europe.

In Switzerland, the reformer **John Calvin** also challenged the Catholic Church. Calvin shared many of Luther's beliefs. However, he preached **predestination,** the idea that God had long ago determined who was saved. Protestants in **Geneva** asked Calvin to lead them. He set up a **theocracy,** or government run by church leaders. Reformers from all over Europe visited Geneva to learn about Calvin's ideas and put them into practice. In the 1600s, some English Calvinists sailed to the Americas to escape persecution.

Review Questions

1. What was the Protestant Reformation?

_____

_____

2. What event caused Luther to write the 95 Theses?

_____

_____

Note Taking Study Guide

REFORMATION IDEAS SPREAD

Focus Question: How did the Reformation bring about two different religious paths in Europe?

As you read this section in your textbook, complete the following flowchart to identify main ideas about the spread of the Protestant Reformation in Europe. Some items have been completed for you.

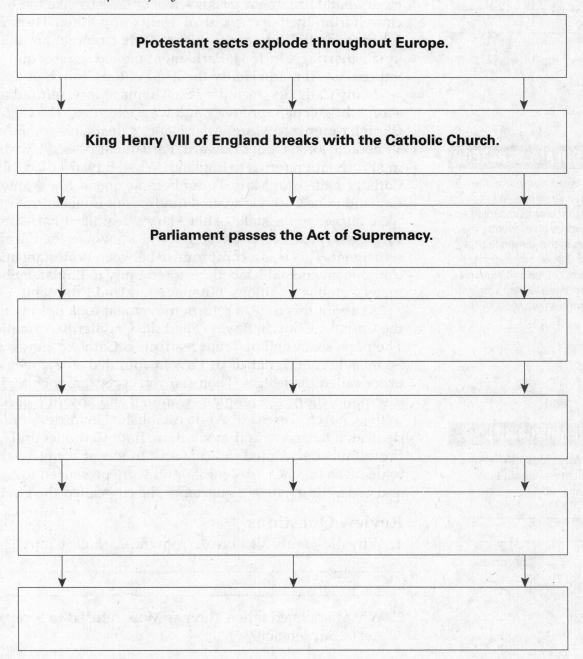

Protestant sects explode throughout Europe.

King Henry VIII of England breaks with the Catholic Church.

Parliament passes the Act of Supremacy.

CHAPTER 1

SECTION 4

Section Summary

REFORMATION IDEAS SPREAD

As the Reformation continued, new Protestant **sects,** or religious groups that had broken away from an established church, sprang up. In England, the break with the Catholic Church came from King **Henry VIII,** who wanted to end his marriage. The pope refused to annul the marriage. Furious, Henry had Parliament pass a series of laws to take the English church from the pope's control. Henry appointed **Thomas Cranmer** archbishop of the new church. Cranmer annulled the king's marriage. In 1534, Parliament passed the Act of Supremacy. It made Henry the head of the Church of England.

Many Catholics, including Sir Thomas More, refused to accept the Act of Supremacy and were executed. The Catholic Church **canonized** More. After Henry's death, his son Edward VI became king. Under Edward, Parliament passed laws bringing Protestant reforms to England. When Edward died, his Catholic half-sister **Mary Tudor** became queen. She wanted England to be Catholic again. Hundreds of English Protestants were burned at the stake. After Mary's death, her half-sister **Elizabeth** ruled. She enforced reforms known as the Elizabethan settlement. This was a **compromise** between Protestant and Catholic practices. Elizabeth restored unity to England. She kept many Catholic traditions, but made England Protestant.

At about this time, a reform movement took hold within the Catholic Church. It was called the Counter Reformation. The pope's **Council of Trent** reaffirmed Catholic views. A Spanish knight, **Ignatius of Loyola,** founded a new religious order called the Jesuits. Their rigorous program included strict discipline, thorough religious training, and absolute obedience to the Church. **Teresa of Avila** established an order of nuns dedicated to prayer and meditation. Both Catholics and Protestants persecuted radical sects. Innocent people were put to death as witches. In Venice, Jews were pressured to convert, and ordered to live in a quarter of the city called the **ghetto.**

Review Questions

1. Why did Henry VIII break from the Catholic Church?

_____

_____

2. What happened when Thomas More refused to accept the Act of Supremacy?

_____

_____

Note Taking Study Guide

CHAPTER 1 SECTION 5

THE SCIENTIFIC REVOLUTION

Focus Question: How did discoveries in science lead to a new way of thinking for Europeans?

As you read this section in your textbook, complete the following chart to identify main ideas about the Scientific Revolution in Europe.

Thinkers of the Scientific Revolution		
Nicolaus Copernicus	Developed sun-centered universe theory	
Tycho Brahe	Provided evidence to support Copernicus's theory	
Johannes Kepler	Calculated the orbits of planets around the sun	
Galileo Galilei		
Francis Bacon		
René Descartes		
Andreas Vesalius		
Ambroise Paré		

Name_____ Class_____ Date_____

Section Summary
THE SCIENTIFIC REVOLUTION

In the mid-1500s, the Scientific Revolution occurred. It changed how people thought about the universe. Before the Renaisance, Europeans believed Earth was the center of everything. In 1543, Polish scholar **Nicolaus Copernicus** suggested that the solar system was **heliocentric,** or centered around the sun. The work of Danish astronomer **Tycho Brahe** supported Copernicus's theory. The German astronomer and mathematician **Johannes Kepler** used Brahe's data to calculate the orbits of the planets. His work also supported Copernicus's theory.

Many scientists built on the foundations laid by Copernicus and Kepler. In Italy, **Galileo** built a telescope and observed that Jupiter's four moons move slowly around that planet. They moved in the way Copernicus said that Earth moves around the sun. Galileo's discoveries caused an uproar. <u>Other scholars attacked him because his observations contradicted ancient views about the world.</u> The Catholic Church condemned him. His ideas challenged the Christian teaching that the heavens were fixed in position to Earth, and perfect.

Despite the Church's objection, a new approach to science emerged. It was based on observation and experimentation. To explain their data, scientists used reasoning to propose a logical **hypothesis,** or possible explanation. This process became known as the **scientific method.** Two giants of this new approach were Englishman **Francis Bacon** and Frenchman **René Descartes.** They used different scientific methods to understand how truth is determined. Bacon stressed experimentation and observation. Descartes emphasized reasoning.

Dramatic changes occurred in many branches of science at this time. English chemist **Robert Boyle** explained that matter is composed of particles that behave in knowable ways. **Isaac Newton** used mathematics to show that a force keeps the planets in orbits around the sun. He called this force **gravity.** He also developed a branch of mathematics called **calculus.**

Review Questions

1. Before the Renaissance, what planet did Europeans believe was the center of the universe?

_____

_____

2. Why did the Church condemn Galileo?

_____

_____

Focus Question: How did the search for spices lead to global exploration?

As you read this section in your textbook, complete the following flowchart to identify causes and effects of European exploration. Some items have been completed for you.

Columbus Sails West

-
-
-

Portugal Leads

- Rounds southern tip of Africa
-
-

Reasons to Explore

- Control trade
- Gain direct access to Asia
-

Name_____ Class_____ Date_____

CHAPTER 2 SECTION 1

Section Summary
THE SEARCH FOR SPICES

READING CHECK

What was the main source of the spices Europeans wanted?

_____

_____

_____

VOCABULARY STRATEGY

Find the word *authority* in the underlined sentence. Sometimes a word will be defined nearby. Clue words or phrases that signal a definition include *which means, also known as,* and *or.* Notice that *authority* is defined within this sentence. Find the clue word that signals the definition. Circle the word in the sentence that could help you figure out what *authority* means.

READING SKILL

Identify Causes and Effects

Identify one cause of European exploration.

_____

_____

_____

Identify one effect of Portugal's explorations along the coast of Africa.

_____

_____

_____

By the 1400s, Europe's demand for trade goods, especially valuable spices, was growing. The chief source of spices was the **Moluccas,** an island chain in present-day Indonesia. Arab and Italian merchants controlled most trade between Asia and Europe. Europeans outside Italy wanted their own access to Asia's trade goods.

Prince Henry encouraged Portuguese sea exploration. He believed that Africa was the source of the riches the Muslim traders controlled. He also hoped to reach Asia by going along the African coast. **Cartographers** prepared maps for the voyages. In 1497, **Vasco da Gama** led four Portuguese ships around the southern tip of Africa. Evenually, they reached the great spice port of Calicut on the west coast of India. Soon, the Portuguese seized ports around the Indian Ocean and created a vast trading empire.

Now others looked for a sea route to Asia. The Italian navigator **Christopher Columbus** persuaded Ferdinand and Isabella of Spain to pay for his voyage. In 1492, Columbus sailed west with three small ships. When the crew finally spotted land, they thought they had reached the Indies, or Southeast Asia. What Columbus had actually found were previously unknown lands.

The Spanish rulers asked Spanish-born Pope Alexander VI to support their authority, or power, to claim the lands of this "new world." The pope set the **Line of Demarcation.** This gave Spain rights to lands west of the line; Portugal had rights to lands east of the line. Both countries agreed to these terms in the **Treaty of Tordesillas.**

Europeans still had not found a quick sea route to Asia, however. In 1519, a Portuguese nobleman named **Ferdinand Magellan** sailed west from Spain to find a way to the Pacific Ocean. In 1520, he found a passageway at the southern tip of South America. Magellan was killed along the way, but the survivors of this voyage were the first to **circumnavigate,** or sail around, the world.

Review Questions

1. Why did European explorers seek a direct sea route to Asia?

_____

_____

2. Who was Vasco da Gama?

_____

_____

CHAPTER 2 SECTION 2

Note Taking Study Guide
TURBULENT CENTURIES IN AFRICA

Focus Question: What effects did European exploration have on the people of Africa?

As you read this section in your textbook, complete the following chart to identify the effects of European exploration in Africa. Some items have been completed for you.

Effects of European Exploration

New African States
- Asante kingdom emerges in the area of present-day Ghana.
-

Slave Trade
- European involvement encourages broader Atlantic slave trade.
-
-

European Footholds
- Portuguese establish forts and trading posts.
- Portuguese attack coastal cities of East Africa.
-

CHAPTER 2 SECTION 2 — Section Summary

TURBULENT CENTURIES IN AFRICA

Which African ruler tried to stop the slave trade?

_____

_____

_____

Find the word *unified* in the underlined sentence. What clue can you find in its prefix, *uni-?* Think of other words that have the same word part, such as *unicycle* or *unicorn.* What do a unicycle and a unicorn have in common? Use the information about the word part *uni-* to help you figure out what *unified* means.

Identify Effects Identify one major effect of the slave trade on African states.

_____

_____

_____

The Portuguese gained footholds on the coast of West Africa by building small forts and trading posts. From there, they sailed around the coast to East Africa. There they continued to build forts and trading posts. They also attacked Arab trading cities in East Africa, such as **Mombasa** and **Malindi.** They eventually took over the East African trade network.

Europeans began to view slaves as the most important part of African trade. By the 1500s, European interest caused the slave trade to grow into a huge moneymaking business. Europeans especially needed workers for their **plantations,** or large estates, in the Americas and elsewhere. Some African leaders tried to slow down or stop the slave trade. The ruler of Kongo, **Affonso I,** was one. He had been taught by Portuguese **missionaries,** and wanted to maintain ties with Europe but stop the slave trade. He was unsuccessful.

The slave trade had major effects on African states. Some small states disappeared forever because of the loss of so many young people. At the same time, new states arose. Their ways of life depended on the slave trade. The **Asante kingdom** emerged in the area of present-day Ghana. In the late 1600s, an able military leader, **Osei Tutu,** won control of the trading city of Kumasi. <u>From there, he conquered neighboring peoples and unified the Asante kingdom.</u> Under Osei Tutu, the Asante kingdom set up a **monopoly,** or sole control, over gold mining and the slave trade. The **Oyo empire** arose as waves of Yoruba people settled in the region of present-day Nigeria. Its leaders used wealth from the slave trade to build a strong army.

By the 1600s, several other European powers had built forts along the west coast of Africa. In 1652, Dutch immigrants arrived at the very tip of the continent. They built **Cape Town,** the first permanent European settlement. Dutch farmers, called **Boers,** settled the lands around the port.

Review Questions

1. How did the Portuguese gain footholds on the coasts of Africa?

_____

_____

2. Who was Osei Tutu?

_____

_____

CHAPTER 2 SECTION 3

Note Taking Study Guide

EUROPEAN FOOTHOLDS IN SOUTH AND SOUTHEAST ASIA

Focus Question: How did European nations build empires in South and Southeast Asia?

As you read this section in your textbook, complete the flowchart below to identify causes and effects of European exploration in South and Southeast Asia. Some items have been entered for you.

Portugal	Netherlands	Spain	Britain
• Builds a rim of trading outposts and controls spice trade between Europe and Asia	• Establishes Cape Town and gains a secure foothold in the region		

Name_____ Class_____ Date_____

After Vasco da Gama's successful voyage to India, the Portuguese returned to the Indian Ocean. They were under the command of **Afonso de Albuquerque.** In 1510, the Portuguese seized the island of **Goa** off the coast of India. Then, they took the trading port of **Malacca.** In less than 50 years, the Portuguese built a trade empire with military and merchant **outposts.** For most of the 1500s, they controlled the spice trade between Europe and Asia.

The Dutch challenged the Portuguese control of Asian trade. In 1599, a Dutch fleet returned from Asia with a cargo of spices. Soon after, the Dutch set up colonies and trading posts around the world. This included their strategic settlement at Cape Town. From Cape Town they could repair and re-supply their ships. In 1602, a group of wealthy Dutch merchants formed the **Dutch East India Company,** which had full **sovereign** powers. This meant that the company could build armies, wage war, negotiate peace treaties, and govern overseas territory. Soon, the Dutch East India Company came to control much of southern Asia. Meanwhile, Spain took over the **Philippines,** which became a key link in its huge empire.

Mughal India was at the center of the valuable spice trade. The **Mughal empire** was larger, richer, and more powerful than any kingdom in Europe. Therefore, Mughal emperors saw no threat in granting trading rights to Europeans. Europeans were permitted to build forts and warehouses in coastal towns.

Over time, the Mughal empire weakened, however, and French and British traders fought for power. Like the Dutch, both the British and the French had formed East India companies. The British used their army of **sepoys,** or Indian troops, to drive out the French. By the late 1700s, the British East India Company had used its great wealth to take over most of India.

Review Questions

1. How did the Portuguese build a trade empire?

_____

_____

2. What are sovereign powers?

_____

_____

CHAPTER 2 SECTION 4

Note Taking Study Guide
ENCOUNTERS IN EAST ASIA

Focus Question: How were European encounters in East Asia shaped by the worldviews of both Europeans and Asians?

As you read this section in your textbook, complete the following chart to understand the effects of European contacts in East Asia. Some items have been completed for you.

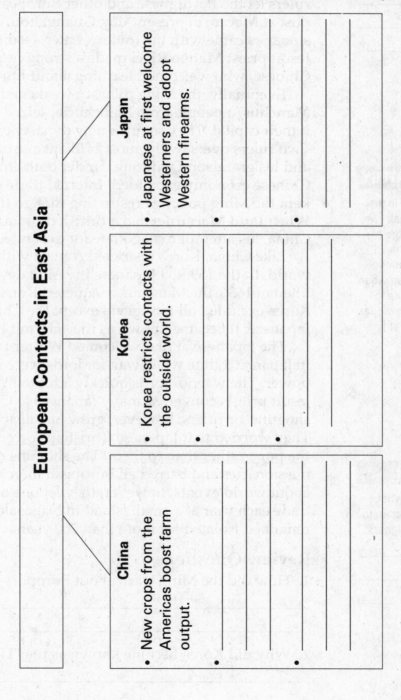

European Contacts in East Asia

Japan
- Japanese at first welcome Westerners and adopt Western firearms.

Korea
- Korea restricts contacts with the outside world.

China
- New crops from the Americas boost farm output.

Name_____ Class_____ Date_____

READING CHECK

What did the Manchus name their new dynasty?

_____

_____

Portuguese traders reached China in 1514. They wanted Chinese silks and porcelains, but the European goods they brought to trade were not as fine as Chinese products. The Chinese, therefore, asked to be paid in gold or silver. The Ming rulers let the Portuguese and other Europeans set up a trading post at **Macao,** in present-day **Guangzhou.** Portuguese missionaries came with the traders. Later, Jesuits arrived, too. The Jesuit priest **Matteo Ricci** made a strong impression on the Chinese, who welcomed learning about Europe.

Eventually, the Ming dynasty weakened. In 1644, the **Manchus,** a people from Manchuria, seized Beijing and made it their capital. They set up a new dynasty called the **Qing.** Two rulers oversaw the most brilliant age of the Qing—Kangxi and his grandson **Qianlong.** Under both emperors, the Chinese economy expanded. Internal trade grew. The Qing kept the Ming policy of restricting foreign traders, however. When **Lord Macartney** led a British diplomatic mission to China, his attempt to negotiate for expanded trade failed.

VOCABULARY STRATEGY

Find the word *allegiance* in the underlined sentence. Think about your prior knowledge of this word. You may say the Pledge of Allegiance at public events. What does it mean when you pledge your *allegiance* to something? Use prior knowledge to help you figure out what *allegiance* means.

Like China, Korea restricted contact with the outside world. In the 1590s, a Japanese invasion devastated Korea. Then in 1636, the Manchus conquered Korea. In response, Korea excluded all foreigners except the Chinese and a few Japanese. It became known as the "Hermit Kingdom."

The Japanese at first welcomed Westerners. Traders arrived in Japan at a time when warrior lords were struggling for power. The warrior lords quickly adopted Western firearms. Jesuit priests converted many Japanese to Christianity. The shoguns, or rulers, however, grew hostile toward foreigners. They worried that Japanese Christians owed their allegiance to the pope rather than to them. The shoguns expelled foreign missionaries and barred all European merchants. To learn about world events, however, they let one or two Dutch ships trade each year at a small island in **Nagasaki** harbor. Japan remained isolated for more than 200 years.

READING SKILL

Identify Effects Explain what caused the shoguns in Japan to grow hostile toward foreigners.

_____

_____

_____

Review Questions

1. How did the Ming learn about Europe?

_____

_____

2. Why did Korea become known as the "Hermit Kingdom"?

_____

_____

Name_____ Class_____ Date_____

Note Taking Study Guide

CONQUEST IN THE AMERICAS

Focus Question: How did a small number of Spanish conquistadors conquer huge Native American empires?

As you read this section of your textbook, fill in the chart below to help you sequence the events that led to European empires in the Americas. Some items have been completed for you.

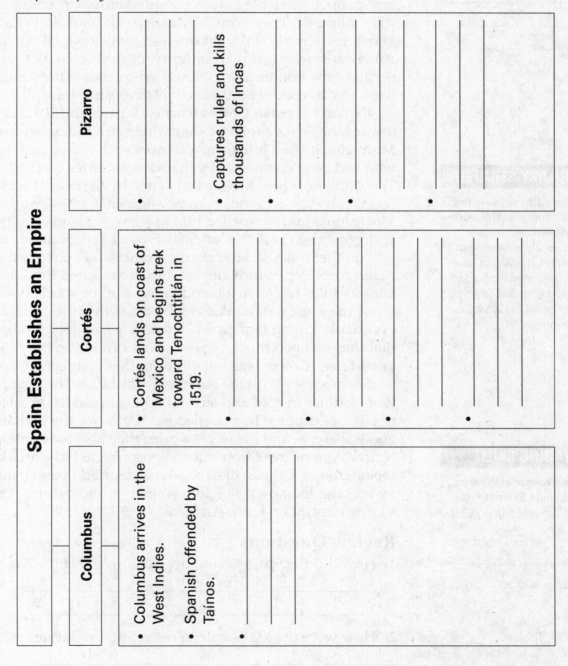

Spain Establishes an Empire

Pizarro
-
- Captures ruler and kills thousands of Incas

Cortés
- Cortés lands on coast of Mexico and begins trek toward Tenochtitlán in 1519.

Columbus
- Columbus arrives in the West Indies.
- Spanish offended by Taínos.

Name_____ Class_____ Date_____

READING CHECK

What was the name of the Aztec capital destroyed by Hernán Cortés?

_____

_____

_____

VOCABULARY STRATEGY

Find the word *compelled* in the underlined sentence. The word is a verb and so describes an action. Do you think Moctezuma was willing or unwilling to do what Cortés wanted him to do? Use the answer to this question to help you figure out what *compelled* means.

READING SKILL

Recognize Sequence What happened two years before Cortés destroyed Tenochtitlán in 1521?

_____

_____

_____

In 1492, Christopher Columbus reached the Caribbean islands in the present-day West Indies. Columbus' first encounter with Native Americans began a cycle of meeting, conquest, and death, which was repeated across the Western Hemisphere.

Columbus first met the Taíno people and claimed their land for Spain. A wave of Spanish **conquistadors,** or conquerors, soon followed. They brought weapons and horses. Without knowing, they also brought diseases, which wiped out Native Americans, who had no **immunity,** or resistance. Within a few decades, the hundreds of Spanish who came to the Americas were able to conquer millions of Native Americans.

Explorer **Hernán Cortés** reached Mexico in 1519 and moved toward the Aztec capital, **Tenochtitlán.** An Indian woman, **Malinche,** helped him form **alliances** with native peoples who had been conquered by the Aztecs. Cortés reached Tenochtitlán, where he was welcomed by the ruler, **Moctezuma.** Soon, however, relations became strained. <u>Cortés imprisoned Moctezuma and compelled him to sign over lands and treasure to the Spanish.</u> In 1521, Cortés destroyed Tenochtitlán.

Another Spanish adventurer, **Francisco Pizarro,** wanted riches from Peru's Inca empire. Pizarro reached Peru in 1532 after its ruler had won a bloody **civil war,** or war between people of the same nation. Pizarro captured the ruler, Atahualpa, eventually killing him. Spanish forces seized Inca lands. After that they claimed much of South America for Spain. A few years later, Pizarro was killed by another Spanish group.

Spain's impact on the Americas was huge. The Spanish took vast fortunes in gold and silver, making Spain the greatest power of Europe. They opened sea routes for the exchange of goods, people, and ideas. However, they also brought death to Native Americans. Many survivors converted to Christianity, seeking hope. Others, like the Maya, resisted Spanish influence by keeping their own religion, language, and culture. This left a large imprint on Latin America.

Review Questions

1. How did the Spanish conquer millions of Native Americans?

_____

_____

2. How were the Maya able to resist Spanish influence?

_____

_____

Name_____ Class_____ Date_____

Focus Question: How did Spain and Portugal build colonies in the Americas?

A. *As you read "Ruling the Spanish Empire," fill in the chart below to record the steps the Spanish took to establish an empire in America. Some items have been completed for you.*

Governing the empire	Catholic Church	Trade	Labor
• Viceroys • _____ _____	• Converted Native Americans to Christianity • _____ _____ • _____ _____	• _____ • Laws passed forbidding colonists from trading with other European nations or even with other Spanish colonies.	• Native Americans forced to work under brutal conditions on plantations and in mines under encomienda system. • _____ • _____

B. *As you read "Colonial Society and Culture" and "Beyond the Spanish Empire," fill in the Venn diagram below to compare and contrast the Spanish and Portuguese empires. Some items have been filled in for you.*

Spanish empire   **Portuguese empire**

- Claimed most of South America
- _____ _____

- Native Americans wiped out by disease.
- _____ _____
- _____ _____

- Claimed Brazil
- _____ _____

CHAPTER 3 SECTION 2

Section Summary

SPANISH AND PORTUGUESE COLONIES IN THE AMERICAS

VOCABULARY STRATEGY

Find the word *drastic* in the underlined sentence. What does *drastic* mean? What clues can you find in nearby words or phrases? Circle any context clues in the paragraph that could help you figure out what *drastic* means.

Spanish settlers followed conquerors into the Americas. There they built colonies and created a culture that blended European, Native American, and African traditions. By the mid-1500s, Spain's empire ran from modern California to South America.

The monarchy appointed **viceroys** to rule. To make the empire profitable, Spain forbade colonists to trade with any nation but Spain. Conquistadors were granted **encomiendas,** or the right to demand work from Native Americans.

Native Americans were forced to work under terrible conditions. Disease, starvation, and cruelty caused a drastic decline in their population. A priest, **Bartolomé de Las Casas,** begged the king to end the abuse. Such laws were passed in 1542. But Spain was too far away to enforce them. Some landlords forced people to become **peons,** or paid workers who were forced to work to repay huge debts. Also, colonists brought in millions of African slaves.

A blending of cultures resulted. Native Americans contributed building styles, foods, and arts. Settlers contributed Christianity and the use of animals, especially horses. Africans contributed farming methods, crops, and arts.

However, society had a strict structure. At the top were **peninsulares,** or people born in Spain. Next were **creoles,** or native-born descendants of Spanish settlers. Below them were the **mestizos,** people of Native American and European descent, and **mulattoes,** people of African and European descent. At the bottom were Native Americans and African slaves.

Portugal, too, had territory in South America in Brazil. As in Spanish colonies, Native Americans in Brazil were nearly wiped out by disease. Brazil's rulers also used African slaves and Native American labor. There, too, a new blended culture developed.

In the 1500s, wealth from the Americas made Spain the most powerful nation in Europe, followed by Portugal. Pirates often attacked treasure ships from their colonies. Some pirates, called **privateers,** even had the approval of their nations' governments.

Review Questions

1. What were encomiendas?

_____

_____

2. How were the Spanish and Portuguese colonies alike?

_____

_____

Focus Question: How did European struggles for power shape the North American continent?

As you read this section of your textbook, complete the following timeline to show the sequence of events in the struggle for North America. Some items have been completed for you.

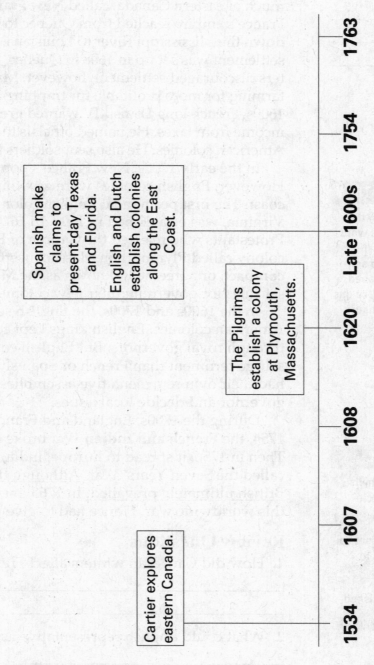

- 1763
- 1754
- Late 1600s — Spanish make claims to present-day Texas and Florida. English and Dutch establish colonies along the East Coast.
- 1620 — The Pilgrims establish a colony at Plymouth, Massachusetts.
- 1608
- 1607
- 1534 — Cartier explores eastern Canada.

CHAPTER 3 SECTION 3 — Section Summary
STRUGGLE FOR NORTH AMERICA

What was the name of the agreement written by the Pilgrims to set the rules for their new colony?

_____

_____

_____

Find the word *prevailed* in the underlined sentence. The word is a verb, so it describes an action. Read the next two sentences to see what happened after England *prevailed.* Use this context clue to help you figure out what *prevailed* means.

Recognize Sequence Which event happened first? Circle your answer.

• French king Louis XIV sent soldiers and more settlers to North America.

• Jamestown was established.

• The Pilgrims started a colony in the Americas.

In the 1600s, the French, Dutch, English, and Spanish competed for lands in North America. By 1700, France and England controlled large parts of North America. Their colonies differed in many ways.

In 1534, Jacques Cartier explored and claimed for the French much of eastern Canada, called **New France.** Eventually, France's empire reached from Quebec to the Great Lakes and down the Mississippi River to Louisiana. The first lasting French settlement was set up in 1608 in Quebec. Hard Canadian winters discouraged settlement, however. Many settlers gave up farming for more profitable fur trapping and fishing. In the late 1600s, French king Louis XIV wanted greater **revenue,** or income from taxes. He named officials to manage his North American colonies. He also sent soldiers and more settlers.

In the early 1700s, New France's population was small. However, English colonies were growing along the Atlantic coast. The first permanent English colony, Jamestown in Virginia, was established in 1607. In 1620, **Pilgrims,** or English Protestants who rejected the Church of England, started a colony called Plymouth in Massachusetts. They wrote a **compact,** or agreement, known as the Mayflower Compact. It set rules for governing their new colony.

In the 1600s and 1700s, the English set up several North American colonies. English kings kept control over them through royal governors. But English colonists had more self-government than French or Spanish colonists. The English had their own representative assemblies that could advise the governor and decide local issues.

During the 1700s, England and France became rivals. In 1754, the **French and Indian War** broke out in North America. Then in 1756, it spread to Europe, India, and Africa and was called the Seven Years' War. Although the war dragged on, the British ultimately prevailed. In 1763, the **Treaty of Paris** ended this worldwide war. France had to give up Canada to Britain.

Review Questions

1. How did Canadian winters affect French settlement?

_____

_____

2. What could English representative assemblies do?

_____

_____

Note Taking Study Guide
THE ATLANTIC SLAVE TRADE

Focus Question: How did the Atlantic slave trade shape the lives and economies of Africans and Europeans?

As you read this section in your textbook, complete the following flowchart to record the sequence of events that led to millions of Africans being brought to the Americas. Some of the items have been completed for you.

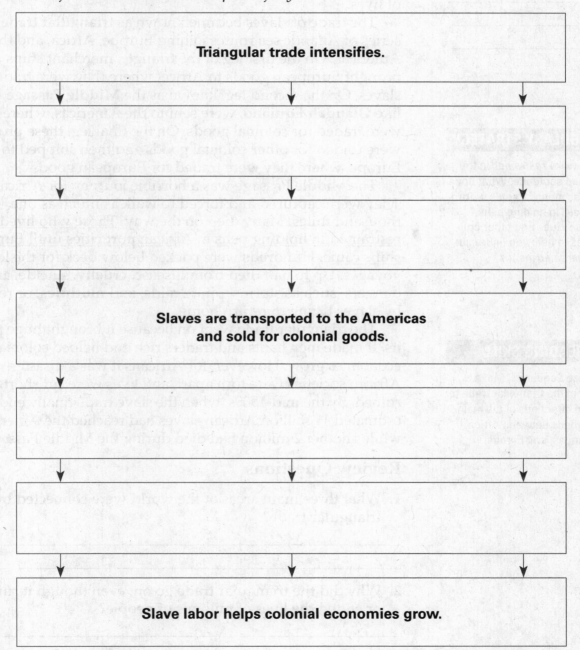

Triangular trade intensifies.

Slaves are transported to the Americas and sold for colonial goods.

Slave labor helps colonial economies grow.

Name_____ Class_____ Date_____

READING CHECK

Which European nation was the first to bring slaves to the Americas?

_____

_____

_____

VOCABULARY STRATEGY

Find the word *restrained* in the underlined sentence. What does *restrained* mean? People were *restrained* "in holding pens." Use these clues and other context clues to help you figure out what *restrained* means.

READING SKILL

Recognize Sequence Make a diagram of the triangular trade to show the directions of the main flow of goods between Africa, the Americas, and Europe.

Empires grew in the 1500s, and trade increased between the Americas and other parts of the world. Spain was the first major nation to buy slaves for its colonies, but the slave trade grew as other European countries set up colonies. Slave labor became a way to make huge profits, but at the cost of millions of lives.

The trade of slaves became known as **triangular trade,** a series of Atlantic sea routes joining Europe, Africa, and the Americas. On the first leg of the triangle, merchant ships brought European goods to Africa, where they were traded for slaves. On the second leg, known as the **Middle Passage,** slaves like **Olaudah Equiano,** were sent to the Americas, where they were traded for colonial goods. On the final leg, these products were traded for other colonial goods and then shipped to Europe, where they were traded for European goods.

The Middle Passage was a horrible journey for Africans. They were captured and forced to walk as much as one thousand miles. Many died on the way. <u>Those who lived were restrained in holding pens in African port cities until European ships came.</u> Hundreds were packed below deck for the long voyages. Up to half died from disease, cruelty, suicide, and dangers, such as storms, pirate raids, and **mutinies,** or revolts, by slaves trying to return home.

The triangular trade went on because it brought huge profits. It made merchants and traders rich and helped colonial economies grow. However, for Africans it was a disaster. African societies were torn apart, and lives were cut short or ruined. By the mid-1800s, when the slave trade finally ended, an estimated 11 million African slaves had reached the Americas, while another 2 million had died during the Middle Passage.

Review Questions

1. What three main areas of the world were connected by the triangular trade?

_____

_____

2. Why did the triangular trade go on, even though it ruined or ended the lives of millions of people?

_____

_____

CHAPTER 3 SECTION 5

Note Taking Study Guide

EFFECTS OF GLOBAL CONTACT

Focus Question: How did the voyages of European explorers lead to new economic systems in Europe and its colonies?

A. *As you read "The Columbian Exchange," complete the following flowchart to record the sequence of events that led to the Columbian Exchange, as well as the effects. Some of the items have been completed for you.*

Causes	Columbian Exchange	Effects
• Age of exploration begins. • _____ • _____	• _____ • _____ • Named for Columbus, whose voyage began the exchange	• _____ • Native American diets improve; horses and donkeys transport goods and people. • _____ • New crops lead to population growth all over the world. • Millions of people migrate. • Populations wiped out by disease and war.

B. *As you read "A Commercial Revolution," complete the following flowchart to record the sequence of events that led to new global economic systems, as well as the effects. Some of the items have been completed for you.*

Causes	New Economic Systems	Effects
• _____ _____ • Growing demand for goods • Fierce competition for trade and empires	• Capitalism • _____ • Mercantilism	• _____ • Putting-out system led to capitalist-owned factories of the Industrial Revolution. • _____ • Merchants and skilled workers prospered. • Middle-class families enjoyed a comfortable life.

Name_____ Class_____ Date_____

What is the name for the global interchange begun by Columbus' first voyage?

_____

_____

_____

Find the word *dispersal* in the underlined sentence. What does *dispersal* mean? What clues to the word's meaning can you find in nearby words or phrases? Circle any context clues that help you figure out what *dispersal* means.

Recognize Sequence Place these events in the correct order:

____ The price revolution takes place.

____ Inflation occurs.

____ Enormous amounts of silver and gold flow into Europe.

Exploration in the 1500s and 1600s led to European control of the globe. By the 1700s, worldwide contact had caused huge changes to people in Europe, Asia, Africa, and the Americas.

When Columbus returned to Europe in 1493, he brought back American plants and animals. He carried European plants, animals, and settlers back to the Americas. A vast global interchange began. Named for Columbus, it was called the **Columbian Exchange.** Sharing different foods and animals helped people around the world. Later, this dispersal of new crops from the Americas led to worldwide population growth.

Another result of global contact was economic change. In the 1500s, **inflation** increased in Europe, due to all the silver and gold from the Americas. Inflation is a rise in prices because of sharp increases in the money supply. This period of rapid inflation in Europe was known as the **price revolution.** Out of these changes came **capitalism,** an economic system of privately owned business. **Entrepreneurs,** or people who take financial risk for profits, were key to the success of capitalism. Europe's entrepreneurs created businesses and joined investors in overseas ventures. This changed local economies into international trading economies. Fierce competition for trade and empires, in turn, led to a new economic system, called **mercantilism.** Under this system, a nation's wealth was measured in gold and silver, and nations had to export more than they imported. Mercantilists also pushed governments to impose **tariffs,** or taxes on imported goods. This would give an advantage to local products by making imports cost more.

Economic changes, however, took centuries to affect most Europeans. However, by the 1700s, many social changes had happened, too. Nobles, whose wealth was in land, were hurt by the price revolution. Merchants who invested in new businesses grew wealthy. Skilled workers in growing cities also prospered, creating a thriving middle class.

Review Questions

1. Why did mercantilists push governments to impose tariffs?

_____

_____

2. By the 1700s, who was being helped by economic changes?

_____

_____

CHAPTER 4 SECTION 1

Note Taking Study Guide

SPANISH POWER GROWS

Focus Questions: How did Philip II extend Spain's power and help establish a golden age?

As you read this section in your textbook, use the outline to identify main ideas and supporting details about Spain's power. Some details have been completed for you.

I. Charles V Inherits Two Crowns

   A. Ruling the Hapsburg empire

      1. Spain

      2. Holy Roman Empire and Netherlands

   B. Charles V abdicates

      1. Charles enters monastery in 1556 and divides empire.

      2. _____

      3. _____

II. Philip II Solidifies Power

   A. Centralizing power

      1. Philip II reigns as an absolute monarch.

      2. Rules by divine right

   B. Battles in the Mediterranean and the Netherlands

      1. Philip fights wars to advance Spanish Catholic power.

      2. Protestant provinces of the Netherlands declare their independence.

   C. The armada sails against England.

      1. Philip considers Elizabeth I of England his enemy.

      2. Spanish armada is defeated.

   D. An empire declines

      1. _____

      2. _____

      3. _____

      4. _____

      5. _____

(Outline continues on the next page.)

Note Taking Study Guide

CHAPTER 4 SECTION 1

SPANISH POWER GROWS

(Continued from page 63)

III. Spain's Golden Age

A. _____

_____

B. _____

_____

C. _____

_____

D. _____

_____

E. _____

_____

Section Summary

SPANISH POWER GROWS

In 1516, **Charles V** was the king of Spain and ruler of the Spanish colonies in the Americas. In 1519, he inherited the **Hapsburg empire.** This included the Holy Roman Empire and the Netherlands. Ruling two empires involved Charles in constant warfare. In addition, the empire's large territory was too cumbersome for Charles to rule well. The difficult and demanding responsibilities led him to give up his throne in 1556. He divided his kingdom between his brother Ferdinand and son Philip.

Philip II was successful in increasing Spanish power in Europe and strengthening the Catholic Church. Philip also ruled as an **absolute monarch**—a ruler with complete authority over the government and the lives of the people. He also declared that he ruled by **divine right.** This meant he believed that his right to rule came from God. Philip was determined to defend the Catholic Church against the Protestant Reformation in Europe. He fought many battles in the Mediterranean and the Netherlands to extend and preserve Spanish Catholic power.

To expand his kingdom, Philip II needed to eliminate his enemies. Elizabeth I of England was his chief Protestant enemy. Philip prepared a huge **armada,** or fleet, to carry an invasion force to England. However, English ships were faster and lighter than Spanish ships. After several disasters, the Spanish sailed home defeated. The defeat of the armada marked the beginning of the end of Spanish power.

While Spain's strength and wealth decreased, the arts in Spain flourished under Philip's support. The years between 1550 and 1650 are often called Spain's *Siglo de Oro,* or "golden century." Among the famous artists of this time was the painter **El Greco.** His work influenced many other artists. This period also produced several remarkable writers. One of the most important was **Miguel de Cervantes.** His *Don Quixote,* which pokes fun at medieval tales of chivalry, was Europe's first modern novel.

Review Questions

1. What territories were included in the Hapsburg empire?

_____

_____

2. Why did Philip fight many battles?

_____

_____

READING CHECK

What is an absolute monarch?

_____

_____

_____

VOCABULARY STRATEGY

Find the word *cumbersome* in the underlined sentence. What does *cumbersome* mean? What clues to its meaning can you find in the surrounding words, phrases, or sentences? Circle the words in the paragraph that could help you figure out what *cumbersome* means.

READING SKILL

Identify Main Ideas and Supporting Details What details in this Summary support the main idea: Spanish power grew in the early 1500s?

_____

_____

_____

CHAPTER
4
SECTION 2

Note Taking Study Guide
FRANCE UNDER LOUIS XIV

Focus Question: How did France become the leading power of Europe under the absolute rule of Louis XIV?

As you read this section in your textbook, complete the concept web to identify supporting details about the rule of King Louis XIV. Some details have been completed for you.

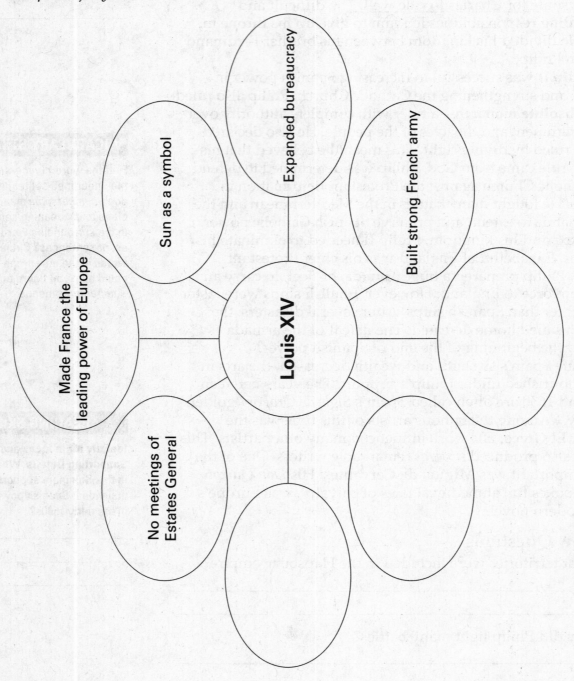

Section Summary

CHAPTER 4 SECTION 2

FRANCE UNDER LOUIS XIV

In the late 1500s, France was torn by religious conflict between French Protestants, called **Huguenots,** and Catholics. During the St. Bartholomew's Day Massacre, thousands of Huguenots were killed. In 1598, **Henry IV** issued the **Edict of Nantes.** This protected Huguenots by allowing them to follow their religion.

After Henry's assassination in 1610, his nine-year old son, Louis XIII, became king. **Cardinal Richelieu** was his chief minister. For 18 years Richelieu worked to make the central government stronger. Then in 1643, five-year-old **Louis XIV** became king. As he grew older, he chose to control the government himself. Louis XIV called himself the Sun King to symbolize his importance.

Louis XIV appointed **intendants** to the royal government. These were royal officials who collected taxes, recruited soldiers, and carried out the king's policies. To boost the country's economy, Louis's finance minister, **Jean Baptiste Colbert,** started expanding business and trade. Taxes helped to finance the king's extravagant lifestyle.

Outside Paris, Louis XIV transformed a hunting lodge into the palace of **Versailles.** This palace represented the king's power and wealth. Ceremonies were held there to emphasize the king's importance. For example, high-ranking nobles would compete to be part of the king's morning ritual known as the *levée,* or rising. These kinds of ceremonies were meant to keep nobles at Versailles with the king. That way, Louis could gain their support and keep them from battling for power.

Under Louis XIV, France became Europe's most powerful state. <u>However, some of Louis's decisions caused the country's prosperity to erode.</u> His lifestyle and the wars he fought were costly. Rival rulers joined together to keep the **balance of power.** They wanted military and economic power spread evenly among European nations. For example, in 1700, when Louis's grandson inherited the throne of Spain, nearby nations fought to prevent the union of France and Spain.

Review Questions

1. What was the Edict of Nantes?

_____

_____

2. What did Versailles symbolize?

_____

_____

READING CHECK

Why did France's economy decline?

_____

_____

_____

VOCABULARY STRATEGY

Find the word *erode* in the underlined sentence. A related word is *erosion.* Think about what happens when a hillside *erodes.* Use your prior knowledge to help you figure out the meaning of *erode.*

READING SKILL

Identify Supporting Details A main idea in this Summary is that Louis XIV increased his power. What details can you find that support this main idea?

_____

_____

_____

Name_____ Class_____ Date_____

Note Taking Study Guide
PARLIAMENT TRIUMPHS IN ENGLAND

Focus Question: How did the British Parliament assert its rights against royal claims to absolute power in the 1600s?

As you read this section in your textbook, complete the flowchart to identify supporting details about the evolution of Parliament. Some details have been completed for you.

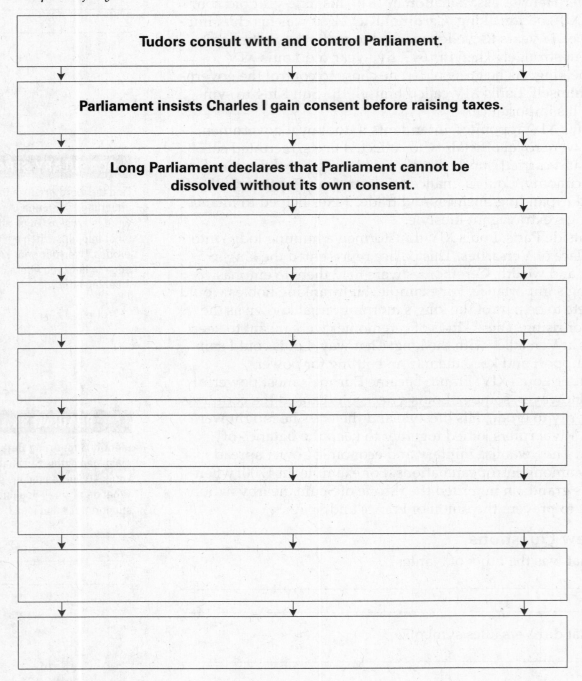

> **Tudors consult with and control Parliament.**

> **Parliament insists Charles I gain consent before raising taxes.**

> **Long Parliament declares that Parliament cannot be dissolved without its own consent.**

CHAPTER 4 SECTION 3

Section Summary

PARLIAMENT TRIUMPHS IN ENGLAND

The first Stuart king, **James I,** inherited the throne in 1603. He claimed absolute power. James clashed with Parliament. He also clashed with **dissenters**—Protestants who disagreed with the Church of England. One such group, the **Puritans,** wanted simpler services and a more democratic church without bishops.

In 1625, James's son **Charles I** inherited the throne. He, too, claimed absolute power. Tensions between Charles and Parliament turned into the English Civil War. It lasted from 1642 to 1651. Supporters of Charles were called Cavaliers. The supporters of Parliament were known as Roundheads. **Oliver Cromwell,** the leader of the Parliament forces, guided them to victory. In January 1649, Parliament had Charles executed.

The House of Commons then abolished the monarchy and declared England a republic, called the Commonwealth. It was ruled by Cromwell. Many new laws were passed, reflecting Puritan beliefs. <u>Cromwell did not tolerate open worship for Catholics.</u> He did respect the beliefs of other Protestants and welcomed Jews back to England. Eventually, people tired of the strict Puritan ways. Cromwell died in 1658. In 1660, Parliament invited Charles II, the son of Charles I, to rule.

Charles II's successor, James II, was forced from the throne in 1688. Protestants feared that he planned to restore the Roman Catholic Church. Parliament offered the crown to James's Protestant daughter, Mary, and her husband, William. This peaceful change of rulers is known as the Glorious Revolution. However, William and Mary first had to accept the **English Bill of Rights.** The Bill of Rights made sure that Parliament had more power than the ruler. This helped establish a **limited monarchy.**

Over time, Britain's government became a **constitutional government**. The law set limits on power. A **cabinet,** or group of parliamentary advisors who set policies, developed. In essence, the British government was an **oligarchy**—a government run by a few powerful people.

Review Questions

1. What was the result of the English Civil War?

_____

_____

2. Who was Oliver Cromwell?

_____

_____

READING CHECK

Why was James II forced from the throne?

_____

_____

_____

VOCABULARY STRATEGY

Find the word *tolerate* in the underlined sentence. What do you think it means? In the next sentence, there is a phrase that means the same thing as *tolerate*. Use that context clue to help you figure out the meaning of *tolerate*.

READING SKILL

Identify Supporting Details The Bill of Rights was a triumph for Parliament. What details in this Summary support that main idea?

_____

_____

_____

CHAPTER 4 SECTION 4

Note Taking Study Guide

RISE OF AUSTRIA AND PRUSSIA

Focus Question: How did the two great empires of Austria and Prussia emerge from the Thirty Years' War and subsequent events?

As you read this section in your textbook, use the table to identify supporting details about the emergence of Austria and Prussia as European powers. Some details have been completed for you.

Rise of Austria	Rise of Prussia
• Austrian ruler keeps title of Holy Roman Emperor. • Ferdinand, Hapsburg king of Bohemia, tries to suppress Protestants and assert power over nobles. • •	• Hohenzollern rulers take over German states. • •

Name_____ Class_____ Date_____

Section Summary
RISE OF AUSTRIA AND PRUSSIA

By the seventeenth century, the Holy Roman Empire had become a mix of many small, separate states. In theory, the Holy Roman emperor, who was chosen by seven leading German princes called **electors,** ruled these states. Yet, the emperor had little power. This lack of power contributed to a series of wars that are together called the Thirty Years' War. It began when **Ferdinand,** the Catholic Hapsburg king of Bohemia, wanted to control Protestants and declare royal power over nobles. This led to a widespread European war.

The Thirty Years' War had a terrible effect on the German states. **Mercenaries,** or soldiers for hire, burned villages, destroyed crops, and killed villagers. There was famine and disease, which caused severe **depopulation,** meaning populations were very low.

It was not until 1648 that a series of treaties known as the **Peace of Westphalia** were set up. <u>These treaties aspired to bring peace to Europe and sought to settle other problems between nations.</u>

While Austria was becoming a strong Catholic state, one of the German states, called **Prussia,** emerged as a new Protestant power. The Prussian ruler **Frederick William I** came to power in 1713. He placed great importance on military values.

In Austria, **Maria Theresa** became empress following her father's death in 1740. That same year, **Frederick II** of Prussia seized the Hapsburg province of Silesia. This led to the **War of the Austrian Succession.** Maria Theresa could not force Frederick out of Silesia. She did, however, preserve her empire and won the support of most of her people. She also strengthened Hapsburg power. She reorganized the government and forced nobles and clergy to pay taxes.

Frederick II continued to use his army to build his country's strength. His acts made Prussia a leading power. By 1750, Austria and Prussia were considered great European powers along with France, Britain, and Russia.

Review Questions
1. Describe the Holy Roman Empire of the seventeenth century.

_____

_____

2. How did Maria Theresa strengthen Austria?

_____

_____

READING CHECK

Who were the great European powers by 1750?

_____

_____

_____

VOCABULARY STRATEGY

Find the word *aspired* in the underlined sentence. The word *strived* is a synonym for *aspired.* Apply what you already know about *strived* to help you learn the meaning of *aspired.*

READING SKILL

Identify Supporting Details
What details support the main idea that the Thirty Years' War had a terrible effect on the German states?

_____

_____

_____

Name_____ Class_____ Date_____

Focus Question: How did Peter the Great and Catherine the Great strengthen Russia and expand its territory?

As you read this section in your textbook, complete the Venn diagram to identify the main ideas about the reigns of Peter the Great and Catherine the Great. Some ideas have been completed for you.

Catherine

- Established warm-water port on Black Sea
-
-

Adopted Western Ideas

Peter

- Visited European countries
- Controlled the Church and nobles
- Created a standing army
-
-

CHAPTER 4 SECTION 5

Section Summary

ABSOLUTE MONARCHY IN RUSSIA

In the early 1600s, Russia was far behind the more advanced western European nations. By the end of that century, however, a new tsar, **Peter the Great,** turned Russia into a leading power.

To modernize Russia, Peter began a new policy of **westernization**—the adoption of Western ideas, technologies, and culture. Many resisted change. To enforce this new policy, Peter became an **autocratic** monarch. This meant that he ruled with unlimited authority.

All Russian institutions were under Peter the Great's control. He executed anyone who resisted the new order. He forced the **boyars**—landowning nobles—to serve the state in civilian or military positions. Peter also stipulated that they shave their beards and wear Western-style clothing.

Peter built up Russia's military power and extended the borders. To increase Russia's trade with the West, the Russians needed a **warm-water port.** The nearest port was on the Black Sea in the Ottoman empire. Peter, however, could not defeat the Ottomans.

Determined to expand Russia's territory, however, Peter fought a long war against Sweden. On the land he won, he built a beautiful capital city, **St. Petersburg.** It became the symbol of modern Russia. When Peter died in 1725, he had expanded Russian territory, gained ports on the Baltic Sea, and created a strong army.

In 1762, **Catherine the Great** followed Peter's lead in embracing Western ideas and expanding Russia's borders. She, too, ruled as an absolute monarch. She was able to defeat the Ottoman empire and finally won the warm-water port on the Black Sea.

In the 1770s, Russia, Prussia, and Austria each wanted Poland as part of their territory. To avoid war, they agreed to **partition,** or divide up, Poland. In 1772, Russia gained part of eastern Poland, while Prussia and Austria took over the west. Poland ceased to exist.

Review Questions

1. Who transformed Russia into a leading power?

_____

_____

2. What kept Peter the Great from gaining a warm-water port?

_____

_____

READING CHECK

What does *westernization* mean?

_____

_____

_____

VOCABULARY STRATEGY

Find the word *stipulated* in the underlined sentence. It comes from a Latin word that means "to bargain." Think about the bargaining process. Usually people have to agree on specific terms. Use this word-origins clue to help you figure out the meaning of *stipulated.*

READING SKILL

Identify Main Ideas Circle the statement below that identifies the main idea of the Summary.

Catherine the Great freed the serfs.

Peter and Catherine enjoyed Western-style clothing.

Peter and Catherine ruled as absolute monarchs.

Name_____ Class_____ Date_____

Focus Question: What effects did Enlightenment philosophers have on government and society?

As you read this section in your textbook, complete the following table to summarize each thinker's works and ideas. Some items have been completed for you.

Thinkers' Works and Ideas	
Hobbes	• *Leviathan*
	• _____
Locke	• *Two Treatises of Government*
	• _____
	• _____
Montesquieu	• _____
	• _____
	• _____
	• _____
	• _____
	• _____
	• _____
	• _____
	• _____
	• _____
	• _____
	• _____
	• _____

<table>
<tr><td>CHAPTER
5
SECTION 1</td><td>## Section Summary
PHILOSOPHY IN THE AGE OF REASON</td></tr>
</table>

In the 1500s and 1600s, the Scientific Revolution changed the way people looked at the world. They began to use reason and science to learn how things worked. For example, they found that rules govern natural forces such as gravity. Scientists and others began to call these rules the **natural law.** They believed that natural law could be used to solve society's problems, too. In this way the Scientific Revolution sparked another revolution in thinking known as the Enlightenment.

Two important English thinkers of the Enlightenment were **Thomas Hobbes** and **John Locke.** Hobbes argued that people were naturally cruel and selfish. They needed to be controlled by a powerful government, such as an absolute monarchy. According to Hobbes, people made an agreement, or **social contract.** In this contract, people gave up their freedom in exchange for an organized society. In contrast, Locke thought that people were basically good. He believed that people had **natural rights,** or rights that belonged to all humans. These are the right to life, liberty, and property. Locke rejected absolute monarchy. He thought a government of limited power was best.

French Enlightenment thinkers, called *philosophes,* also believed that people could use reason to improve government, law, and society. These thinkers included Baron de **Montesquieu, Voltaire,** Denis **Diderot,** and Jean-Jacques **Rousseau.** Montesquieu, for example, developed the ideas of separation of powers and of checks and balances. These ideas would be used by the Framers of the United States Constitution. In a set of books called the *Encyclopedia,* Diderot explained the new ideas on the topics of government, philosophy, and religion.

Other thinkers, including **Adam Smith,** focused on using natural law to reform the economy. Instead of government control, they urged the policy of **laissez faire.** This allowed the free market to regulate business.

Review Questions

1. What is the natural law?

_____

_____

2. Which of Montesquieu's ideas appear in the U.S. Constitution?

_____

_____

READING CHECK

Who were the *philosophes*?

_____

_____

_____

VOCABULARY STRATEGY

Find the word *philosophy* in the underlined sentence. The word *philosophy* comes from a Greek word that means "love of wisdom." *Philosophe,* which means "philosopher," comes from the same ancient Greek word. Reread the paragraph about the *philosophes.* Use the word-origin clues to help you figure out what *philosophy* means.

READING SKILL

Summarize What did Thomas Hobbes believe about people and the government?

_____

_____

_____

Name_____ Class_____ Date_____

Focus Question: As Enlightenment ideas spread across Europe, what cultural and political changes took place?

A. *As you read "New Ideas Challenge Society" and "Arts and Literature Reflect New Ideas," complete the following concept web to categorize how Enlightenment ideas spread. Some items have been completed for you.*

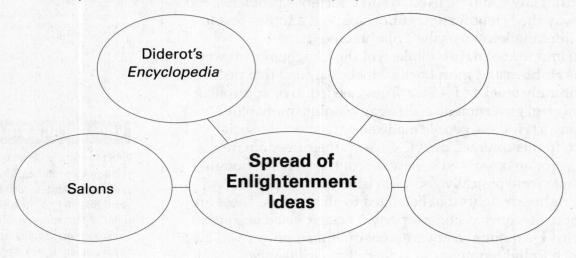

B. *As you read "Enlightened Despots Embrace New Ideas" and "Lives of the Majority Change Slowly," complete the following concept web to summarize information about enlightened despots and their contributions. Some items have been completed for you.*

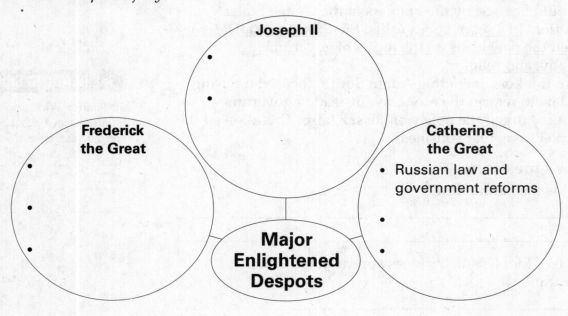

CHAPTER 5 SECTION 2

Section Summary
ENLIGHTENMENT IDEAS SPREAD

Enlightenment ideas flowed from France, across Europe and beyond. Before the Enlightenment, society was based on old ways of doing things. These included divine-right rule, a strict class system, and a belief in heavenly reward for earthly suffering. Enlightenment ideas challenged traditional beliefs and customs. In response, government and church leaders practiced **censorship.** They banned and burned books containing new ideas they did not like. They put writers in prison. Censorship, however, did not stop the spread of ideas. Writers disguised their ideas in works of fiction. Ideas continued to spread in **salons,** or informal social gatherings. There, writers, artists, and *philosophes* shared ideas about new literature, the arts, science, and philosophy.

In the 1600s and 1700s, the arts also evolved to meet the changing tastes and the new Enlightenment ideals. In art and in music, there was a shift from the heavy style of **baroque** to the more charming style of **rococo.** Later, composers wrote works in an elegant style called classical. New forms of literature developed, also. For example, new kinds of books called novels were being written for the growing group of middle-class readers.

Some changes happened in government, too. *Philosophes* tried to persuade European rulers to accept Enlightenment ideas. Some monarchs did. These **enlightened despots** used their power to bring about some political and social changes. In Prussia, **Frederick the Great** allowed a free press. He also urged religious tolerance. **Catherine the Great** of Russia abolished torture. In Austria, **Joseph II** traveled in disguise among his subjects to learn of their problems. Even though ideas of the Enlightenment spread, the lives of most Europeans changed slowly.

Review Questions

1. How did government and church leaders censor Enlightenment ideas?

_____

_____

2. What new art and musical styles developed during the Enlightenment?

_____

_____

READING CHECK

Name one European ruler who was an enlightened despot.

_____

_____

_____

VOCABULARY STRATEGY

Find the word *evolved* in the underlined sentence. What surrounding words or phrases can you find that might give you clues about its meaning? Circle the context clues in the paragraph that helped you to learn what *evolved* means.

READING SKILL

Summarize How were Enlightenment ideas spread across Europe?

_____

_____

_____

Name_____ Class_____ Date_____

Focus Question: How did ideas of the Enlightenment lead to the independence and founding of the United States of America?

As you read this section in your textbook, complete the following timeline with events that led to the formation of the United States. Some items have been completed for you.

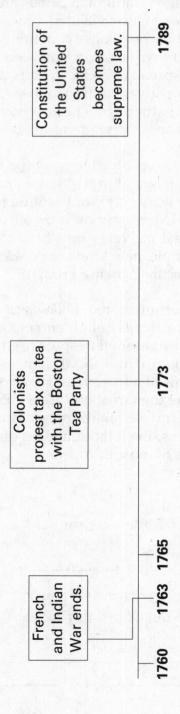

Constitution of the United States becomes supreme law. — 1789

Colonists protest tax on tea with the Boston Tea Party — 1773

1765

French and Indian War ends. — 1763

1760

CHAPTER 5 SECTION 3

Section Summary

BIRTH OF THE AMERICAN REPUBLIC

In the mid-1700s, Britain was a global power. The new king, George III, wanted to assert his leadership and expand his rule. Britain's huge territories included colonies in North America. However, society and politics in these colonies developed in their own way. Some colonists began to feel that maybe they would do better if they did not belong to Britain.

Tensions between the colonists and Britain grew. The British Parliament passed laws, such as the **Stamp Act,** that increased colonists' taxes. The colonists felt they should not be taxed because they had no one to speak for them in the British Parliament. A series of violent clashes with British soldiers strengthened the colonists' anger. Leaders from each colony, including **George Washington,** met in a Continental Congress to decide what to do. In April 1775, however, tensions exploded into war. The American Revolution began.

On July 4, 1776, American leaders adopted the Declaration of Independence. Written mostly by **Thomas Jefferson,** it includes John Locke's ideas about the rights to "life, liberty, and property." It outlines the reasons for wanting to be free of British rule and claims **popular sovereignty.** This principle states that all government power comes from the people.

At first, it did not look like the Americans could win. Britain had trained soldiers and a huge fleet. However, later France and other European nations joined the American side, and helped bring about the British surrender at **Yorktown, Virginia.** In 1783, the **Treaty of Paris** ended the war.

Leaders of the new American nation, such as **James Madison** and **Benjamin Franklin,** wrote the Constitution creating a **federal republic.** The new government was based on the separation of powers, an idea borrowed from Montesquieu, an Enlightenment thinker. The Constitution included the Bill of Rights, which listed basic rights that the government must protect.

Review Questions

1. Why did colonists feel they should not be taxed?

_____

_____

2. What ideas of John Locke are in the Declaration of Independence?

_____

_____

READING CHECK

What kind of government did the Constitution create?

_____

_____

_____

VOCABULARY STRATEGY

Find the word *assert* in the underlined sentence. What context clues can you find in the surrounding words, phrases, or sentences that hint at its meaning? Think about what a king would do if he wanted to *assert* his leadership. Circle the word below that has the same meaning as *assert*.

1. declare

2. deny

READING SKILL

Recognize Sequence Place the following events in order:

• Declaration of Independence written

• Continental Congress meets

• Treaty of Paris signed

• Parliament passes Stamp Act.

1._____

2._____

3._____

4._____

Name_____ Class_____ Date_____

Focus Question: What led to the storming of the Bastille, and therefore, to the start of the French Revolution?

As you read this section in your textbook, complete the following chart by identifying the multiple causes of the French Revolution. Some items have been completed for you.

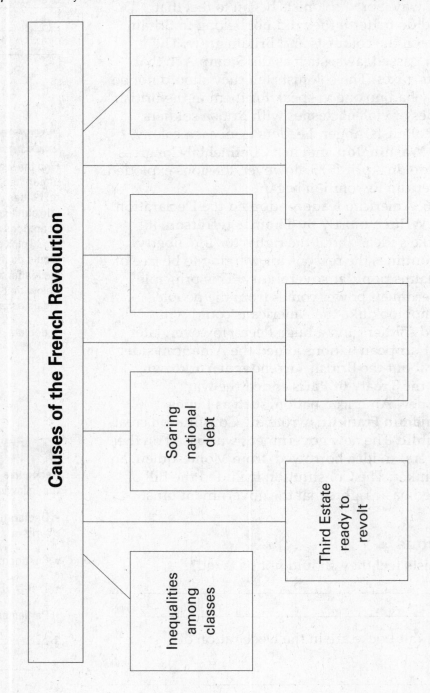

Causes of the French Revolution

Soaring national debt

Inequalities among classes

Third Estate ready to revolt

CHAPTER 6 SECTION 1

Section Summary

ON THE EVE OF REVOLUTION

Under France's **ancien régime**, there were three social classes, or **estates**. The clergy made up the First Estate. The nobles made up the Second Estate. Everyone else, including the **bourgeoisie,** or middle class, belonged to the Third Estate. Most of the Third Estate was made up of rural peasants. Its poorest members were urban workers.

Members of the Third Estate resented the privileges enjoyed by the other classes. The First and Second Estates, for example, paid almost no taxes. Yet peasants paid taxes on many things. People began to question this inequality.

Economic troubles added to France's social problems. France was deeply in debt because of **deficit spending.** Bad harvests sent food prices soaring. **Louis XVI** chose **Jacques Necker** as his financial advisor. Necker proposed taxing the First and Second Estates, but the nobles and high clergy forced the king to dismiss him. As 1788 ended, France was nearly bankrupt. Louis XVI called for the **Estates-General** to meet at Versailles. The Estates-General was the lawmaking body made up of the three classes. Before the meeting, the king had all three estates prepare **cahiers**, or notebooks, listing their complaints. The long lists of problems showed how deeply the Third Estate resented the other two estates.

The Estates-General met in May 1789. Delegates of the Third Estate took a daring step. They claimed to represent the people of France and formed a new National Assembly. Locked out of their meeting place, the delegates took their famous **Tennis Court Oath.** They swore never to separate until they had established a just constitution.

On July 14, 1789, the streets of Paris buzzed with rumors that royal troops were going to occupy the city. A crowd gathered outside the **Bastille,** a grim fortress used as a prison. They demanded weapons that were stored there. When the commander refused, the angry mob stormed the Bastille, sparking the French Revolution.

Review Questions

1. What were the three classes during France's ancien régime?

_____

_____

2. Why was France in debt?

_____

_____

READING CHECK

Which social classes paid the least in taxes?

_____

_____

_____

VOCABULARY STRATEGY

Find the word *urban* in the underlined sentence. Notice that the word *rural* appears in the previous sentence. *Rural* means "country." *Rural* is an antonym of *urban,* so it has the opposite meaning. Use what you know about the word *rural* to help you figure out what *urban* means.

READING SKILL

Recognize Multiple Causes List two causes of the French Revolution.

_____

_____

_____

CHAPTER 6 SECTION 2

Note Taking Study Guide

THE FRENCH REVOLUTION UNFOLDS

Focus Question: What political and social reforms did the National Assembly institute in the first stage of the French Revolution?

As you read this section in your textbook, complete the following outline by identifying the main ideas and supporting details in this section. Some items have been completed for you.

I. Political crisis leads to revolt

    A. The Great Fear

        1. Inflamed by famine and rumors

        2. _____

    B. Paris Commune comes to power.

        1. _____

        2. _____

II. The National Assembly acts

    A. Special privilege ends.

        1. _____

        2. _____

    B. Declaration of the Rights of Man

        1. _____

        2. _____

    C. _____

        1. _____

        2. _____

III. The National Assembly presses onward

    A. The Church is placed under state control.

        1. _____

        2. _____

    B. _____

        1. _____

        2. _____

    C. _____

        1. _____

        2. _____

(Outline continues on the next page.)

CHAPTER 6 SECTION 2

Note Taking Study Guide

THE FRENCH REVOLUTION UNFOLDS

(Continued from page 82)

IV. _____
- A. _____
  - 1. _____
  - 2. _____
- B. _____
  - 1. _____
  - 2. _____
- C. _____
  - 1. _____
  - 2. _____
- D. _____
  - 1. _____
  - 2. _____

CHAPTER 6 SECTION 2	**Section Summary**
	THE FRENCH REVOLUTION UNFOLDS

READING CHECK

What kind of government did the sans-culottes want?

_____

_____

_____

In France, the political crisis of 1789 happened at the same time as a famine. Starving peasants took out their anger on the nobles. Many **factions,** or dissenting groups of people, struggled for power. Moderates looked to the **Marquis de Lafayette** for leadership. However, a more radical group, the Paris Commune, took over the city's government.

The storming of the Bastille and the peasant revolts forced the National Assembly to act. Nobles gave up their privileges. In late August, the Assembly issued the Declaration of the Rights of Man and the Citizen. It proclaimed that all male citizens were equal. However, it did not grant equal rights to women. Journalist **Olympe de Gouges** wrote a declaration that did, but the Assembly did not accept it.

VOCABULARY STRATEGY

Find the word *proclaimed* in the underlined sentence. What do you think it means? The words *proclamation, declaration,* and *announcement* are all synonyms of *proclaimed.* They are words with similar meanings. Use what you know about these synonyms to figure out the meaning of *proclaimed.*

In the meantime, the king hesitated to accept reforms. His queen, **Marie Antoinette,** angered many for spending money while people starved. Thousands of women marched to Versailles, where the royal family lived. They demanded the king return to Paris. The National Assembly soon drafted the Constitution of 1791. It reflected Enlightenment goals, stating that all male citizens were equal under the law, and placing the Church under state control.

Events in France caused debate all over Europe. Some praised the reforms. European rulers, however, feared the French Revolution. They worried that the rebellion would spread. The horror stories told by French **émigrés** who fled the revolution added to the fear.

In October 1791, the newly elected Legislative Assembly took power. However, it did little to improve conditions. Working-class men and women called **sans-culottes** pushed for more radical action. Some demanded a **republic.** The **Jacobins,** a revolutionary political club, supported the sans-culottes. The radicals soon controlled the Legislative Assembly. They were eager to spread the revolution and declared war against Austria and other European monarchies.

READING SKILL

Identify Supporting Details
Identify two Enlightenment goals that are found in the Constitution of 1791.

_____

_____

_____

Review Questions

1. Who was Olympe de Gouges?

_____

_____

2. Why did European rulers fear the French Revolution?

_____

_____

Name_____ Class_____ Date_____

Focus Question: What events occurred during the radical phase of the French Revolution?

As you read this section in your textbook, complete the following timeline to show the sequence of events that took place during the radical phase of the French Revolution. Some dates have been completed for you.

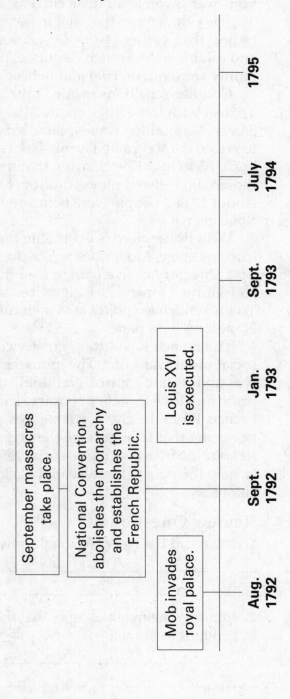

September massacres take place.

National Convention abolishes the monarchy and establishes the French Republic.

Louis XVI is executed.

Mob invades royal palace.

1795

July 1794

Sept. 1793

Jan. 1793

Sept. 1792

Aug. 1792

CHAPTER 6 SECTION 3

Section Summary

RADICAL DAYS OF THE REVOLUTION

In 1793, the revolution entered a dangerous and bloody phase. Tensions rose between revolutionaries and those hoping to restore the king's power. On August 10, 1792, a mob stormed the royal palace. Radicals called for the election of a new legislature called the National Convention. **Suffrage,** or the right to vote, was given to all male citizens, not just property owners.

The Convention that met in September 1792 was more radical than earlier assemblies. It voted to end the monarchy and establish the French Republic. Louis XVI and most of his family were put on trial and beheaded.

Counter-rebellions inside France worried the Convention. To deal with these, they created the Committee of Public Safety. Maximilien **Robespierre** led the Committee. He helped to create the **Reign of Terror.** The Terror lasted from September 1793 to July 1794. During that time, courts held trials for those who resisted the revolution. Many were falsely accused. About 17,000 people were beheaded by **guillotine,** including Robespierre.

With Robespierre's death, the revolution entered a less-extreme stage. Moderates wrote the Constitution of 1795. It set up a Directory of five men to lead the nation, and a two-house legislature. However, rising prices and corruption remained. To prevent chaos politicians then turned to military hero **Napoleon** Bonaparte.

The French Revolution greatly changed France. The old social order was gone. The monarchy was gone. The Church was under state control. **Nationalism,** or strong feelings of pride and love for one's country, had spread throughout France. From the city of **Marseilles,** troops marched to a new song that later became the French national anthem. Revolutionaries also made social reforms. They set up systems to help the poor. They also ended slavery in some French colonies.

Review Questions

1. What did the New National Convention do in 1792?

_____

_____

2. Identify one major change that the French Revolution brought to France.

_____

_____

Name_____ Class_____ Date_____

Focus Question: Explain Napoleon's rise to power in Europe, his subsequent defeat, and how the outcome still affects Europe today.

As you read this section in your textbook, complete the flowchart to list the main ideas about Napoleon's rise to power and his defeat. Some items have been completed for you.

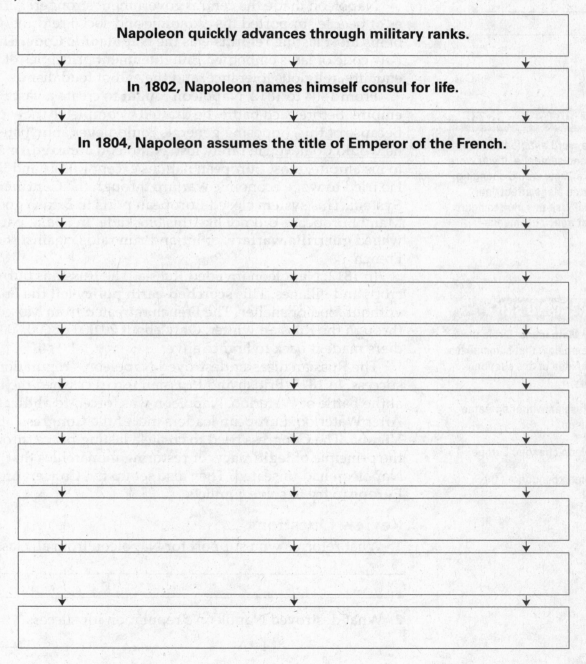

Napoleon quickly advances through military ranks.
In 1802, Napoleon names himself consul for life.
In 1804, Napoleon assumes the title of Emperor of the French.

CHAPTER 6
SECTION 4

Section Summary
THE AGE OF NAPOLEON

The last phase of the revolution is known as the Age of Napoleon. Napoleon Bonaparte started his rise to power as a young officer. By 1804, he had become emperor of France. At each step on his rise, Napoleon held a **plebiscite.** People voted, but Napoleon always kept absolute power.

Napoleon made the central government stronger. All classes of people supported his economic and social reforms. One of his most lasting reforms was the **Napoleonic Code.** This new code of laws embodied Enlightenment principles of equality, religious tolerance, and the end of feudalism.

From 1804 to 1812, Napoleon fought to create a vast French empire. Before each battle, he drafted a completely new plan. <u>Because of this, opposing generals could never anticipate what he would do next.</u> He rarely lost. Napoleon **annexed,** or added to his empire, most European nations except Russia and Britain. He tried to wage economic warfare through the **Continental System.** This system closed European ports to British goods. Many Europeans did not like this blockade. In Spain, patriots waged **guerrilla warfare,** or hit-and-run raids, against the French.

In 1812, Napoleon invaded Russia. The Russians burned crops and villages. This **scorched-earth policy** left the French without food or shelter. The French retreated from Moscow through the Russian winter. Only about 20,000 of 600,000 soldiers made it back to France alive.

The Russian disaster destroyed Napoleon's reputation for success. In 1815, British and Prussian forces crushed the French at the Battle of Waterloo. Napoleon was forced to **abdicate.** After Waterloo, European leaders met at the **Congress of Vienna.** The Congress tried to create a lasting peace through the principle of **legitimacy,** or restoring monarchies that Napoleon had unseated. They also set up the **Concert of Europe** to try to solve conflicts.

Review Questions

1. What reforms won support for Napoleon from all classes?

_____

_____

2. What destroyed Napoleon's reputation for success?

_____

_____

Name_____ Class_____ Date_____

Focus Question: What events helped bring about the Industrial Revolution?

As you read this section in your textbook, complete the following flowchart to list multiple causes of the Industrial Revolution. Some items have been completed for you.

New technologies
- New sources of energy such as steam and coal emerge.

Growing labor force

Agricultural revolution
- Farming methods improve.

Industrial Revolution

CHAPTER 7 SECTION 1

Section Summary

DAWN OF THE INDUSTRIAL AGE

The Industrial Revolution started in Britain. In 1750, most people worked on the land using handmade tools. When the Industrial Revolution began, the rural way of life in Britain started to disappear. By the 1850s, many country villages had grown into industrial towns and cities. New inventions and scientific "firsts" appeared each year. For example, an American dentist first used an **anesthetic** during surgery.

A series of related causes helped spark the Industrial Revolution. It was made possible, in part, by another revolution—in agriculture. This agricultural revolution improved the quality and quantity of food. Farmers mixed different kinds of soils or tried new kinds of crop rotation to get higher yields. Meanwhile, rich landowners pushed ahead with **enclosure.** Enclosure is the process of taking over and consolidating land once shared by peasant farmers. As millions of acres were enclosed, farm output and profits rose. The agricultural revolution created a surplus of food, so fewer people died from hunger. Statistics show that the agricultural revolution contributed to a rapid growth in population.

Agricultural progress, however, had a human cost. Many farm laborers lost jobs. They then migrated to towns and cities. There, they became the labor force that operated the new machines of the Industrial Revolution.

Other factors that helped trigger the Industrial Revolution were new technologies and new sources of energy and materials. One vital power source was coal, used to develop the steam engine. In 1764, Scottish engineer **James Watt** improved the steam engine. Watt's engine became a key power source. Coal was also used to produce iron. Iron was needed to make machines and steam engines. In 1709, Adam Darby used coal to **smelt** iron, or separate iron from its ore. Darby's experiments led to the production of less expensive and better-quality iron.

Review Questions

1. How did the Industrial Revolution change rural life in Britain?

_____

_____

2. What other revolution contributed to the start of the Industrial Revolution?

_____

_____

Name_____ Class_____ Date_____

Focus Question: What key factors allowed Britain to lead the way in the Industrial Revolution?

As you read this section in your textbook, complete the following concept webs to identify causes and effects of Britain's early lead in industrialization. Fill in the first concept web with causes. Fill in the second concept web with effects. Some items have been completed for you.

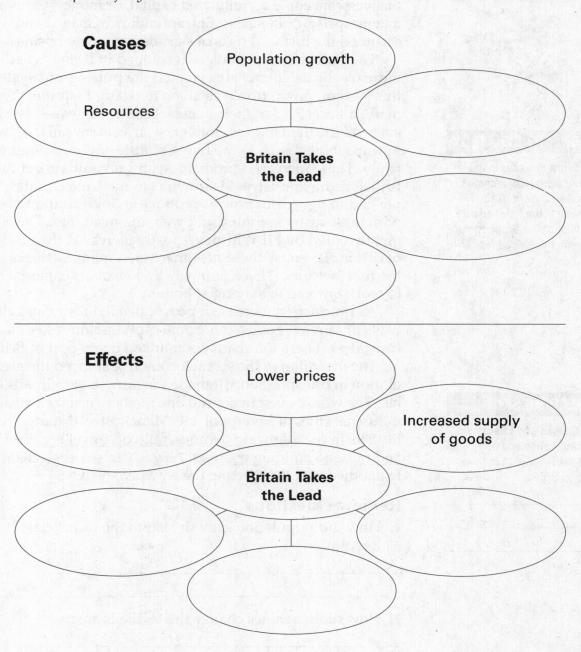

Causes

Population growth

Resources

Britain Takes the Lead

Effects

Lower prices

Increased supply of goods

Britain Takes the Lead

CHAPTER 7

SECTION 2

Section Summary
BRITAIN LEADS THE WAY

VOCABULARY STRATEGY

Find the word *decades* in the underlined sentence. It comes from the Greek word *deka*, which means "ten." Based on the meaning of the Greek root, what do you think *decades* means?

READING SKILL

Identify Causes and Effects
Identify one cause and one effect of the revolution in transportation in Britain.

_____

_____

_____

The Industrial Revolution began in Britain for several reasons. Population growth was one. Another was Britain's plentiful natural resources, such as rivers, coal, and iron. Also, the growing population and ready workforce increased the demand for goods. To increase production of goods, however, another key ingredient was needed—money. Money was necessary to start businesses. People accumulated **capital,** or money, to invest in an **enterprise,** or business. **Entrepreneurs** managed and assumed the financial risks of starting these new businesses.

The Industrial Revolution developed in Britain's textile industry. British merchants created the **putting-out system.** In this system, raw cotton was given to peasant families. They made it into cloth, in their homes. Production was slow, however. As the demand for cloth grew, inventors came up with new machines, such as the flying shuttle and the spinning jenny. These increased production and revolutionized the British textile industry. Meanwhile, in the United States, people had to figure out how to produce enough cotton to keep up with these faster spinning and weaving machines. The cotton gin, invented by **Eli Whitney,** greatly increased the production of cotton. To house these new machines, manufacturers built the first factories. There, spinners and weavers came each day to work, instead of staying at home.

As production increased, people needed faster and cheaper ways of moving goods, too. Some capitalists invested in **turnpikes.** These toll roads soon linked every part of Britain.

The invention of the steam locomotive spurred the great revolution in transportation. It made the growth of railroads possible. The world's first major rail line ran between the British industrial cities of **Liverpool** and **Manchester.** It started running in 1830. <u>In the following decades, railroad travel became faster and railroad building boomed.</u> As you can see, each change led to another, rapidly affecting the way people lived.

Review Questions

1. How did population growth lead to the Industrial Revolution?

   _____

   _____

2. How did machines change the textile industry?

   _____

   _____

CHAPTER 7
SECTION 3

Note Taking Study Guide

SOCIAL IMPACT OF THE INDUSTRIAL REVOLUTION

Focus Question: What were the social effects of the Industrial Revolution?

As you read this section in your textbook, complete the following table to understand the effects of industrialization. Some items have been filled in for you.

Industrialization	
Benefits	**Challenges**
• Created jobs	• Crowded cities
• Wealthy middle class	• Pollution
•	• Struggle for survival in slums
	•
•	
	•
•	

CHAPTER 7 SECTION 3

Section Summary

SOCIAL IMPACT OF THE INDUSTRIAL REVOLUTION

What new social class emerged during the Industrial Revolution?

_____

_____

_____

Find the word *contaminated* in the underlined sentence. What clues to the word's meaning can you find in the surrounding words, phrases, or sentences? How do the words *sewage* and *awful stench* help you figure out what *contaminated* means?

Understand Effects Explain three effects of the Industrial Revolution on the lives of the workers.

_____

_____

_____

The Industrial Revolution brought **urbanization,** or the movement of people to cities. Masses of people moved from farms to cities because of changes in farming, soaring population growth, and demand for workers. Almost overnight, small villages around mines grew into cities. Other cities grew up around the factories that were built in once-quiet market towns.

Those who benefited most from the Industrial Revolution were entrepreneurs. They made up a new middle class created by the Industrial Revolution. The wealthy and the middle class lived in nice neighborhoods. The poor lived in crowded tiny rooms in **tenements,** multistory buildings divided into apartments. These tenements had no running water and no sewage or sanitation system. <u>Sewage rotted in the streets or was dumped into rivers, which contaminated drinking water and created an awful stench.</u> This led to the spread of diseases.

Working in a factory system was very different from working on a farm. In rural villages, people worked hard, but the amount of work varied with each season. The factory system was a harsh new way of life. Working hours were long. Shifts lasted from twelve to sixteen hours, six or seven days a week. Tired workers were injured by machines that had no safety devices. Working conditions in mines were even worse than in the factories. Factories and mines also hired many boys and girls. These children often started working at age seven or eight, a few as young as five.

The early industrial age brought terrible hardships. In time, however, reformers pressed for laws to improve working conditions. **Labor unions,** or workers' organizations, won the right to ask for better wages, hours, and working conditions.

Despite the social problems created by the Industrial Revolution, it did have some positive effects. More jobs were created and wages rose. As the cost of railroad travel fell, people could travel farther for less money than ever before.

Review Questions

1. Why did people migrate from farms to cities during the Industrial Revolution?

_____

_____

2. What were working conditions like in factories?

_____

_____

CHAPTER
7
SECTION 4

Note Taking Study Guide
NEW WAYS OF THINKING

Focus Question: What new ideas about economics and society were fostered as a result of the Industrial Revolution?

As you read this section in your textbook, complete the following outline to identify main ideas about the new economic and social theories. Some items have been completed for you.

I. Laissez-faire economics

    A. Adam Smith and free enterprise

        1. _____

        2. _____

II. Malthus on population

    A. Malthus holds bleak view.

        1. Population will outpace food supply.

        2. _____

        3. _____

    B. Ricardo shares view.

        1. _____

        2. _____

III. Utilitarians for limited government

    A. Goal of society should be "the greatest happiness for the greatest number."

        1. _____

        2. _____

IV. Socialist thought emerges

    A. Focus should be on the good of society in general, not on individual rights.

        1. _____

        2. _____

    B. Socialists establish utopian communities.

        1. Hoped that equality among people would end conflict

        2. Utopian industrialist Robert Owen sets up a model community in Scotland.

(Outline continues on next page.)

CHAPTER 7 SECTION 4

Note Taking Study Guide
NEW WAYS OF THINKING

(Continued from page 95)

V. Karl Marx explains class struggle
  A. _____
    1. _____
    2. _____
VI. _____
  A. _____
    1. _____
    2. _____
    3. _____
  B. Marxism loses appeal.
    1. _____
    2. _____

CHAPTER 7 SECTION 4

Section Summary

NEW WAYS OF THINKING

Many thinkers tried to understand the great changes taking place in the early Industrial Age. Middle-class business leaders supported the laissez-faire, or "hands-off" approach. They believed that a free market would help everyone, not just the rich. However, one British laissez-faire economist, **Thomas Malthus,** thought the poor would always suffer. He believed population would grow faster than the food supply. He did not think the government should help the poor. He believed people should improve their own lives through hard work and have fewer children.

Other thinkers sought to soften laissez-faire doctrines. They felt some government help was needed. The British philosopher and economist **Jeremy Bentham** supported **utilitarianism.** He believed that the goal of society should be the "greatest happiness for the greatest number" of citizens. Other thinkers, such as John Stuart Mill, strongly believed in individual freedom, but wanted the government to step in to prevent harm to workers.

To end poverty and injustice, some offered a radical solution—**socialism.** Under socialism, the **means of production**—the farms, factories, railways, and other businesses—would be owned by the people as a whole, not by individuals. Some early socialists, such as **Robert Owen,** set up communities in which all work and property were shared. They were called Utopians.

The German philosopher **Karl Marx** formulated a new theory. His theory predicted a struggle between social classes that would end in a classless society that he called communist. Marx wrote that the struggles of the **proletariat,** or working class, would end because wealth and power would be equally shared. In practice, **communism** later referred to a system in which a small elite controlled the economy and politics. In the 1860s, German socialists adapted Marx's beliefs to form **social democracy,** which called for a slow transition from capitalism to socialism.

Review Questions

1. Why did middle-class leaders support laissez-faire economics?

_____

_____

2. What did Jeremy Bentham believe the goal of society should be?

_____

_____

READING CHECK

What group of early socialists formed communities in which all work and property were shared?

_____

_____

_____

VOCABULARY STRATEGY

Find the word *formulated* in the underlined sentence. Note that the base word is *form.* What does it mean "to form" something? Think of synonyms of the word *form,* such as *plan, shape.* Use the meaning of the word *form* and the synonyms you think of to help you learn what *formulated* means.

READING SKILL

Identify Main Ideas What are the main ideas of Karl Marx's theory?

_____

_____

_____

Name_____ Class_____ Date_____

Note Taking Study Guide
AN AGE OF IDEOLOGIES

Focus Question: What events proved that Metternich was correct in his fears?

A. *As you read "Conservatives Prefer the Old Order" and "Liberals and Nationalists Seek Change," fill in the table to identify main ideas about conservatism, liberalism, and nationalism. Some items have been completed for you.*

Conservatism	Liberalism	Nationalism
• Supports a return to world before 1789 • Supports restoration of royal families to power • _____ • _____ • _____ • _____	• Supports government based on written constitutions • Supports separation of powers within the government • _____ • _____ • _____	• _____ _____ _____

B. *As you read "Central Europe Challenges the Old Order," use the table to identify supporting details about revolts in Serbia, Greece, and other countries. Some items have been entered for you.*

Serbia	Greece	Other Revolts
• Karageorge leads war against Ottomans from 1804 to 1813; leads to sense of Serbian identity. • _____ • _____	• Greeks revolt against the Ottomans in 1821. • _____ • _____	• Rebels in Spain, Portugal, and some Italian states • _____ • _____

CHAPTER 8 SECTION 1

Section Summary
AN AGE OF IDEOLOGIES

After the Congress of Vienna, clashes among different **ideologies,** or belief systems, caused more than 30 years of turmoil in Europe. Conservatives wanted to return to the way things were before 1789. This group included kings, nobles, and church leaders. Their agreement to work together was called the Concert of Europe. They wanted to restore royal families that Napoleon had displaced. They supported a social system in which lower classes respected those above them. Also, they backed established churches and opposed constitutional governments. Conservative leaders such as Prince Metternich of Austria wanted to crush revolutionary ideas.

Liberals and nationalists challenged the conservatives. The Enlightenment and the French Revolution had inspired them. Liberals generally included business owners, bankers, lawyers, politicians, and writers. They wanted governments based on written constitutions. They opposed monarchies and the established churches. They believed that liberty, equality, and property were natural rights. Later, liberals supported **universal manhood suffrage,** allowing all adult men to vote.

Nationalism gave people with a common heritage a sense of identity. It also gave them the goal of creating their own homeland. In the 1800s, nationalist groups within the Austrian and Ottoman empires set out to create their own states. Rebellions began in the Balkans. The Serbs were the first to revolt. By 1830, they had won **autonomy,** or self-rule, within the Ottoman empire. In 1821, the Greeks revolted. By 1830, Greece was independent from the Ottomans. Revolts spread to Spain, Portugal, and Italy. Metternich urged conservative leaders to crush the revolts. In response, French and Austrian troops smashed revolts in Spain and Italy.

Demands from the new industrial working class were soon added to liberal and nationalist demands. <u>By the mid-1800s, social reformers and agitators were urging workers to support socialism or other ways of reorganizing property ownership.</u>

Review Questions

1. What type of social system did conservatives support?

_____

_____

2. Why did liberals and nationalists challenge conservatives?

_____

_____

READING CHECK

What is autonomy?

_____

_____

_____

VOCABULARY STRATEGY

Find the word *agitators* in the underlined sentence. What do you think it means? Note that the *agitators* were "<u>urging</u> workers to support socialism." To *urge* people to do something means "to encourage or pressure" them. Use this context clue to figure out the meaning of *agitators*.

READING SKILL

Identify Main Ideas What two groups challenged conservatives for political control after the Congress of Vienna?

_____

_____

_____

Name_____ Class_____ Date_____

Note Taking Study Guide
REVOLUTIONS OF 1830 AND 1848

Focus Question: What were the causes and effects of the revolutions in Europe in 1830 and 1848?

As you read this section, fill in the table below with a country, date, and main idea for each revolution of 1830 and 1848. Some of the items have been completed for you.

Revolutions of 1830 and 1848	Radicals force king to abdicate.			Revolution leads to election of Louis Napoleon as president.					Frankfurt Assembly offers the king the throne of a united Germany, but he refuses.
	1830			1848					1848
	France			France					Germany

CHAPTER 8 SECTION 2

Section Summary

REVOLUTIONS OF 1830 AND 1848

Louis XVIII died in 1824, and Charles X inherited the French throne. In 1830, Charles suspended the legislature and limited the right to vote. Angry rebels soon controlled Paris. They were led by liberals and **radicals.** When Charles X gave up the throne, radicals hoped to set up a republic. However, liberals insisted on a constitutional monarchy. **Louis Philippe** was called the "citizen king" because he owed his throne to the people.

The Paris revolts led to other revolts in Europe. Most failed, but they led to reforms. One successful revolution took place in Belgium. It gained its independence from Holland in 1831. Nationalists also revolted in Poland, but they failed to win widespread support. Russian forces soon crushed the rebels there.

In the 1840s, radicals, socialists, and liberals denounced Louis Philippe's government. A **recession** made the French people even more unhappy. The government tried to silence critics. Angry crowds then took to the streets in February 1848. The turmoil spread, and Louis Philippe gave up the throne. Liberals, radicals, and socialists proclaimed the Second Republic. By June, the upper and middle classes had won control of the government. Workers again took to the streets of Paris. At least 1,500 people were killed before the government crushed the rebellion. By the end of 1848, the National Assembly issued a constitution. This constitution gave the right to vote to all adult men. An election for president was held, and Louis Napoleon, the nephew of Napoleon Bonaparte, won. By 1852, however, he had declared himself Emperor **Napoleon III.**

The uprising in Paris in 1848 led to more revolutions across Europe. Revolts broke out in Vienna, and Metternich resigned. Hungarian nationalists led by **Louis Kossuth** demanded a government independent of Austria. The Czechs made similar demands. The Italian states also revolted, and the German states demanded national unity. Some of the rebellions were successful at first, but most of them had failed by 1850.

Review Questions

1. What country became independent in 1831?

_____

_____

2. How did Louis Napoleon become Emperor Napoleon III?

_____

_____

READING CHECK

Who was the "citizen king"?

_____

_____

_____

VOCABULARY STRATEGY

Find the word *denounced* in the underlined sentence. What do you think it means? Reread the sentences that follow the underlined sentence. Were the French people happy or unhappy with Louis Philippe's government? Use this context clue to decide which word below has a similar meaning to *denounced.*

1. criticized

2. supported

READING SKILL

Identify Main Ideas What is the main idea of the last paragraph in the Summary? Remember that the first sentence of a paragraph often contains the main idea.

_____

_____

_____

CHAPTER 8 SECTION 3 — Note Taking Study Guide
REVOLTS IN LATIN AMERICA

Focus Question: Who were the key revolutionaries to lead the movements for independence in Latin America, and what were their accomplishments?

As you read this section, fill in the table below with a country, a date, and a main idea for each revolt in Latin America. Some of the items have been completed for you.

Revolts in Latin America

Main idea	Toussaint L'Ouverture leads an army of former slaves and ends slavery there.			Simón Bolívar suprises the Spanish at Bogotá.			United Provinces of Central America breaks into separate republics.
Date	1791			1819			1838
Country	Haiti			Colombia			Guatemala, El Salvador, Honduras, Nicaragua, Costa Rica

Name_____ Class_____ Date_____

Section Summary
REVOLTS IN LATIN AMERICA

By the late 1700s, the desire for revolution had spread to Latin America. There, the social system had led to discontent. Spanish-born *peninsulares* made up the highest social class. They controlled the government and the Church. Creoles, mestizos, and mulattoes resented their lower status. **Creoles** were people of European descent who were born in Latin America. **Mestizos** were people of Native American and European descent. **Mulattoes** were people of African and European descent. The Enlightenment and the French and American revolutions had inspired creoles. When Napoleon invaded Spain in 1808, Latin American leaders decided to demand independence.

Revolution had already begun in Hispaniola in 1791. In that year, **Toussaint L'Ouverture** led a slave rebellion there. The rebellion ended slavery and gave Toussaint control of the island. Napoleon's army tried to retake the island, but failed. In 1804, the island became the independent country of Haiti.

In 1810, **Father Miguel Hidalgo** called for Mexican independence. After some successes, he was captured and killed. **Father José Morelos** took up the cause, but he, too, was killed. Finally, in 1821, revolutionaries led by Agustín de Iturbide overthrew Spanish rule and declared independence for Mexico. Central American colonies soon declared independence, too.

In the early 1800s, discontent and revolution spread across all of South America. **Simón Bolívar** led an uprising in Venezuela. Although his new republic was soon overthrown, Bolívar did not give up. He marched his army across the Andes and took the city of Bogotá from the surprised Spanish. Then he moved south to free Ecuador, Peru, and Bolivia. There, he joined forces with another great leader, **José de San Martín.** San Martín helped Argentina and Chile win freedom from Spain. The wars of independence ended in 1824, but power struggles among South American leaders led to civil wars. However, in Brazil, **Dom Pedro** became emperor and proclaimed independence for that colony in 1822.

Review Questions

1. What led to discontent in Latin America by the late 1700s?

_____

_____

2. When did Mexico gain its independence?

_____

_____

READING CHECK

Which group in Latin America made up the highest social class?

_____

_____

_____

VOCABULARY STRATEGY

Find the word *proclaimed* in the underlined sentence. What do you think it means? *Proclaim* comes from the Latin word *proclamare.* The prefix *pro-* means "before" and *clamare* means "to cry out" or "shout." Use this information about word origins to help you decide which of the following words means the same as *proclaimed.*

1. announced

2. denied

READING SKILL

Identify Main Ideas Circle the sentence below that states a main idea from the Summary.

- The social system in Latin America led to discontent.

- Spanish-born *peninsulares* were the highest social class.

- Creoles were people of European descent who were born in Latin America.

- Mestizos were people of Native American and European descent.

- Mulattoes were people of African and European descent.

Name_____ Class_____ Date_____

Focus Question: How did science, technology, and big business promote industrial growth?

As you read this section in your textbook, complete the following chart to identify main ideas about the major developments of the Industrial Revolution. Some items have been completed for you.

The Second Industrial Revolution

Transportation/Communication
- The automobile age begins.
-
-
-

Industry/Business
- Technology sparks industrial growth.
-
-
-
-
-

New Powers
- Germany, France, and United States have more natural resources than Britain.
-
-

CHAPTER 9 SECTION 1

Section Summary
THE INDUSTRIAL REVOLUTION SPREADS

For a while, Britain was the world's industrial leader. By the mid-1800s, however, Germany and the United States had become the new leaders. These nations had much more coal, iron, and other natural resources than Britain did. They also were able to use British experts and technology. As in Britain, cities in the new industrial nations grew quickly.

Technology helped industry grow. **Henry Bessemer** invented a new way to make steel from iron. **Alfred Nobel** invented dynamite for use in construction. **Michael Faraday** created the first **dynamo,** a machine that makes electricity. Soon electricity replaced steam as the main power source for industry. In the 1870s, the American inventor **Thomas Edison** developed the electric light bulb. Soon entire cities were lit with electric lights. Factories could now operate at night and produce more goods. The use of **interchangeable parts** and the **assembly line** made production faster and cheaper, too.

Technology also changed transportation and communication. Steamships replaced sailing ships. Trains quickly connected cities and brought raw materials to factories. The invention of the internal combustion engine led to the mass production of automobiles. In 1903, **Orville and Wilbur Wright** launched the air age by flying a plane for a few seconds. The telegraph and telephone made the exchange of information nearly instantaneous. **Guglielmo Marconi** invented the radio, a big part of today's global communication network.

These new technologies needed large amounts of money. To get this money, owners sold **stock,** or shares in their companies, to investors. These businesses became giant **corporations**. Others formed business groups called **cartels.** By the late 1800s, what we call "big business" came to dominate industry.

Review Questions

1. How did Germany and the United States become industrial leaders?

_____

_____

2. What new form of energy changed cities and factories?

_____

_____

READING CHECK

What invention changed life in the cities?

_____

_____

_____

VOCABULARY STRATEGY

What do you think the word *dominate* means in the underlined sentence? It is a verb, so it describes an action. However, it comes from a Latin word that means "lord" or "master." Use the word's origin to help you figure out what *dominate* means.

READING SKILL

Identify Main Ideas How did transportation change during the Industrial Revolution?

_____

_____

_____

CHAPTER
9
SECTION 2

Note Taking Study Guide
THE RISE OF THE CITIES

Focus Question: How did the Industrial Revolution change life in the cities?

As you read this section in your textbook, complete the following outline to identify main ideas and supporting details about how the Industrial Revolution changed life in the cities. Some items have been completed for you.

  I. Medicine and the population explosion

    A. The fight against disease

      1. _____

      2. _____

    B. Hospital care improves.

      1. _____

      2. _____

 II. Life in the cities

    A. City landscapes change.

      1. _____

      2. _____

    B. _____

      1. _____

      2. _____

    C. _____

      1. _____

      2. _____

    D. _____

      1. _____

      2. _____

III. Working-class struggles

    A. _____

      1. _____

      2. _____

    B. _____

      1. _____

      2. _____

CHAPTER 9 SECTION 2 | Section Summary
THE RISE OF THE CITIES

Between 1800 and 1900, the population of Europe more than doubled. This was due to advances in medicine that slowed death rates. In the fight against disease, scientists studied **germ theory.** They believed that certain germs might cause specific diseases. In 1870, French chemist **Louis Pasteur** showed the link between germs and disease. German doctor **Robert Koch** identified the cause of tuberculosis, a deadly lung disease. British hospital reformer **Florence Nightingale** raised standards of care and cleanliness. British surgeon **Joseph Lister** discovered that antiseptics prevent disease. As people understood what causes disease, they practiced better hygiene. Disease decreased and fewer people died.

At this time, cities underwent big changes in Europe and the United States. The largest **urban renewal** project took place in Paris in the 1850s. Old, crowded areas of the city were replaced with wide avenues and grand public buildings. Steel made it possible to build tall buildings called skyscrapers. Paved streets helped make cities more livable. Electric streetlights illuminated the night and increased safety. Huge new sewage systems made cities healthier. City planners knew they needed to provide clean water. These acts helped cut death rates.

Despite these efforts, cities were still harsh places for the poor. In the worst slums, whole families lived in a single room. However, millions of people still moved to the cities. They came to get work, for entertainment, and for an education.

Most people worked long hours in factories, in unsafe circumstances for low wages. Workers protested these terrible conditions. They formed **mutual-aid societies** to help sick or injured workers. They also organized unions. Pressured by unions, reformers, and working-class voters, governments passed laws that improved working conditions. Wages varied, but overall, the **standard of living** for most workers did rise.

Review Questions
1. How did advances in medicine increase population?

_____

_____

2. How did new sewage systems make city life healthier?

_____

_____

READING CHECK
Who showed the link between germs and disease?

_____

_____

_____

VOCABULARY STRATEGY
What does the word *illuminated* mean in the underlined sentence? The root of this word is *lumen*, which is Latin for "light." What other word in this sentence includes the word *light*? Use the word root and the word *streetlight* to help you figure out the meaning of *illuminated*.

READING SKILL
Identify Supporting Details
What were working conditions like for most factory workers?

_____

_____

CHAPTER
9
SECTION 3

Note Taking Study Guide

CHANGING ATTITUDES AND VALUES

Focus Question: How did the Industrial Revolution change the old social order and long-held traditions in the Western world?

As you read this section in your textbook, complete the following table. List new issues in the first column and write two supporting details for each issue in the second column. Some items have been completed for you.

Changes in Social Order and Values	
Issue	**Change**
• New social order	• Upper class: old nobility, new industrialists, business families • Growing middle class develops its own way of life. •
• Rights for women	• •
• Growth of public education	• •
• New directions in science	• •
•	• •

CHAPTER 9 SECTION 3

Section Summary

CHANGING ATTITUDES AND VALUES

In the late 1800s, many new issues challenged the old social order. For centuries, mainly the two classes had been nobles and peasants. Now a more complex social structure developed with several social classes. The new upper class included very rich business families. Below the upper class was a growing middle class and then a struggling lower middle class. At the bottom were workers and peasants. The middle class had its own values and way of life, including a **cult of domesticity.** This encouraged women to stay home and care for the family.

Demands for women's rights also challenged the old social order. Women sought fairness in marriage, divorce, and property laws. In the United States, reformers such as **Elizabeth Cady Stanton** and **Sojourner Truth** worked for **women's suffrage,** or the right to vote. Women's groups also supported the **temperance movement,** a campaign to limit or ban the use of alcoholic beverages.

Attitudes toward education changed, too. People believed that education would create better workers. Reformers persuaded many governments to set up public schools and require basic education. Because of this, more children got an education.

New ideas in science also brought change. **John Dalton** developed atomic theory. However, the most controversial new idea came from British naturalist **Charles Darwin.** It upset many people, who disagreed with his theory. Darwin thought that all forms of life evolve over millions of years. His theory of natural selection explains how members of each species compete to survive. Some people used a twisted version of Darwin's theory, called Social Darwinism, to support **racism.**

Religion continued to be a force in Western society. Life in industrial societies could be very cruel for some. Religious groups tried to help the working poor. For example, the **social gospel** movement urged Christians to work to improve society.

Review Questions

1. Who was included in the new upper class of the late 1800s?

_____

_____

2. What rights did women want?

_____

_____

READING CHECK

Who developed the new scientific theory of natural selection?

_____

_____

_____

VOCABULARY STRATEGY

Find the word *controversial* in the underlined sentence. What do you think it means? The word begins with the prefix *contro-*, which means "against." Use the meaning of the prefix and the context clues in the paragraph to help you figure out what *controversial* means.

READING SKILL

Identify Supporting Details Why did more children begin to get an education in the late 1800s?

_____

_____

_____

Name_____ Class_____ Date_____

Note Taking Study Guide

ARTS IN THE INDUSTRIAL AGE

Focus Question: What artistic movements emerged in reaction to the Industrial Revolution?

As you read this section in your textbook, complete the following table. Identify supporting details about the major features of artistic movements of the 1800s. Some items have been completed for you.

Major Artistic Movements of the 1800s		
Movement	**Goals/Characteristics**	**Major Figures**
Romanticism	• Rebellion against reason • Emphasis on imagination, freedom, and emotion • Use of direct language, intense feelings, glorification of nature • • •	• William Wordsworth • William Blake • Samuel Taylor Coleridge • • • •
Realism	• To represent the world as it was, without romantic sentiment • • •	• Charles Dickens • Victor Hugo • • •
Impressionism	• To capture the first fleeting impression made by a scene or object on the viewer's eye •	• •
Postimpressionism	•	• • •

Name_____ Class_____ Date_____

From about 1750 to 1850, a cultural movement called **romanticism** emerged. It was a reaction against the ideas of the Enlightenment. Romanticism emphasized imagination, freedom, and emotion. <u>The works of romantic writers included direct language, intense feelings, and a glorification of nature.</u> **William Wordsworth, William Blake,** and **Lord Byron** were major romantic poets. Romantic writers, such as **Victor Hugo,** were inspired by history, legend, and folklore. Composers also tried to stir deep emotions. The passionate music of **Ludwig van Beethoven** used an exciting range of sound. Painters, too, broke free from the formal styles of the Enlightenment. They used bold brush strokes and colors to capture the beauty and power of nature.

However, in the mid-1800s, an art movement called **realism** took hold. Realists wanted to portray the world as it truly was. They rejected romantic beauty. Their works made people aware of the often bleak life of the Industrial Age. Many realists wanted to improve life for their subjects. The novels of **Charles Dickens,** for example, shocked readers with images of poverty, mistreatment of children, and urban crime. Painters, such as **Gustave Courbet**, painted ordinary working-class men and women.

A new art form, photography, also developed. **Louis Daguerre** made some of the first successful photographs. Photography made some artists question the purpose of realist paintings when a camera made exact images. By the 1870s, one group started a new movement called **impressionism**. Artists such as **Claude Monet** wanted to capture the first impression made by a scene on the viewer's eye. By focusing on visual impressions, artists showed familiar subjects in unfamiliar ways. Later, the postimpressionist painter **Vincent van Gogh** experimented with sharp brush lines and bold colors.

Review Questions

1. What qualities did romantics include in their works?

_____

_____

2. What was the goal of the impressionist artists?

_____

_____

READING CHECK

What cultural movement was a reaction to the Enlightenment?

_____

_____

_____

VOCABULARY STRATEGY

What does the word *intense* mean in the underlined sentence? Look for clues in the surrounding words, phrases, or sentences. Circle the words in the paragraph that could help you figure out the meaning of *intense*.

READING SKILL

Identify Supporting Details Identify two details that support this main idea: Realist artists and writers made people more aware of the harshness of life in the Industrial Age.

_____

_____

_____

**CHAPTER
10
SECTION 1**

Note Taking Study Guide

BUILDING A GERMAN NATION

Focus Question: How did Otto von Bismarck, the chancellor of Prussia, lead the drive for German unity?

As you read this section in your textbook, complete the following chart to record the sequence of events that led to German unification. Some items have been completed for you.

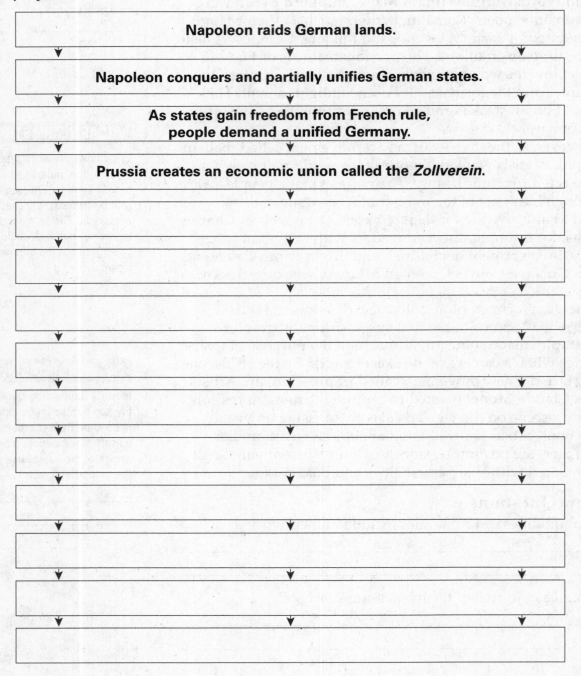

Napoleon raids German lands.

Napoleon conquers and partially unifies German states.

As states gain freedom from French rule, people demand a unified Germany.

Prussia creates an economic union called the *Zollverein*.

CHAPTER
10
SECTION 1

Section Summary
BUILDING A GERMAN NATION

In the early 1800s, German-speaking people did not live in one nation. They were scattered among several German states, parts of Prussia, and the Austrian empire. Napoleon dissolved the Holy Roman Empire and organized some German states into the Rhine Confederation. Napoleon's actions helped develop German national identity. Not everyone wanted French rule. They fought to free their lands and began to demand one German nation for all German-speaking people. After Napoleon's defeat, the Congress of Vienna created the German Confederation, a weak alliance of German states headed by Austria. In the 1830s, Prussia created an economic union called the *Zollverein*. This union removed tariffs between German states. Still, the German people did not live in one, unified German nation.

In 1862, King William I named **Otto von Bismarck** as the **chancellor** of Prussia. Bismarck wanted to unite the German states under Prussian rule. He was very skillful at **Realpolitik,** or practical politics based on the needs of the state. First, Bismarck built up the Prussian army. He led Prussia into three wars, gaining land for Prussia in each one.

In 1864, Bismarck formed an alliance with Austria. In 1866, however, he made up an excuse to attack Austria. After its victory, Prussia **annexed,** or took control of, several northern German states. This angered the French ruler, Napoleon III. Bismarck rewrote and released to the press a telegram that reported on a meeting between William I of Prussia and the French ambassador. <u>Bismarck's editing made it seem that William I had insulted the French.</u> Furious, Napoleon III declared war on Prussia. This is what Bismarck had wanted. Supported by troops from other German states, Prussia defeated the French.

Delighted by the victory, German princes asked William I to take the title **kaiser,** or emperor. He agreed. In 1871, Germans celebrated the birth of the Second **Reich,** or empire.

Review Questions
1. What was the *Zollverein* and what did it accomplish?

_____

_____

2. How did Bismarck use war to strengthen Prussia?

_____

_____

READING CHECK
Who was Otto von Bismarck?

_____

_____

_____

VOCABULARY STRATEGY
Find the word *editing* in the underlined sentence. What clues to its meaning can you find in the surrounding words, phrases, or sentences? For example, what does the word *rewrote* suggest? Circle the words in the paragraph that could help you figure out what *editing* means.

READING SKILL
Recognize Sequence Place the following actions of Bismarck in the correct sequence:

____ He annexes several North German states.

____ He forms an alliance with Austria.

____ He attacks Austria.

____ He builds up Prussia's army.

Name_____ Class_____ Date_____

Focus Question: How did Germany increase its power after unifying in 1871?

As you read this section in your textbook, complete the following chart to record the causes and effects of a strong German nation. Some items have been completed for you.

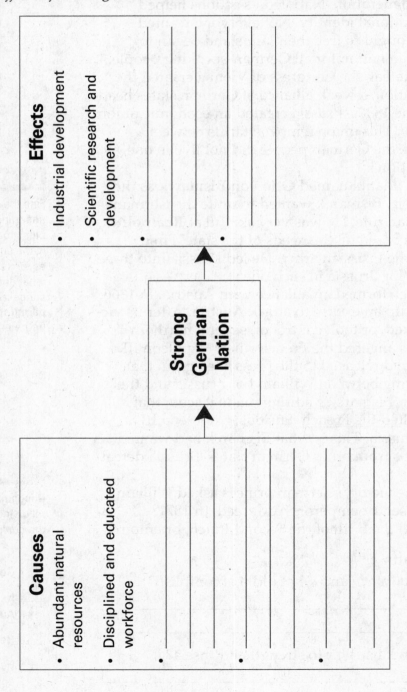

Causes
- Abundant natural resources
- Disciplined and educated workforce

Strong German Nation

Effects
- Industrial development
- Scientific research and development

CHAPTER 10 SECTION 2

Section Summary

GERMANY STRENGTHENS

After 1871, the new German empire became an industrial giant. There are several reasons why this was possible. Germany had large iron and coal resources. These are the basic ingredients for industrial development. It also had a disciplined and educated workforce. The middle class helped create a productive and efficient society, too. The country's growing population also provided a huge home market for goods. It also created a supply of workers.

Industrialists saw the value of science in business. They developed new products, such as synthetic chemicals and dyes. Both industrialists and the government encouraged scientific research and development. The German government also supported economic development. It issued a single form of money and reorganized the banking system. The leaders of the new empire were determined to maintain a strong economy.

As chancellor, Bismarck had several foreign-policy goals. He wanted to keep France weak. He also wanted to build strong ties with Austria and Russia. At home, Bismarck believed the Socialists and the Catholic Church threatened the new empire. He worried that Socialists would turn workers toward revolution. He thought Catholics would be more loyal to the Church than to the state. Bismarck tried to repress both groups. His efforts, however, backfired. For example, he launched the *Kulturkampf,* or "battle for civilization." It was meant to make Catholics give their loyalty to the state first, above the Church. Instead, Catholics rallied behind the Church.

In 1888, **William II** became the new kaiser. He shocked Europe by asking Bismarck to resign. William II believed that his right to rule came from God. Not surprisingly, he resisted democratic reforms. However, his government still provided many **social welfare** programs to help certain groups of people. He also provided cheap transportation and electricity.

Review Questions

1. What are two reasons why the new German empire became an industrial giant?

_____

_____

2. What were Bismarck's foreign-policy goals?

_____

_____

READING CHECK

What two groups did Bismarck believe threatened the new German state?

_____

_____

_____

VOCABULARY STRATEGY

Find the word *synthetic* in the underlined sentence. *Natural* is an antonym of *synthetic*. Use what you know about the word *natural* to help you figure out what *synthetic* means.

READING SKILL

Recognize Sequence After Bismarck introduced the *Kulturkampf,* what happened next?

_____

_____

_____

Name_____ Class_____ Date_____

Note Taking Study Guide

UNIFYING ITALY

Focus Question: How did influential leaders help create a unified Italy?

As you read this section in your textbook, complete the following timeline to show the sequence of events that led to Italian unification. Some dates have been completed for you.

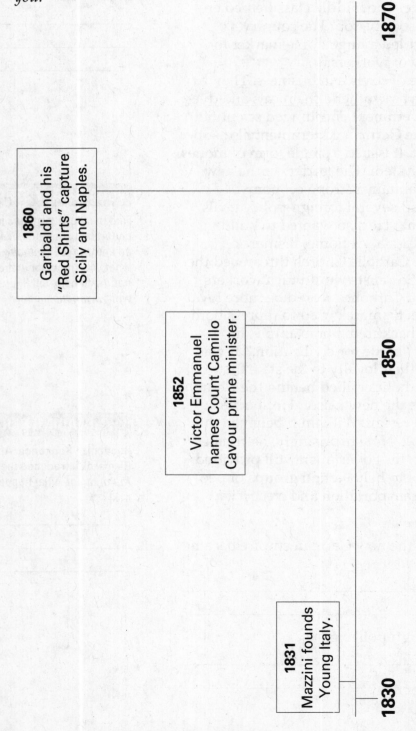

1870

1860
Garibaldi and his "Red Shirts" capture Sicily and Naples.

1852
Victor Emmanuel names Count Camillo Cavour prime minister.

1850

1831
Mazzini founds Young Italy.

1830

Name_____ Class_____ Date_____

Section Summary
UNIFYING ITALY

The people of the Italian peninsula spoke the same language and shared a common history. However, the region had not been united since Roman times. By the 1800s, however, patriots were determined to unite Italy. First, Napoleon's invasions had sparked dreams of nationalism. Then, Giuseppe Mazzini founded Young Italy. <u>The goal of this secret society was "to constitute Italy, one, free, independent, republican nation."</u> A united country made economic sense because it would end trade barriers among the states. It also would encourage industrial development.

Victor Emmanuel II was the king of Sardinia. He wanted to join other Italian states with his own. Victor Emmanuel made Count **Camillo Cavour** his prime minister. Cavour wanted to end Austrian power in Italy. With help from France, Sardinia defeated Austria and annexed Lombardy. Also, Austrian-backed leaders in northern states were overthrown.

In southern Italy, **Giuseppe Garibaldi** was also fighting for unification. He had recruited a force of 1,000 red-shirted volunteers. Garibaldi and his "Red Shirts" quickly won control of Sicily. They then crossed to the mainland and seized Naples. Garibaldi gave both regions to Victor Emmanuel. In 1861, Victor Emmanuel II became king of Italy. By 1870, France had withdrawn its troops from Rome, and Italy acquired Venetia. For the first time since the fall of the Roman empire, Italy was united.

The new nation faced many problems, and tensions grew. There were strong differences between the north and south. The north was richer and had more cities. In contrast, the south was poor and rural. **Anarchists,** people who wanted to abolish all government, turned to violence. Despite these problems, Italy's economy developed. As the population grew, however, **emigration** offered a chance for a better life. Many Italians left for the United States, Canada, and Latin American nations.

Review Questions
1. What sparked dreams of national unity in Italy?

_____

_____

2. Why did a unified Italy make economic sense?

_____

_____

READING CHECK
Who was Camillo Cavour?

_____

_____

_____

VOCABULARY STRATEGY
Find the word *constitute* in the underlined sentence. In this sentence, the word is used as a verb. A verb describes an action. Ask yourself: *What action were the nationalists trying to take?* Use the answer to this question to help you figure out what *constitute* means.

READING SKILL
Recognize Sequence What happened after France withdrew its troops from Rome?

_____

_____

_____

Name_____ Class_____ Date_____

Focus Question: How did the desire for national independence among ethnic groups weaken and ultimately destroy the Austrian and Ottoman empires?

As you read this section in your textbook, complete the following table to record some major events in Austrian history during the 1800s. Some dates have been completed for you.

Events in Austrian History				
By this time, factories spring up in Austrian cities, along with worker discontent and stirrings of socialism.	Nationalist revolts break out, but are crushed by the Hapsburg government.			
1840	**1848**	**1859**	**1866**	**1867**

CHAPTER 10 SECTION 4

Section Summary

NATIONALISM THREATENS OLD EMPIRES

In 1800, the Hapsburgs were the longest-reigning family in Europe. Their Austrian empire was home to many ethnic groups, including German-speaking Austrians, Slavs, Hungarians, and Italians.

By the 1840s, the empire faced many problems associated with industrial life. Also, nationalism threatened the empire. The Hapsburgs ignored these issues as long as they could. When revolts broke out in 1848, the government crushed them. During this time of unrest, 18-year-old **Francis Joseph** came to the Hapsburg throne. In an attempt to strengthen the empire, he granted some limited reforms. He also created a constitution, but the majority of power remained with German-speaking Austrians. This did not satisfy most of the other ethnic groups.

Austria's defeat in the 1866 war with Prussia brought even more pressure for change, especially from Hungarians within the empire. **Ferenc Deák** helped work out a compromise known as the **Dual Monarchy** of Austria-Hungary. Under the agreement, Austria and Hungary became separate states. Each had its own constitution. However, Francis Joseph still ruled both nations. Hungarians welcomed the compromise, but other groups resented it. Unrest grew among the Slavs. Some nationalists called on fellow Slavs to unite in "fraternal solidarity." By the early 1900s, nationalist unrest often kept the government from addressing political and social problems.

The Ottomans ruled an empire that stretched from Eastern Europe and the Balkans, to the Middle East and North Africa. It also included many different ethnic groups. During the 1800s, various peoples revolted against the Ottomans. They wanted their own independent states. With the empire weakened, European powers scrambled to divide up the Ottoman lands. A series of crises and wars occurred in the Balkans. By the early 1900s, that region became known as the "Balkan powder keg." The "explosion" came in 1914 and helped set off World War I.

Review Questions

1. How did the Hapsburgs respond when nationalist revolts broke out?

_____

_____

2. Why were the Balkans known as a "powder keg"?

_____

_____

READING CHECK

What new government did Ferenc Deák help set up?

_____

_____

_____

VOCABULARY STRATEGY

Find the word *fraternal* in the underlined sentence. The word comes from the Latin word *frater,* which means "brother." Look for clues in the surrounding text, such as *unite* and *solidarity.* Use the word's origin and context clues to help you figure out what *fraternal* means.

READING SKILL

Recognize Sequence What are two events that happened after the Ottoman empire weakened?

1._____

_____

2._____

_____

Name_____ Class_____ Date_____

Focus Question: Why did industrialization and reform come more slowly to Russia than to Western Europe?

As you read this section in your textbook, complete the following timeline to show the sequence of events in Russia during the late 1800s and early 1900s. Some events have been added for you.

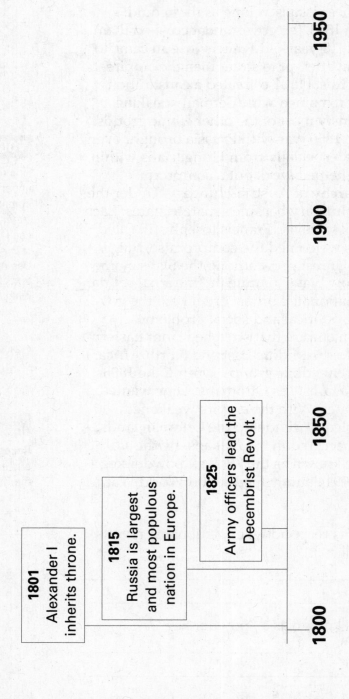

1801
Alexander I inherits throne.

1815
Russia is largest and most populous nation in Europe.

1825
Army officers lead the Decembrist Revolt.

1800

1850

1900

1950

CHAPTER 10 SECTION 5

Section Summary

RUSSIA: REFORM AND REACTION

By 1815, Russia was the largest nation in Europe. The Russian **colossus,** or giant, had vast natural resources. Reformers hoped to free the country from autocratic rule, economic backwardness, and social injustice. A rigid social structure, however, presented an obstacle to progress. Also, the tsars had ruled with absolute power for centuries.

Alexander II became tsar during the **Crimean War.** His reign followed the pattern of reform and repression of previous tsars. When Russia lost the war, it showed the country's backwardness and inefficiency. People demanded changes. The tsar agreed to some reforms. He ordered the **emancipation,** or freedom, of serfs. He set up elected assemblies, called **zemstvos.** Then he made legal reforms, which included trial by jury. However, these changes did not satisfy many Russians. <u>As radicals insisted on even greater changes and more reforms, the tsar moved toward repression.</u> This angered radicals. Terrorists killed Alexander II in 1881. In response to his father's death, Alexander III brought back repressive rule. He suppressed the cultures of non-Russian peoples. Official persecution fueled **pogroms,** or violent mob attacks on Jewish people. Many Jews left Russia and became **refugees,** seeking safety elsewhere.

Russia entered the industrialized age under Alexander III and his son Nicholas II. However, industrialization caused political and social problems to build. On Sunday, January 22, 1905, a peaceful protest calling for reforms turned deadly. The tsar's troops killed and wounded hundreds of people. Following this "Bloody Sunday," unrest exploded across Russia. Nicholas was forced to make many reforms. He agreed to call a **Duma,** or an elected national legislature. He also named **Peter Stolypin** as prime minister. Stolypin recognized that Russia needed reform. Unfortunately, the reforms he introduced were too limited. By 1914, Russia was still an autocracy, but simmering with discontent.

Review Questions

1. What was the obstacle to progress in Russia in the 1800s?

_____

_____

2. What did Alexander III do in response to his father's death?

_____

_____

READING CHECK

What event occurred on January 22, 1905?

_____

_____

_____

VOCABULARY STRATEGY

Find the word *radicals* in the underlined sentence. The word *radicals* is a noun for a kind of people. Ask yourself: "Why were radicals dissatisfied with Alexander II's reforms?" Use that information to help you figure out who *radicals* are.

READING SKILL

Recognize Sequence Which political reform occurred first? Circle your answer.

• setting up elected assemblies

• calling a Duma

• suppressing non-Russian cultures

CHAPTER 11 SECTION 1

Note Taking Study Guide
DEMOCRATIC REFORM IN BRITAIN

Focus Question: How did political reform gradually expand suffrage and make the British Parliament more democratic during the 1800s?

As you read this section in your textbook, complete the outline below to identify the main ideas in the section. Some items have been completed for you.

I. Reforming Parliament

   A. Reformers press for change.

      1. _____

      2. _____

   B. Reform Act of 1832

      1. Large towns and cities gain representation.

      2. _____

      3. _____

   C. The Chartist movement

      1. _____

      2. _____

II. The Victorian Age

   A. Symbol of a nation's values

      1. _____

      2. _____

   B. A confident age

      1. _____

      2. _____

III. A New Era in British Politics

   A. Expanding suffrage

      1. _____

      2. _____

      3. Britain becomes a parliamentary democracy.

   B. Limiting the Lords

      1. _____

      2. _____

Section Summary
DEMOCRATIC REFORM IN BRITAIN

In 1815, Britain was a constitutional monarchy with a Parliament. However, it was not very democratic. The House of Commons was controlled by wealthy nobles and squires. The House of Lords could veto any bill passed by the House of Commons. Catholics and Protestants outside the Church of England could not vote. The **rotten boroughs** still had members in Parliament, even though they had lost most of their voters during the Industrial Revolution. <u>At the same time, new industrial cities had no seats allocated in Parliament.</u>

In 1832, the Great Reform Act redistributed seats in the House of Commons. It also enlarged the **electorate,** or the people who could vote. However, it kept a property requirement for voting. Protesters called the Chartists demanded reforms, such as universal male suffrage and a **secret ballot.** In time, Parliament passed most of these reforms.

From 1837 to 1901, the great symbol in British life was **Queen Victoria.** She set the tone for the Victorian age. Victorian values, which she represented, included duty, thrift, honesty, hard work, and respectability. Under Victoria, the British empire grew even larger.

In the 1860s, British politics began to change. **Benjamin Disraeli** turned the Tories into the modern Conservative Party. The Whigs, led by **William Gladstone,** developed into the Liberal Party. Both leaders served as prime minister and fought for important reforms. The Conservative Party pushed through the Reform Bill of 1867. This bill gave the vote to many working-class men. In the 1880s, the Liberals passed reforms that gave the vote to farm workers and most other men.

By the end of the century, Britain was a **parliamentary democracy.** In this form of government, the prime minister and cabinet are chosen by their fellow members of the parliament and are responsible to it. In 1911, Parliament passed a bill that greatly lessened the power of the House of Lords. Since then, it has been a mostly ceremonial body.

Review Questions
1. What form of government did Britain have in 1815?

_____

_____

2. Name two important prime ministers of the Victorian age.

_____

_____

READING CHECK

Who was the great symbol in British life from 1837 to 1901?

_____

_____

VOCABULARY STRATEGY

Find the word *allocated* in the underlined sentence. What does it mean? Note that the Great Reform Act of 1832 "redistributed" seats in the House of Commons. This redistribution meant that seats were now allocated fairly. Use this context clue to help you figure out the meaning of the word *allocated*.

READING SKILL

Identify Main Ideas Which of the following sentences states the main idea of the first paragraph of this Summary? Circle it.

- The House of Commons was controlled by wealthy nobles and squires.

- Catholics and non-Church of England Protestants could not vote.

- Britain was a constitutional monarchy, but it was not very democratic.

- The House of Lords could veto any bill passed by the House of Commons.

CHAPTER 11 SECTION 2

Note Taking Study Guide
SOCIAL AND ECONOMIC REFORM IN BRITAIN

Focus Question: What social and economic reforms were passed by the British Parliament during the 1800s and early 1900s?

As you read this section in your textbook, complete the chart below by listing reforms in Britain during the 1800s and early 1900s. Some items have been completed for you.

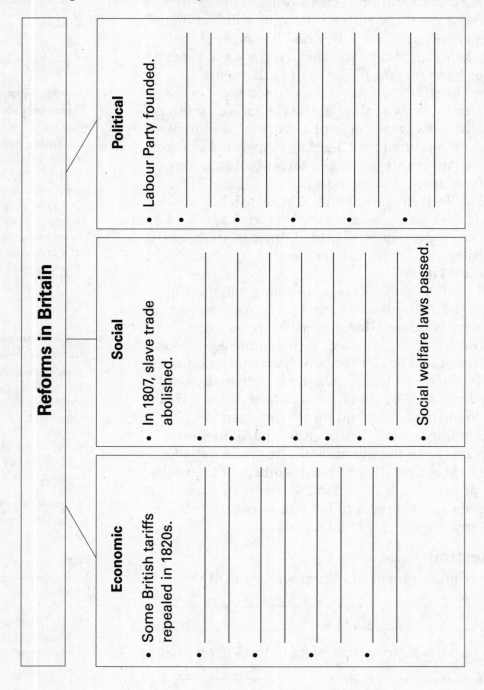

Reforms in Britain

Political
- Labour Party founded.
-
-
-
-
-

Social
- In 1807, slave trade abolished.
-
-
-
-
-
-
-
- Social welfare laws passed.

Economic
- Some British tariffs repealed in 1820s.
-
-
-
-

CHAPTER 11 SECTION 2

Section Summary

SOCIAL AND ECONOMIC REFORM IN BRITAIN

During the 1800s, Parliament passed important laws. One issue was **free trade,** or trade without restrictions between countries. The Corn Laws caused strong debate. These laws placed high tariffs on imported grain. This helped British farmers and landowners but made bread more expensive. In 1846, Parliament **repealed,** or cancelled, the Corn Laws. The **abolition movement** brought about laws that ended the slave trade and banned slavery in all British colonies. Other reforms reduced the number of **capital offenses,** or crimes punishable by death. Instead of being put to death, many criminals were shipped to **penal colonies** in Australia and New Zealand.

Working conditions in the industrial age were grim and often dangerous. Gradually, Parliament passed laws to improve conditions in factories and mines. Other laws set minimum wages and maximum hours of work. An education act called for free elementary education for all children. Trade unions became legal in 1825, and worked to improve the lives of workers. The Labour Party was formed in 1900 and soon became one of Britain's major parties. In the early 1900s, Parliament passed laws to protect workers with old-age pensions and accident, health, and unemployment insurance.

Women struggled to win the right to vote. When peaceful efforts brought no results, Emmeline Pankhurst and other suffragists turned to more drastic, violent protest. In 1918, Parliament finally granted the vote to women over 30.

Throughout the 1800s, Britain faced the "Irish Question." The Irish resented British rule. Many Irish peasants lived in poverty. They paid high rents to **absentee landlords** living in England. Irish Catholics also had to pay tithes to the Church of England. The potato famine made thing worse. Irish leader Charles Stewart Parnell and others argued for **home rule,** or self-government, but this was debated for decades. Under Gladstone the government stopped Irish tithes and passed laws to protect the rights of Irish tenant farmers.

Review Questions

1. What laws did the abolition movement inspire?

_____

_____

2. Name two reasons why the Irish resented British rule.

_____

_____

READING CHECK

What is free trade?

_____

_____

_____

VOCABULARY STRATEGY

Find the word *drastic* in the underlined sentence. What do you think it means? Note that the suffragists first tried "peaceful efforts" before turning to "more *drastic,* violent protest." Which of the following words do you think has the same meaning as *drastic?*

1. moderate

2. extreme

READING SKILL

Categorize Group the laws that were passed to help workers into the following three categories: working conditions and wages, education, and insurance.

_____

_____

_____

Name_____ Class_____ Date_____

Focus Question: What democratic reforms were made in France during the Third Republic?

As you read this section in your textbook, complete the timeline below by labeling the main events described in this section. Some items have been completed for you.

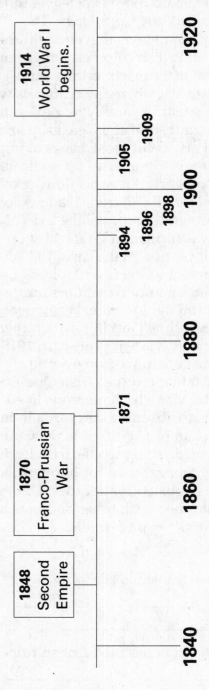

1914
World War I begins.

1920

1909

1905

1900

1898

1896

1894

1880

1871

1870
Franco-Prussian War

1860

1848
Second Empire

1840

CHAPTER
11
SECTION 3

Section Summary
DIVISION AND DEMOCRACY IN FRANCE

In 1852 **Napoleon III** set up the Second Empire in France. At first, he ruled like a dictator. In the 1860s, however, he gave the legislature more power. He encouraged industry and building projects. During his reign, a Frenchman organized the building of the **Suez Canal.** Unfortunately, Napoleon had major failures in foreign affairs. He tried to take control of Mexico by putting Austrian archduke Maximilian on the throne, but this failed. France and Britain won the Crimean War, but France suffered huge losses. The worst disaster was the Franco-Prussian War. In the end, the Prussians captured Napoleon. This ended his rule.

The Republicans in Paris set up a **provisional,** or temporary, government. This government became the Third Republic. In 1871, rebels in Paris created the Paris Commune. Their goal was to save the Republic from royalists. However, the government sent troops to stop the rebellion, and thousands were killed. The new French government had a two-house legislature and a president. However, the **premier** had the real power. France had many political parties, and no one party could take control. So parties had to form **coalitions,** or alliances, to rule. The coalition governments were unstable.

Scandals in the late 1800s caused people to lose trust in the government. The most serious scandal was the **Dreyfus affair.** Alfred Dreyfus was a Jewish army officer. He was wrongly accused of spying for Germany. When writer Émile Zola accused the army and government of hiding the truth, he was convicted of **libel.** The Dreyfus affair showed that there were strong anti-Jewish feelings in France. This led Theodor Herzl to start a movement to create a Jewish homeland—**Zionism.**

In the early 1900s, France passed labor laws to improve wages, working hours, and safety conditions. It also set up free public elementary schools. <u>The French tried to repress Church involvement in government, too.</u> In 1905, it passed a law to separate church and state.

Review Questions
1. How did Napoleon III's rule end?

_____

_____

2. What movement resulted from the Dreyfus affair?

_____

_____

READING CHECK

What are coalitions?

_____

_____

VOCABULARY STRATEGY

Find the word *repress* in the underlined sentence. What does it mean? Reread the sentence that follows the underlined sentence. What did France do to *repress* Church involvement in government? Did this increase or decrease Church involvement? Which of the words below is closest in meaning to *repress*?

1. limit

2. increase

READING SKILL

Recognize Sequence Arrange the three French governments described in this section (provisional government, Second Empire, Third Republic) in the correct chronological order.

_____

_____

Name_____ Class_____ Date_____

Note Taking Study Guide
EXPANSION OF THE UNITED STATES

Focus Question: How did the United States develop during the 1800s?

As you read this section in your textbook, complete the chart below by listing key events under the appropriate headings. Some items have been completed for you.

Civil War	
Before	**After**
• Western expansion	• Fifteenth Amendment extends voting rights to all adult male citizens.
• _____	• _____
_____	_____
• _____	• _____
_____	_____
• _____	• _____
_____	_____
	• _____
	_____
	• _____
	_____
	• _____
	_____
	• Nineteenth Amendment extends voting rights to all adult women.

Section Summary
EXPANSION OF THE UNITED STATES

In the 1800s, the United States followed a policy of **expansionism,** or extending the nation's boundaries. In 1803, the **Louisiana Purchase** nearly doubled the size of the country. More territory was soon added in the West and South. Americans believed in **Manifest Destiny.** This is the idea that their nation was destined to spread across the entire continent.

Voting, slavery, and women's rights were important issues. In 1800, only white men who owned property could vote. By the 1830s, most white men had the right to vote. William Lloyd Garrison, Frederick Douglass, and other abolitionists called for an end to slavery. Lucretia Mott, Elizabeth Cady Stanton, Susan B. Anthony, and other women began to seek equal rights.

Economic differences, as well as slavery, divided the country into the North and the South. When Abraham Lincoln was elected in 1860, most Southern states **seceded,** or left the Union. This started the American Civil War. Southerners fought fiercely but finally surrendered in 1865.

During the war, Lincoln issued the Emancipation Proclamation. This declared that the slaves in the South were free. After the war, slavery was banned throughout the nation. African Americans were granted some political rights. However, African Americans still faced **segregation.** Some state laws prevented African Americans from voting, too.

After the Civil War, the United States became a world leader in industrial and agricultural production. By 1900, giant monopolies controlled whole industries. <u>For example, John D. Rockefeller's Standard Oil Company dominated the world's petroleum industry.</u> Big business enjoyed huge profits, but not everyone benefited. Unions sought better wages and working conditions for factory workers. Farmers and city workers formed the Populist Party to seek changes. Progressives worked to ban child labor, limit working hours, regulate monopolies, and give voters more power. Progressives also worked to get women the right to vote. This finally happened in 1920.

Review Questions

1. What started the American Civil War?

_____

_____

2. What reforms did Progressives want?

_____

_____

READING CHECK

What effect did the Louisiana Purchase have on the size of the United States?

_____

_____

_____

VOCABULARY STRATEGY

Find the word *dominated* in the underlined sentence. What does it mean? The previous sentence states that giant monopolies *controlled* whole industries. The word *control* is a synonym for *dominate*. How does this sentence help you understand the meaning of *dominated*?

READING SKILL

Categorize Group the reforms described in this section by the people who did or would benefit from them: white men, African Americans, workers, and women.

_____

_____

_____

_____

CHAPTER 12 SECTION 1 — Note Taking Study Guide

BUILDING OVERSEAS EMPIRES

Focus Question: How did Western nations come to dominate much of the world in the late 1800s?

As you read this section in your textbook, complete the chart below showing the multiple causes of imperialism in the 1800s. Some items have been completed for you.

Event

The New Imperialism

Causes

- Need for natural resources
- Desire for new markets
- Bankers sought to invest their profits.
- Colonies offered an outlet for Europe's population.

CHAPTER
12
SECTION 1

Section Summary
BUILDING OVERSEAS EMPIRES

Many Western countries built overseas empires in the late 1800s. This expansion is called **imperialism.** It is the domination by one country of another country or region. In the 1800s Europeans began an aggressive expansion called the "new imperialism." The new imperialism had many causes. The Industrial Revolution was one. Manufacturers needed natural resources such as rubber and petroleum. They needed new markets to sell their goods. Colonies provided a place for Europe's growing population to live, too.

Nationalism played an important role, as well. Europeans felt that ruling a global empire increased a nation's prestige and influence. If one country began claiming Asian or African lands, rival nations would move in to claim nearby lands. Many in Europe were concerned about people overseas; they believed they had a duty to spread Western medicine, law, and religion. But there was also a growing sense that Europeans were racially superior to non-Westerners. Many Westerners used Social Darwinism to justify dominating other societies. As a result, millions of non-Westerners were robbed of their cultural heritage.

Africans and Asians strongly resisted Western expansion. Some people fought the invaders, but the Europeans had superior weapons and technology, such as machine guns, the telegraph, and riverboats. Others tried to strengthen their societies by reforming their own religious traditions. Many Western-educated Africans and Asians organized nationalist movements to expel the imperialists.

The imperial powers had several ways to control colonies. The French practiced direct rule. They sent officials from France to run the colony. The British often used indirect rule, governing through local rulers. In a **protectorate,** local rulers were left in place but were expected to follow the advice of Europeans. In a **sphere of influence,** an outside power claimed exclusive investment or trading privileges, but did not rule the area. Europeans did this to prevent conflicts among themselves.

Review Questions
1. What kinds of technology aided imperialism?

_____

_____

2. How is a protectorate different from a sphere of influence?

_____

_____

READING CHECK

How did the Industrial Revolution help to cause the new imperialism?

_____

_____

_____

VOCABULARY STRATEGY

Find the word *prestige* in the underlined sentence. Notice that the word *increased* is in the same sentence. What would a nation gain from a global empire? Think about why nations wanted to have colonies. How would Europeans feel if their rivals had larger empires? Use these context clues to help you figure out the meaning of *prestige.*

READING SKILL

Multiple Causes List the causes of imperialism found in this Section Summary.

_____

_____

_____

Name_____ Class_____ Date_____

Focus Question: How did imperialist European powers claim control over most of Africa by the end of the 1800s?

As you read this section in your textbook, complete the chart below by identifying the causes and effects of the partition of Africa by European nations. Some items have been completed for you.

Cause
- Explorers and missionaries increase contact.
-
-
- Berlin Conference

Event

Partition of Africa

Effect
- Europeans establish new borders in Africa.

CHAPTER 12 SECTION 2

Section Summary

THE PARTITION OF AFRICA

Before the 1800s, the Ottoman empire ruled much of North Africa. In West Africa, **Usman dan Fodio** set up a successful Islamic state inspiring other Muslim reform movements. Islam and trade influenced East Africa. In southern Africa, the Zulus emerged as a major force. They were led by **Shaka,** a ruthless and brilliant leader. His conquests set off huge migrations of conquered people to other areas and caused new wars.

European contact with Africans increased when European explorers pushed into the interior. Missionaries followed the explorers. They built schools, churches, and medical clinics. However, they took a **paternalistic** view of Africans, treating them like children. One explorer and missionary, **Dr. David Livingstone,** spent so many years in Central Africa that the journalist **Henry Stanley** was sent to find him.

About 1871, **King Leopold II** of Belgium hired Stanley to arrange trade treaties with African leaders. Leopold's interest caused Britain, France, and Germany to join in a scramble for African land. To stop conflict, Europeans met in Berlin to divide up the continent of Africa for themselves. As the years passed, Europeans took more and more of Africa's resources, and rarely allowed Africans any role in government. When gold and diamonds were discovered in southern Africa, the British fought the **Boer War.** The Boers were descendents of Dutch settlers.

Africans tried to resist European imperialism. **Samori Touré** fought French forces in West Africa. **Yaa Asantewaa** was an Asante queen who led the fight against the British. Another female leader was **Nehanda** of the Shona in Zimbabwe. Most efforts failed, except in Ethiopia. <u>Earlier, Ethiopia had been divided up among rival princes who then ruled their own domains.</u> However, **Menelik II** modernized his country. His army fought the Italians. The nation remained independent.

During this time, a Western-educated, upper-class African **elite** developed. By the early 1900s, African nationalists had begun to work for independence.

Review Questions

1. What did King Leopold hire Stanley to do?

_____

_____

2. Why did Europeans meet in Berlin?

_____

_____

READING CHECK

Which African country kept its independence?

_____

_____

_____

VOCABULARY STRATEGY

Find the word *domains* in the underlined sentence. Use context clues to figure out its meaning. Think about what a prince rules. When you divide a country, what are you dividing? Use these context clues to help you figure out the meaning of *domains*.

READING SKILL

Cause and Effect What caused Europeans to meet in Berlin? What was the effect on Africa?

_____

_____

_____

Name_____ Class_____ Date_____

Focus Question: How did European nations extend their power into Muslim regions of the world?

As you read this section in your textbook, complete the concept web below to understand the effects of European imperialism on Muslim regions. Some items have been completed for you.

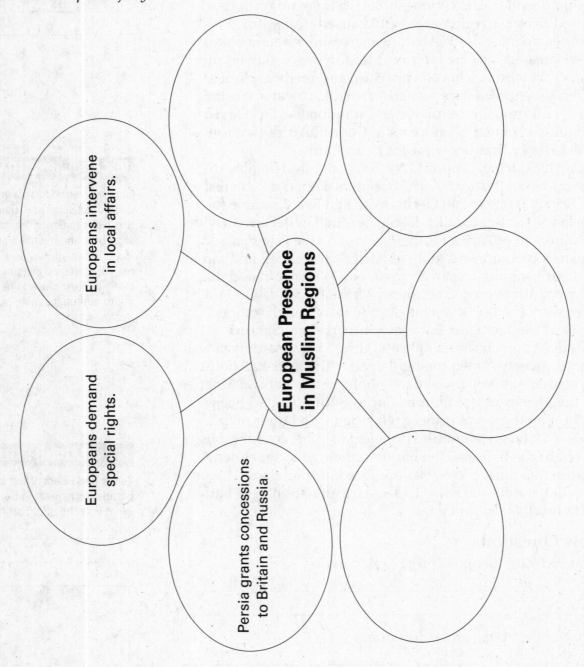

Europeans intervene in local affairs.

Europeans demand special rights.

European Presence in Muslim Regions

Persia grants concessions to Britain and Russia.

CHAPTER 12 SECTION 3

Section Summary
EUROPEAN CLAIMS IN MUSLIM REGIONS

In the 1500s, there were three great Muslim empires—the Ottomans in the Middle East, the Safavids in Persia, and the Mughals in India. By the 1700s, all three were in decline due to corruption and discontent. In response, Muslim reform movements arose. They stressed spiritual devotion and strict rules on how to act. Some also opposed foreign expansion in Muslim areas. For example, in the Sudan, **Muhammad Ahmad** said that he was the **Mahdi,** the long-awaited savior of the faith. The Mahdi and his followers fiercely fought British expansion.

At its height, the Ottoman empire extended across parts of North Africa, Southeastern Europe, and the Middle East. When ideas of nationalism spread from Western Europe, people within the empire began to rebel. Ambitious **pashas** wanted more power. Some leaders looked to the West for ideas on reforming the government and its rigid rules. In the early 1700s, they reorganized the bureaucracy. Repressive **sultans** usually rejected reform. Another problem was tension between Turkish nationalists and minority groups. This led to a brutal **genocide** of Christian Armenians when Turks thought that Armenians were supporting Russia against Turkey.

In the early 1800s, Egypt was a semi-independent province of the Ottoman empire. **Muhammad Ali** is sometimes called the "father of modern Egypt" because he introduced a number of political and economic reforms. He conquered the neighboring lands of Arabia, Syria, and Sudan. Before he died in 1849, he had set Egypt on the road to becoming a major Middle Eastern power. His successors lacked his skills, however. In 1882, Egypt became a protectorate of Britain.

Like the Ottoman empire, Persia—now Iran—faced major challenges. Foreign nations, especially Russia and Britain, wanted to control Iran's oil fields. They were granted special rights called **concessions,** and even sent in troops to protect their interests. These actions outraged Iranian nationalists.

Review Questions

1. Why did Muslim reform movements arise?

_____

_____

2. Why is Muhammad Ali sometimes called the "father of modern Egypt"?

_____

_____

READING CHECK

Who was the Mahdi?

_____

_____

_____

VOCABULARY STRATEGY

Find the word *bureaucracy* in the underlined sentence. *Bureau* is a French word that means "office." The suffix *-cracy* means "type of government." A *bureaucrat* is an official who works in a *bureaucracy.* Use these word-origin clues to help you figure out what *bureaucracy* means.

READING SKILL

Understanding Effects What was the effect of the foreign troops stationed in Iran?

_____

_____

_____

Name_____ Class_____ Date_____

Focus Question: How did Britain gradually extend its control over most of India despite opposition?

As you read this section in your textbook, complete the flowchart below to identify the causes and effects of British colonial rule in India. Some items have been completed for you.

Effect

- India's once prosperous hand-weaving industry is ruined.
- Massive deforestation

Event

British Colonial Rule in India

Cause

- Mughal empire lacks strong rulers.
- British East India Company increases influence.

CHAPTER 12 SECTION 4

Section Summary

THE BRITISH TAKE OVER INDIA

Mughal rulers once had a powerful Muslim empire in India. The British East India Company had trading rights on the edges of the empire. The main goal of the East India Company was to make money. As Mughal power declined, the East India Company gained power. The British were able to conquer India because Indians were not able to unite against the British.

The British felt that Western religion and culture was more advanced than Indian religions and culture. In the 1850s, the East India Company made several unpopular moves. The most serious caused the Sepoy Rebellion. Indian soldiers, or **sepoys,** were told to bite off the tips of their rifle cartridges. This caused a rebellion because the cartridges were greased with animal fat, violating local religious beliefs. The British crushed the revolt, killing thousands of Indians.

After the rebellion, Parliament ended the rule of the East India Company. Instead, a British **viceroy** governed India in the name of the monarch. <u>In this way, the overall British economy could benefit from trade with India.</u> However, this trade favored the British. Also, although the British built railroads and telegraph networks, they ruined India's hand-weaving industry. Encouraging Indian farmers to grow cash crops led to **deforestation** and famines.

Some educated Indians wanted India to become more modern. Others felt they should stay with their own Hindu or Muslim cultures. In the early 1800s, **Ram Mohun Roy** combined both views. Roy condemned child marriage and **sati,** which called for a widow to throw herself on her husband's funeral fire. He opposed **purdah,** or the isolation of women. He also set up educational societies to help revive pride in Indian culture. Most British felt that Western-educated Indians would be happy with British rule. Instead, Indian nationalists formed the Indian National Congress in 1885 and began pressing for self-rule.

Review Questions

1. How were the British able to conquer India?

_____

_____

2. What caused the Sepoy Rebellion?

_____

_____

READING CHECK

What British official ruled India in the name of the monarch?

_____

_____

_____

VOCABULARY STRATEGY

Find the word *overall* in the underlined sentence. *Overall* is a compound word. That means it is a word formed from two other words. Circle the two words that form *overall*. Use the meanings of these two words to figure out what *overall* means.

READING SKILL

Identify Causes and Effects
What happened when the British encouraged Indians to grow cash crops?

_____

_____

_____

Name______________________ Class__________________ Date________

CHAPTER 12 SECTION 5

Note Taking Study Guide

CHINA AND THE NEW IMPERIALISM

Focus Question: How did Western powers use diplomacy and war to gain power in Qing China?

As you read this section in your textbook, complete the chart below by listing the multiple causes of the decline of Qing China. Some items have been completed for you.

Event

Decline of Qing China

Cause

- Opium trade disrupts economy.
- Opium War with Britain
- Treaty of Nanjing forces China to make concessions to British.
-
-
-
-
-
-
-
-
-
- Two-year-old boy inherits the throne; China slips into chaos.

CHAPTER 12 SECTION 5	Section Summary
	CHINA AND THE NEW IMPERIALISM

For centuries, China had a favorable **balance of trade,** because of a **trade surplus.** Westerners had a **trade deficit** with China, buying more from the Chinese than they sold to them. Then the British began trading opium grown in India in exchange for Chinese tea. The Chinese asked Britain to stop this drug trade. The British refused, and this led to the **Opium War** in 1839. Without modern weapons and fighting methods, the Chinese were easily defeated. Under the Treaty of Nanjing, which ended the war, Britain received a huge **indemnity** and British citizens gained the right of **extraterritoriality.** Afterward, France, Russia, and the United States each made specific demands on China. <u>China felt pressure to sign treaties stipulating the opening of more ports and allowing Christian missionaries into China.</u>

China had other problems too. Peasants hated the corrupt Qing government. Their rebellion, known as the **Taiping Rebellion,** almost toppled the Qing dynasty. Another problem was that educated Chinese did not agree about modernizing. Some felt Western ideas and technology threatened Confucianism. Reformers who wanted to adopt Western ways did not have government support.

Meanwhile, China's defeat in the **Sino-Japanese War** of 1894 encouraged European nations to carve out spheres of influence in China. The United States feared that America might be shut out. The United States called for an **Open Door Policy,** making trade in China open to everyone. Concerned that China's problems were due to not modernizing, the emperor **Guang Xu** launched the Hundred Days of Reform in 1898. However, conservatives imprisoned the emperor.

Many Chinese were angry about the presence of foreigners. Some formed a secret group known to Westerners as the Boxers. A group known as the Boxers tried to kill foreigners in the **Boxer Uprising** in 1900. Although the Boxers failed, nationalism increased. Reformers began calling for a republic. One of them, **Sun Yixian,** became president of the new Chinese republic when the Qing dynasty fell in 1911.

Review Questions

1. What caused the Opium War?

_____

_____

2. What caused the Boxer Rebellion?

_____

_____

READING CHECK

Who became president of China in 1911?

_____

_____

_____

VOCABULARY STRATEGY

Find the word *stipulating* in the underlined sentence. What clues can you find in the surrounding words, phrases or sentences? Ask yourself what France, Russia, and the United States demanded or asked of China. Use these context clues to help you figure out what *stipulating* means.

READING SKILL

Recognize Multiple Causes List two causes of the Open Door Policy.

_____

_____

Name_____ Class_____ Date_____

Focus Question: How did Japan become a modern industrial power, and what did it do with its new strength?

As you read this section in your textbook, complete the chart below to identify causes and effects of the Meiji Restoration. Some items have been completed for you.

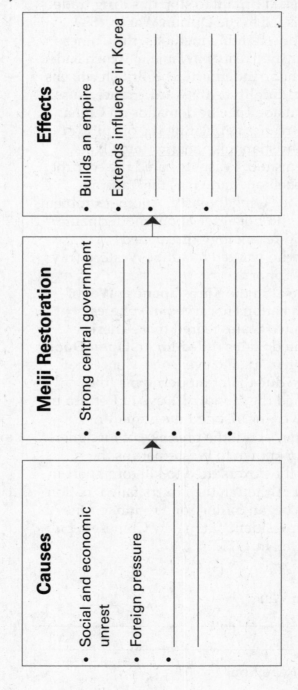

Causes
- Social and economic unrest
- Foreign pressure
-

Meiji Restoration
- Strong central government
-
-
-

Effects
- Builds an empire
- Extends influence in Korea
-
-

CHAPTER 13 SECTION 1

Section Summary

JAPAN MODERNIZES

In 1603, shoguns seized power in Japan and closed it to foreigners. For more than 200 years, Japan was isolated from the world. Over time, many Japanese became discontent. They suffered financial hardship and had no political power. The government responded by trying to revive old ways. <u>They tried emphasizing farming over commerce.</u> These efforts had little success. The shoguns' power weakened.

Then, in 1853, a fleet of well-armed U.S. ships arrived. They were led by Commodore **Matthew Perry,** who demanded that Japan open its ports. Japan was unable to defend itself, so it was forced to sign treaties that gave the United States trading rights. Disgraced by the terms of these treaties, daimyo and samurai revolted. The revolt unseated the shogun and restored the emperor Mutsuhito to power. Mutsuhito moved to the shogun's palace in the city of Edo, which was renamed **Tokyo.** This began a long reign known as the **Meiji Restoration.**

The Meiji reformers wanted to create a new political and social system. Their constitution made all citizens equal. A legislature, or **Diet,** was formed. Meiji leaders also wanted to build a modern industrial economy. The government supported powerful families, known as **zaibatsu.** These families ruled over industrial empires. Japan modernized very quickly. This was partly due to Japan's strong sense of identity caused by its **homogeneous society.** Its people shared a common culture and language.

Japan needed natural resources for industry. This need and the desire to equal the West pushed Japan to build an empire. First, Japan forced Korea to open its ports for trade. Next, competition between Japan and China in Korea led to the **First Sino-Japanese War,** which Japan won. Japan gained ports in China and won control over Taiwan. Then, Japan successfully battled Russia in the **Russo-Japanese War.** By the early 1900s, Japan was the strongest power in Asia.

Review Questions

1. What caused the daimyo and samurai to revolt?

_____

_____

2. What right did all citizens gain under the Meiji constitution?

_____

_____

READING CHECK

Why did Japan have a strong sense of identity?

_____

_____

_____

VOCABULARY STRATEGY

Find the word *emphasizing* in the underlined sentence. What does it mean? Look for context clues in the surrounding words. For example, what clue does the word *over* provide about the relationship of farming to commerce? To what does "old ways" refer here? Use these clues to help you figure out what *emphasizing* means.

READING SKILL

Identify Causes and Effects
What was one cause and one effect of the coming to Japan of Perry's fleet?

_____

_____

_____

CHAPTER 13 SECTION 2

Note Taking Study Guide
IMPERIALISM IN SOUTHEAST ASIA AND THE PACIFIC

Focus Question: How did industrialized powers divide up Southeast Asia, and how did the colonized peoples react?

As you read this section in your textbook, complete the flowchart below to identify causes, events, and effects of imperialism in Southeast Asia and the Pacific. Some items have been completed for you.

Effects
- Europeans introduce modern technology.
- Europeans expand commerce and industry.

↑

Events
- Dutch dominate the Dutch East Indies (now Indonesia).
- The British annex Burma.
- The French seize Indochina.

↑

Causes
- Sea lanes opened between India and China.
- Profitable crops of coffee, indigo, spices
- Natural resources

CHAPTER 13 SECTION 2

Section Summary

IMPERIALISM IN SOUTHEAST ASIA AND THE PACIFIC

In the 1800s, European merchants began to colonize much of Southeast Asia. The Dutch, for example, took over all of the Dutch East Indies (now Indonesia). The British expanded from India into Burma and Malaya. The Burmese resisted British rule but suffered terrible defeats. The French invaded Vietnam. The Vietnamese fought fiercely, but lost against European weapons. The French took over all of Vietnam, Laos, and Cambodia. They called these holdings **French Indochina.** Meanwhile, the king of Siam, **Mongkut,** was able to keep his country from becoming a European colony. To do so, he accepted some unequal treaties. By the 1890s, Europeans controlled most of Southeast Asia.

The Philippines had been under Spanish rule since the 1500s. In 1898, the **Spanish-American War** broke out. During the war, U.S. battleships destroyed the Spanish fleet in the Philippines. Filipino rebel leaders declared independence from Spain. They joined the U.S. fight against Spain. In return for their help, the Filipino rebels expected the United States to recognize their independence. Instead, in the treaty that ended the war, the United States gave Spain $20 million for control of the Philippines. The Filipino rebels were bitterly disappointed. They renewed their struggle for independence, but the United States crushed the rebellion. <u>The United States, however, did promise Filipinos a slow transition to self-rule sometime in the future.</u>

In the 1800s, the industrialized powers also began to take an interest in the many Pacific islands. American sugar growers, for example, pressed for power in the Hawaiian Islands. When the Hawaiian queen **Liliuokalani** tried to reduce foreign influence, American planters overthrew her. In 1898, the United States annexed Hawaii. Supporters of annexation argued that if the United States did not take Hawaii, other rival countries would. By 1900, the United States, Britain, France, or Germany had claimed nearly every island in the Pacific.

Review Questions

1. How did the king of Siam keep his country from becoming a European colony?

_____

_____

2. What had Filipino rebels expected in return for helping the United States during the Spanish-American War?

_____

_____

READING CHECK

What did the French call their holdings of Vietnam, Laos, and Cambodia?

_____

_____

_____

VOCABULARY STRATEGY

Find the word *transition* in the underlined sentence. Note that the word begins with the prefix *trans-*, which means "across" or "through." Use the meanings of the word's prefix to help you figure out what the word *transition* means.

READING SKILL

Identify Causes and Effects Identify one cause and one effect of Liliuokalani's attempts to reduce foreign influence in Hawaii.

_____

_____

_____

Name_____ Class_____ Date_____

Focus Question: How were the British colonies of Canada, Australia, and New Zealand settled, and how did they win self-rule?

As you read this section in your textbook, complete the chart below to identify the causes and effects of events in the British colonies of Canada, Australia, and New Zealand. Some items have been completed for you.

Cause	Event	Effect				
Loyalist Americans flee to Canada.	Up to 30,000 loyalists settle in Canada.	Ethnic tensions arise between English- and French-speaking Canadians.				
The British hurry to put down the rebellions in Upper and Lower Canada.	British Parliament passes the Act of Union.	The act joins the two Canadas into one province and gives them an elected legislature.				
Canada grows as thousands of English, Scottish, and Irish people immigrate to the country.						
Britain needs prisons for its convicts.						

CHAPTER 13 SECTION 3

Section Summary

SELF-RULE FOR CANADA, AUSTRALIA, AND NEW ZEALAND

In 1791, Britain created two provinces in Canada: English-speaking Upper Ganada and French-speaking Lower Canada. <u>When unrest grew in both colonies, the British sent Lord Durham to compile a report on the causes.</u> In response to his report, Parliament joined the two Canadas into one colony.

As the country grew, Canadian leaders urged **confederation,** or unification, of Britain's North American colonies. They felt that this would strengthen the new nation against the United States and help the economy. British Parliament passed a law that made Canada a **dominion,** or self-governing nation. Canada continued to grow. As Canada expanded westward, the Native American way of life was destroyed. The **métis**—people of mixed Native American and French Canadian descent—tried to resist. Government troops, however, put down their revolts.

In 1770, Captain James Cook claimed Australia for Britain. Australia had long been inhabited by other people. These **indigenous,** or original, people are called Aborigines. When white settlers arrived in Australia, the Aborigines suffered terribly. Britain needed prisons for its criminals. So, it made Australia into a **penal colony,** or faraway jail. Then, Britain encouraged non-criminal citizens to move to Australia by offering them land and tools. Like Canada, Australia was made up of separate colonies scattered around the continent. To keep away other European powers and to boost development, Britain agreed to Australian demands for self-rule. In 1901, the colonies united into the independent Commonwealth of Australia.

Captain James Cook also claimed New Zealand for Britain. The indigenous people of New Zealand are the **Maori.** They were determined to defend their land. In 1840, Britain annexed New Zealand. Colonists took more and more of the land. This led to fierce wars with the Maori. Many Maori died. By the 1870s, Maori resistance had crumbled. Like settlers in Australia and Canada, white New Zealanders wanted self-rule. In 1907, they won independence.

Review Questions

1. Why did Britain agree to make Canada a dominion?

_____

_____

2. Why did the British agree to self-rule in Australia?

_____

_____

READING CHECK

What indigenous people suffered when European settlers arrived in Australia?

_____

_____

_____

VOCABULARY STRATEGY

Find the word *compile* in the underlined sentence. The word *compile* comes from a Latin word that means "to heap together." Use this clue to help you learn what *compile* means.

READING SKILL

Identify Causes and Effects
Identify the causes and effects of the Maori fight against New Zealand colonists.

_____

_____

_____

CHAPTER 13 SECTION 4

Note Taking Study Guide

ECONOMIC IMPERIALISM IN LATIN AMERICA

Focus Question: How did Latin American nations struggle for stability, and how did industrialized nations affect them?

A. *As you read this section in your textbook, complete the chart below to identify multiple causes of instability in Latin America. Then, give an example of how each cause affected Mexico. Some items have been completed for you.*

Instability in Latin America	
Causes	**Mexican Example**
Colonial legacy leaves deep-rooted inequalities after independence.	Large landowners, army leaders, and the Catholic Church dominate Mexican politics.
Efforts for reform are crushed.	

B. *As you read "The Economics of Dependence" and "The Influence of the United States," complete the chart below to identify effects of foreign influence on Latin America. Some items have been completed for you.*

Effects of Foreign Influence

Cycle of economic dependence continues.		

CHAPTER 13 SECTION 4

Section Summary
ECONOMIC IMPERIALISM IN LATIN AMERICA

Many factors kept democracy from taking hold in Latin America's newly independent nations. Constitutions guaranteed equality before the law, but inequalities remained. These nations did not have a tradition of unity. Therefore, **regionalism,** or loyalty to a local area, weakened them. Local strongmen, called *caudillos,* formed private armies to resist the central government.

Mexico is an example of the struggle to build stable governments in Latin America at this time. Large landowners, army leaders, and the Catholic Church dominated Mexican politics. The ruling elite was divided between conservatives and liberals. Conservatives defended tradition. <u>Liberals saw themselves as enlightened supporters of progress.</u> Battles between these two groups led to revolts and the rise of dictators. When **Benito Juárez** and other liberals gained power, they began an era of reform known as **La Reforma.** Juárez offered hope to the oppressed people of Mexico. After Juárez died, however, General Porfirio Díaz ruled as a harsh dictator. Many Indians and mestizos fell into **peonage,** to work off advances on their wages.

Under colonial rule, Latin America was economically dependent on Spain and Portugal. This prevented Latin America from developing its own economy. After independence, this pattern changed very little. Britain and the United States replaced Spain as Latin America's chief trading partners.

Meanwhile, the United States expanded across North America. U.S. leaders wanted to discourage any new European colonies in the Americas, so they issued the **Monroe Doctrine.** To protect U.S. investments in Latin America, the United States sent troops. This made the United States a target of resentment and rebellion. Then the United States built the **Panama Canal** across Central America. The canal boosted trade and shipping worldwide. To people in Latin America, however, the canal was another example of "Yankee imperialism."

Review Questions

1. What three groups dominated Mexican politics?

_____

_____

2. After independence, on which countries did the new Latin American republics depend economically?

_____

_____

READING CHECK

Who were the caudillos?

_____

_____

_____

VOCABULARY STRATEGY

Find the word *enlightened* in the underlined sentence. Break the word down into its smaller parts. Note that the root word of *enlightened* is *light. Light* is sometimes used to mean "information," as in the phrase, "Let's shed some light on the subject." Use this word-part clue to help you figure out what *enlightened* means.

READING SKILL

Identify Causes and Effects Identify what caused the United States to issue the Monroe Doctrine. Then, identify one effect it had on Latin America.

_____

_____

_____

Name_____ Class_____ Date_____

Focus Question: Why and how did World War I begin in 1914?

As you read this section in your textbook, complete the following chart to summarize the events that led to the outbreak of World War I. Some items have been completed for you.

The War Begins

- Archduke of Austria assassinated by Serbian nationalist.

Tensions Rise

- Powers want to protect status.
- Compete overseas for colonies

Alliances Form

- Triple Alliance, 1882— Germany, Austria, Italy

CHAPTER 14 SECTION 1

Section Summary
THE GREAT WAR BEGINS

Although powerful forces were pushing Europe towards war, the great powers had made non-binding agreements, called **ententes,** to try to keep the peace. The Triple Alliance was made up of Germany, Austria-Hungary, and Italy. Russia, France, and Britain made up the Triple Entente. During World War I, Germany and Austria fought on the same side. They were called the Central Powers. Russia, France, and Britain were known as the Allies.

In the period before the war, European powers competed. They wanted to protect their status. <u>Overseas rivalries divided them.</u> They fought for new colonies in Africa and elsewhere. They began to build up their armies and navies. The rise of **militarism** helped to feed this arms race.

Nationalism also caused tensions to grow. Germans were proud of their military and economic power. The French wanted **Alsace and Lorraine** back from Germany. Pan-Slavism led Russia to support fellow Slavs in Serbia. Austria and Ottoman Turkey were afraid that they would lose territory, especially in the Balkans. Soon, unrest made that region a "powder keg." Then, a Serbian nationalist shot to death the heir to the Austrian throne at Sarajevo, Bosnia.

Some Austrian leaders saw this as a chance to crush Serbia. They sent Serbia an **ultimatum,** or set of demands, which Serbia partly refused to follow. Austria, with Germany's full support, declared war on Serbia in July 1914.

Soon, the network of agreements drew other great powers into the fight. Russia began to **mobilize** its army to support Serbia. Germany then declared war on Russia. France said it would keep to its treaty with Russia, so Germany declared war on France, too. When Germany invaded Belgium to get to France, it ended Belgium's **neutrality.** This caused Britain to declare war on Germany. World War I had begun.

Review Questions

1. How did the network of European agreements cause World War I to start?

_____

_____

2. What act caused Britain to declare war?

_____

_____

READING CHECK

Which countries made up the Central Powers?

_____

_____

_____

VOCABULARY STRATEGY

What does the word *overseas* mean in the underlined sentence? What clues can you find in the surrounding words, phrases, or sentences? Circle the words in the paragraph that could help you learn what *overseas* means.

READING SKILL

Summarize What events led Austria to declare war on Serbia?

_____

_____

_____

CHAPTER 14 SECTION 2

Note Taking Study Guide

A NEW KIND OF WAR

Focus Question: How and where was World War I fought?

A. *As you read "Stalemate on the Western Front," "Battle on Other European Fronts," and "War Around the World," record important details about World War I events in the flowchart below. Some items have been completed for you.*

Western Front
- Stalemate
- First battle of the Marne prevented a quick German victory.
- Soldiers fought from trenches.
- _____

Eastern Front
- Battle lines shifted.
- _____
- _____

Elsewhere in Europe
- Bulgaria joined the Central Powers and helped defeat its old Balkan rival Serbia.
- _____
- _____

Ottoman Empire
- Joined the Central Powers
- _____

Colonies
- European colonies were drawn into the war.

B. *As you read "Technology of Modern Warfare," complete the following concept web to summarize information about the technology of World War I. Some items have been completed for you.*

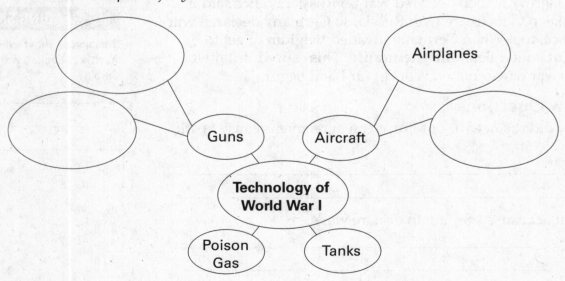

CHAPTER 14 SECTION 2	**Section Summary**
	A NEW KIND OF WAR

World War I was the largest conflict in history up to that time. Millions of French, British, Russian, and German soldiers went to battle. Germany wanted to defeat France quickly, but Belgian forces resisted Germany's advance. Both sides dug deep trenches on the battlefront to protect their armies from enemy fire. This conflict on the Western Front turned into a long, deadly **stalemate,** or deadlock that neither side could break.

New technology made World War I different from earlier wars. Modern weapons were able to kill more soldiers than ever before. In 1915, first Germany then the Allies began using poison gas. New machines like tanks, airplanes, and submarines were used in this war. In 1915, Germany flew **zeppelins** to bomb the English coast. Both sides equipped airplanes with machine guns. <u>Pilots known as "flying aces" confronted each other in the skies.</u> However, their "dog fights" had little effect on the ground war. German submarines called **U-boats** attacked Allied ships. To defend against them, the Allies organized **convoys,** or groups of merchant ships protected by warships.

Battle lines shifted back and forth on Europe's Eastern Front. War deaths were higher than on the Western Front. Russia was not ready to fight a modern war. When pushing into eastern Germany, Russian armies were badly defeated. In 1915, Italy declared war on Austria-Hungary and Germany. In 1917, the Austrians and Germans attacked the Italians.

Although most of the fighting took place in Europe, World War I was a global conflict. Japan used the war to seize German outposts in China and islands in the Pacific. The Ottoman empire joined the Central Powers. Its strategic location enabled it to cut off Allied supplies to Russia through the **Dardanelles,** a vital strait. The Ottoman Turks were hard hit in the Middle East. Arab nationalists rebelled against their rule. The British sent **T.E. Lawrence,** or Lawrence of Arabia, to aid them. European colonies in Africa and Asia were also drawn into World War I.

Review Questions

1. Why did a stalemate develop on the Western Front?

_____

_____

2. What caused the great number of deaths during World War I?

_____

_____

READING CHECK

Which of the European powers was not ready to fight a modern war?

_____

_____

_____

VOCABULARY STRATEGY

What does the word *confronted* mean in the underlined sentence? What clues or examples can you find in the surrounding words, phrases, or sentences that hint at its meaning? For example, think about the meaning of the phrase "dog fights." Circle the words in the paragraph that could help you learn what *confronted* means.

READING SKILL

Identify Supporting Details Identify two differences between the Western Front and the Eastern Front.

_____

_____

_____

Note Taking Study Guide

CHAPTER 14 SECTION 3

WINNING THE WAR

Focus Question: How did the Allies win World War I?

As you read this section in your textbook, complete the following outline to summarize the content of this section. Some items have been completed for you.

I. **Waging total war**

   A. Economies committed to war production.

      1. Conscription

      2. Rationing

      3. Price controls

   B. Economic warfare

      1. _____

      2. _____

      3. _____

   C. Propaganda war

      1. _____

      2. _____

      3. _____

   D. Women join war effort.

      1. _____

      2. _____

      3. _____

II. **Morale collapses.**

   A. War fatigue

      1. _____

      2. _____

      3. _____

   B. _____

      1. _____

      2. _____

      3. _____

(Outline continues on the next page.)

CHAPTER 14
SECTION 3

Note Taking Study Guide

WINNING THE WAR

(Continued from page 152)

III. United States declares war.

A. _____

   1. _____

   2. _____

   3. _____

B. _____

   1. _____

   2. _____

   3. _____

C. _____

   1. _____

   2. _____

   3. _____

IV. _____

A. _____

B. _____

C. _____

CHAPTER 14 SECTION 3 | Note Taking Study Guide

WINNING THE WAR

What did both sides use to control public opinion?

_____

_____

_____

VOCABULARY STRATEGY

What does the word *eroded* mean in the underlined sentence? You can use prior knowledge to figure it out. Think about what you might already know about this word in another form: *erosion*. What does *erosion* mean? Use what you might know about *erosion* as a clue to what *eroded* means.

READING SKILL

Summarize Describe how World War I was a total war.

_____

_____

_____

World War I was the first **total war.** Nations put all their resources into the war effort. Both sides set up systems to recruit, arm, transport, and supply their armies. Nations set up military **conscription,** or "the draft." This required all young men to be ready to fight. Women played an important role, too. They took over the jobs of millions of men who had left to fight.

International law allowed wartime blockades to seize **contraband,** such as weapons or other illegal goods. British blockades, however, kept ships from carrying other supplies, such as food, in and out of Germany. In response, German U-boats torpedoed the British passenger liner the *Lusitania.* Both sides used **propaganda** to control public opinion. They printed tales of **atrocities.** Some were true and others were not.

After a time, war fatigue set in. Long casualty lists, food shortages, and the failure to win led to calls for peace. The morale of troops and civilians plunged. <u>In Russia, stories of unfit generals and corruption eroded public confidence and led to revolution.</u>

In 1917, the United States joined the fight by declaring war on Germany. Many factors led to this decision. Germany kept up its submarine attacks. Also, many Americans supported the Allies because of cultural ties. By 1918, about two million fresh American soldiers had joined the tired Allied troops. Earlier in that year, President Wilson had issued his **Fourteen Points.** This list of terms for ending this and future wars included **self-determination** for the peoples of Eastern Europe.

In March of 1918, a final showdown on the Western Front began. American troops and Allies drove back German forces. German generals told the kaiser that the war could not be won. The kaiser stepped down and the new German government asked for an **armistice** to end the fighting. At 11 A.M. on November 11, 1918, World War I came to an end.

Review Questions

1. What effect did years of war have on morale?

_____

_____

2. What are two reasons why the United States entered the war?

_____

_____

CHAPTER 14 SECTION 4

Note Taking Study Guide

MAKING THE PEACE

Focus Question: What factors influenced the peace treaties that ended World War I and how did people react to the treaties?

A. *As you read "The Costs of War," complete this concept web to summarize the costs of World War I. Some items have been completed for you.*

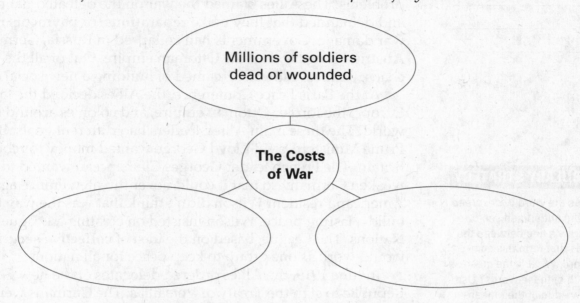

B. *As you read "The Paris Peace Conference," "The Treaty of Versailles," and "Outcome of the Peace Settlements," use this table to categorize issues and problems that resulted from postwar agreements. Some items have been completed for you.*

Issue	Treaty Settlement	Problems
War Debt	Because of the treaty, the new German Republic had to make large payments to pay for damage caused by the war.	These payments would hurt an already damaged German economy.
Fear of German Strength	The treaty limited the size of the German military.	
Nationalism		
Colonies and Other Non-European Territories		
League of Nations		

CHAPTER **14** SECTION 4	**Note Taking Study Guide**
	MAKING THE PEACE

The costs of World War I were huge in several ways. There was a great loss of life made worse by an influenza **pandemic.** In addition, raising the money to cover war debts and to rebuild homes, farms, factories and roads would create new economic problems. The Allies blamed the war on the defeated nations and demanded that they make **reparations,** or payments for war damage. Governments had collapsed in Russia, Germany, Austria-Hungary, and the Ottoman empire. Out of all the chaos, political **radicals** dreamed of building a new social order.

At the Paris Peace Conference, the Allies decided the fate of Europe, the former Ottoman empire, and colonies around the world. The three main Allied leaders had different goals. British Prime Minister David Lloyd George wanted money to rebuild Britain. The French leader Georges Clemenceau wanted to weaken Germany so that it could never threaten France again. American President Wilson didn't think that was the way to build a lasting peace. Wilson insisted on creating a League of Nations. The League, based on the idea of **collective security,** would work as one group to keep peace for all nations.

In June 1919, the Allies ordered delegates of the new German Republic to sign the Treaty of Versailles. The Germans were upset that the treaty forced Germany to take the blame for causing the war, cut the size of Germany's military, and burdened the German economy with war reparations.

The Allies then drew up treaties with the other Central Powers. <u>Like the Treaty of Versailles, these treaties left widespread dissatisfaction.</u> Many nations felt betrayed by the peacemakers—especially people in colonies who had hoped for an end to imperial rule. Outside Europe, the Allies added to their overseas empires by creating a system of **mandates.** However, the Paris Peace Conference did offer one ray of hope by starting the League of Nations. Unfortunately, the failure of the United States to support the League weakened it.

Review Questions
1. What were the high costs of World War I?

_____

_____

2. Why were the leaders of the new German Republic upset over the Treaty of Versailles?

_____

_____

Name_____ Class_____ Date_____

Focus Question: How did two revolutions and a civil war bring about Communist control of Russia?

As you read this section in your textbook, fill in the following timeline with dates and facts about the series of events that led to Communist control of Russia. Some items have been included for you. Then write two sentences summarizing the information in the timeline.

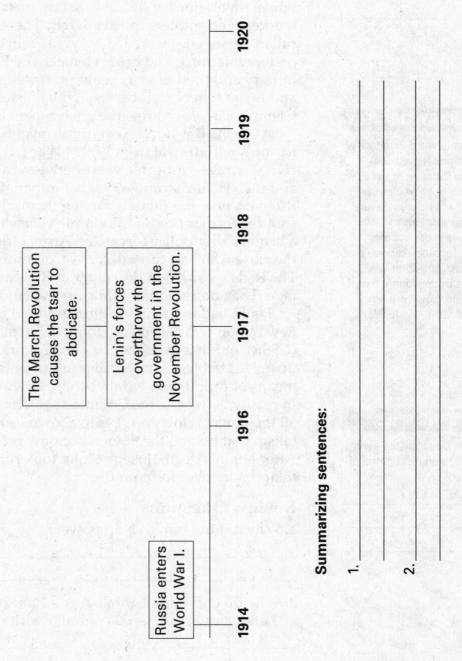

Summarizing sentences:

1. _____

2. _____

1920
1919
1918
The March Revolution causes the tsar to abdicate.
Lenin's forces overthrow the government in the November Revolution.
1917
1916
Russia enters World War I.
1914

CHAPTER 14 SECTION 5 — Note Taking Study Guide
REVOLUTION AND CIVIL WAR IN RUSSIA

What was the name of the new Communist nation?

_____

_____

_____

What does the word *withdrawal* mean in the underlined sentence? How is the word used? Look at other context clues in the sentence to help you figure out what the word means. The context clues in the second underlined sentence tell you that after the Russian withdrawal, the Russian troops fought a civil war, meaning they were no longer involved in World War I.

Summarize Describe the events that led to Communist control of Russia.

_____

_____

_____

By the early 1900s Russia had many problems. Tsar Nicholas II resisted change. Marxists tried to start a revolution among the **proletariat** factory workers and urban wage earners. World War I strained Russian resources. By March 1917, disasters on the battlefield and shortages at home caused the tsar to give up his power. Politicians set up a temporary government. Meanwhile, revolutionary socialists set up their own councils of workers and soldiers called **soviets.** These radical socialists, called Bolsheviks, were led by V. I. Lenin. Lenin believed only revolution could bring change. The Russian people were hungry and tired of war. Lenin promised them "Peace, Land, and Bread." In November 1917, the Bolsheviks, renamed Communists, overthrew the government and seized power.

After the Bolshevik Revolution, events in Russia led to the nation's withdrawal from World War I. After the withdrawal, civil war raged for three years between the Communist "Reds" and the "White" armies of tsarist imperial officers. The Russians now fought only among themselves. The Communists shot the former tsar and his family. They organized the **Cheka,** a brutal secret police force. Red Army officers were kept under the close watch of **commissars**—Communist Party officials. The Reds' position in the center of Russia gave them an advantage. They defeated the White armies, and the civil war ended.

Lenin had to rebuild the government and economy. The new nation was called the Union of Soviet Socialist Republics (USSR), or Soviet Union. The new Communist constitution set up an elected legislature. All political power, resources, and means of production would belong to workers and peasants. In reality, however, the Communist Party, not the people, had all the power. However, Lenin allowed some features of capitalism that helped the Soviet economy recover from the wars. After Lenin's death, Joseph Stalin took ruthless steps to win total power over the country.

Review Questions
1. Why did the tsar give up power?

_____

_____

2. Why do you think Lenin's revolutionary slogan—"Peace, Land, and Bread"—was popular with the Russian people?

_____

_____

Name_____ Class_____ Date_____

Note Taking Study Guide
STRUGGLE IN LATIN AMERICA

Focus Question: How did Latin Americans struggle for change in the early 1900s?

A. *As you read "The Mexican Revolution" and "Revolution Leads to Change," list the causes and effects of the Mexican Revolution. Some items have been completed for you.*

Causes
- Díaz ruled for nearly 35 years.
- Foreign investors controlled many of the natural resources.
-
-
-

Mexican Revolution

Effects
- Venustiano Carranza was elected president of Mexico in 1917.
- A new constitution was approved; it called for nationalization of foreign-owned interests.
-
-
-
-

B. *As you read "Nationalism at Work in Latin America," complete the following chart by listing the effects of nationalism in Latin America. Some items have been completed for you.*

Effects of Nationalism in Latin America

Economic
- Governments supported businesses and factories to produce goods.
-
-

Political
- People lost trust in governments.
-

Cultural
- Traditional art forms enjoyed renewed interest.
-

Name_____ Class_____ Date_____

In the early 1900s, Latin America enjoyed business success. However, investors from other countries controlled much of the region's natural resources. Peasants and workers had little say in the government. Military leaders or wealthy landowners held most of the power. Therefore, only a few people benefited from the growing economy. Most Mexicans lived in poverty. Peasants worked on **haciendas,** or large farms owned by the rich. Eventually, people demanded a say in government. Faced with rebellion, the dictator Porfirio Díaz left office in 1911. A struggle for power, called the Mexican Revolution, began.

In 1917, Venustiano Carranza was elected Mexico's president. He approved a new constitution that included land and labor reform. The constitution strengthened government control over the economy. One way it did this was through **nationalization,** the takeover of natural resources. The government took over some foreign-owned oil companies. Fighting continued until the Institutional Revolutionary Party (PRI) was formed. The PRI took control, allowing some reforms while keeping most of the power.

As was the case elsewhere, the Great Depression hurt Latin American economies. As a result, **economic nationalism,** or home control of the economy, became popular. Some nations also took over foreign-owned properties and businesses. Stronger leaders emerged. Another change was the growth of **cultural nationalism,** and the rejection of European influences. Artists such as Diego Rivera revived mural painting, an art form of the Aztecs and Maya, to depict the people's struggles. At this time, the United States was often involved in Latin America, intervening when U.S. interests were in danger. This created anti-American feeling. In response, President Franklin Roosevelt developed the **Good Neighbor Policy.** This meant that the United States promised to stay out of Latin American politics. The result was better relations between the United States and Latin American countries.

Review Questions

1. Who became president of Mexico in 1917?

_____

_____

2. What was the impact of the Good Neighbor Policy?

_____

_____

Name_____ Class_____ Date_____

Focus Question: How did nationalism contribute to changes in Africa and the Middle East following World War I?

As you read this section in your textbook, complete the following table to identify causes and effects of the rise of nationalism. Some boxes have been filled in for you.

Rise of Nationalism

Region	Reasons for Rise	Effects
Africa	• Oppressed by European colonialism • More than one million Africans fought on behalf of colonial rulers in World War I with hopes of more rights. • •	• Europeans increased their control in some areas; the apartheid system was adopted in South Africa. • The African National Congress protested unfair laws.
Turkey and Persia	• Collapse of Ottoman empire after World War I •	• Atatürk established Turkey as a secular republic. • • •
Middle East	• Growth of Pan-Arabism • Feelings of betrayal at Paris Peace Conference after World War I • •	• Ongoing Arab resentment of Westerners •

CHAPTER 15 SECTION 2 — Section Summary

NATIONALISM IN AFRICA AND THE MIDDLE EAST

Who ended Ottoman rule and set up a republic in Turkey?

_____

_____

_____

Find the word *advocated* in the underlined sentence. It is from the Latin word *advocare,* which means "to call to one's aid." Use this word-origins clue to help you figure out what *advocated* means.

Identify Causes and Effects
What effect did European rule have on African farmers?

_____

_____

_____

During the early 1900s, Europeans controlled most of Africa. They kept the best lands for themselves or forced African farmers to grow cash crops instead of food. Some Africans had to work in mines or on plantations and then pay taxes to the colonial governments. In South Africa, blacks lost the right to vote and were kept from certain jobs. This repression and segregation became even harsher under **apartheid.**

During the 1920s, the movement known as **Pan-Africanism** called for the unity of Africans around the world. The activist W.E.B. DuBois organized the first Pan-African Congress in 1919. He asked world leaders to approve more rights for Africans. Meanwhile the **négritude movement,** made up of artists and writers in West Africa and the Caribbean, celebrated African pride and protested colonial rule. For example, the poet Léopold Senghor celebrated Africans' tribal past. These movements, however, brought little real change.

In **Asia Minor,** Mustafa Kemal overthrew the Ottoman ruler and created the republic of Turkey. He encouraged business by building railroads and factories. His success in modernizing Turkey inspired nationalists in Persia. Reza Khan overthrew the Persian shah. As the new ruler, he modernized the country and convinced British oil companies to give Persia a bigger share of profits. Both rulers replaced Islamic traditions with Western ways that Muslim leaders condemned.

Arab nationalism grew in the Middle East. **Pan-Arabism** was built on a common history among Arabs living from the Arabian Peninsula to North Africa. After World War I, Arabs had hoped to gain independence but felt betrayed when the French and British took control of their lands. Meanwhile, Jewish nationalists dreamed of a homeland in Palestine. To show support for European Jews, Britain issued the **Balfour Declaration.** This statement advocated a homeland for Jews in Palestine. Arabs felt that the declaration favored the Jews. Ever since, Arabs and Jews have fought for control of Palestine.

Review Questions

1. What were the two African nationalist movements?

_____

_____

2. How were Mustafa Kemal and Reza Khan alike?

_____

_____

CHAPTER
15
SECTION 3

Note Taking Study Guide

INDIA SEEKS SELF-RULE

Focus Question: How did Gandhi and the Congress party work for independence in India?

As you read this section in your textbook, complete the chart with the causes and effects of Gandhi's leadership on India's independence movement. Some items have been filled in for you.

Effects

- Gandhi called for a boycott of British goods, especially cotton textiles.
- Gandhi's Salt March inspired other Indians to join his protest of the British monopoly on salt.
-
-
-

↑

Gandhi Leads Independence Movement

↑

Causes

- Millions of Indians served in World War I for Britain, based on the promise of greater self-rule.
- Limited British reforms after World War I frustrated Indians.
-
-
-
-

CHAPTER 15 SECTION 3

Section Summary

INDIA SEEKS SELF-RULE

In April 1919, British soldiers killed and wounded hundreds of peaceful Indian protestors. This event was called the **Amritsar massacre**. It was a turning point in India's history because it convinced Indians that their country should be independent of Britain. The tragedy was the result of frustration that had been growing since World War I. During the war, Britain had promised India greater self-government. Afterwards, it made only a few small changes. The Congress party of India began calling for independence. This mostly middle-class party had little in common with the poor Indian peasants. In the 1920s, Mohandas Gandhi came forward as a new leader. Gandhi had experience opposing unfair treatment and prejudice. For 20 years, he had fought laws in South Africa that discriminated against Indians.

Gandhi inspired people of all religions and backgrounds. He preached **ahimsa**. This is a belief in nonviolence and respect for all life. Gandhi spoke out against harsh treatment of the **untouchables,** or Hindu society's lowest group. Henry David Thoreau's ideas about **civil disobedience** influenced Gandhi. This was the idea that people should not obey unjust laws. Gandhi began a program of civil disobedience. He led a series of nonviolent protests against British rule. For example, he called for Indians to **boycott,** or refuse to buy, British goods.

Another important event was Gandhi's stand against the British salt monopoly. Although salt was available for free in the sea, Indians were forced to buy salt from the British. When Gandhi marched 240 miles to the sea to get salt, thousands of followers joined him. He waded into the water and picked up a lump of sea salt. He was arrested. Newspapers around the world criticized Britain. Stories reported police brutality against peaceful marchers. Thousands of Indians were jailed when they continued to gather salt. Slowly, Gandhi's actions and the British reactions forced the British to give some power to Indians.

Review Questions

1. What did the British promise India during World War I?

_____

_____

2. What is ahimsa?

_____

_____

Note Taking Study Guide

UPHEAVALS IN CHINA

Focus Question: How did China cope with internal division and foreign invasion in the early 1900s?

A. *As you read "The Chinese Republic in Trouble," complete the following chart by listing the multiple causes of upheaval in the Chinese Republic.*

Causes of Upheaval

Warlord Uprisings	Foreign Imperialism	Nationalism
• Disorder in provinces	•	•
•	•	•
		•

B. *As you read "Struggle for a New China" and "Japanese Invasion," complete the chart to sequence the fighting among the Guomindang, the warlords, the Chinese Communists, and the Japanese. Some items have been filled in for you.*

1926
• Guomindang and Communists defeat warlords.

→

1927
• Civil war between Guomindang and Communists begins.

1934–35
• The Communists retreat

→

1936
•

Name_____ Class_____ Date_____

CHAPTER
15
SECTION 4

Section Summary
UPHEAVALS IN CHINA

What was the May Fourth Movement?

_____

_____

_____

Find the word *intellectual* in the first underlined sentence. The word has two word parts: the root word *intellect* means "ability to think," and *–ual* means "relating to." Use the meanings of the word parts and the context clues in the second underlined sentence to help you figure out the meaning of *intellectual*.

Recognize Multiple Causes
Why did Chinese peasants support the Communists?

_____

_____

_____

After the Qing dynasty collapsed, Sun Yixian became president of China's new republic. He hoped to rebuild China. Instead, China fell into chaos as warlords battled for control, and Sun Yixian stepped down as president. When the economy fell apart, millions of peasants suffered severe hardships. Also, foreign powers tried to dominate China. During World War I, Japan issued the **Twenty-One Demands.** This was intended to give Japan control over China. China was too weak to refuse all the demands, and gave up some power to Japan. Then, after World War I, the Allies gave Japan power over some former German lands in China. This angered many students. They began a cultural and intellectual reform movement known as the **May Fourth Movement.** These reformers looked to Western knowledge to make China strong. Others turned to Marxism. The Soviet Union trained some Chinese to become the **vanguard**, or leaders, of a communist revolution.

In 1921, Sun Yixian's **Guomindang,** or Nationalist party, formed a new government. After Sun's death, Jiang Jieshi became the party leader. By joining with the Communists, he defeated the warlords. However, Jiang feared the Communists were a threat to his power. He killed thousands of Communist Party members and their supporters. Led by Mao Zedong, the Communists retreated to northern China. The Guomindang attacked Mao's forces throughout the **Long March,** from 1934 to 1935. During the difficult march, Mao's soldiers treated peasants kindly, paid for goods, and made sure they did not destroy crops. Many peasants, who had suffered under the Guomindang, welcomed the Communists.

In 1937, Japan invaded China, bombed several cities, and killed hundreds of thousands of Chinese. In response, Jiang and Mao formed an alliance to fight the invaders. They were able to work together until the Japanese threat was gone.

Review Questions

1. List three ways in which Japan affected China.

_____

_____

2. Why did the Communists and Guomindang unite?

_____

_____

CHAPTER 15 SECTION 5

Note Taking Study Guide
CONFLICTING FORCES IN JAPAN

Focus Question: How did Japan change in the 1920s and 1930s?

As you read this section in your textbook, complete the table by listing the effects of liberalism and militarism in Japan during the 1920s and 1930s. Some items have been listed for you.

Conflicting Forces in Japan	
Liberalism in the 1920s	**Militarism in the 1930s**
• Greater democracy	• Depression causes unrest.
•	•
•	•
•	•
	•

CHAPTER 15 SECTION 5

Section Summary

CONFLICTING FORCES IN JAPAN

The Japanese economy grew during World War I, based on the export of goods to the Allies and increased production. At this time, Japan also expanded its presence in East Asia and sought further rights in China. Additionally, Japan gained control of some former German possessions in China after the war. **Hirohito** became emperor of Japan in 1926.

During the 1920s, Japan had a more liberal government. The elected members of the Japanese parliament exercised power. The right to vote was extended to all adult men. Western ideas about women's rights brought some changes. Despite increased democracy, the zaibatsu, a group of powerful business leaders, manipulated politicians. These business leaders donated money to political parties. The group used its influence to push for laws that supported trade and favored their businesses.

The military leaders and **ultranationalists,** or extreme nationalists, were angry with the government for giving in to Western demands and for accepting payoffs from the zaibatsu. The military and nationalists wanted to expand the empire. They looked to northern China for its raw materials. In 1931, the army set explosives to blow up railroad tracks in the Chinese province of **Manchuria,** blaming it on the Chinese. This provided an excuse to conquer the region. Japanese politicians objected, but the people supported the military. The League of Nations also protested the invasion. As a result, Japan left the League.

The military and ultranationalists increased their power throughout the 1930s. Extremists murdered some politicians and business leaders. To please the ultranationalists the government limited some democratic freedoms. Also, Japan took advantage of China's civil war. Military leaders expected to conquer China within a few years. Instead, when World War II broke out in Europe, the fighting quickly spread to Asia. In September 1940, Japan signed an agreement with Italy and Germany. The three nations formed the Axis Powers.

Review Questions

1. How did Japan benefit from World War I?

_____

_____

2. What were the effects of Japan's liberal government in the 1920s?

_____

_____

Name_____ Class_____ Date_____

Note Taking Study Guide
POSTWAR SOCIAL CHANGES

Focus Question: What changes did Western society and culture experience after World War I?

As you read this section in your textbook, complete the concept web below to identify supporting details related to "Changes to Society" and "Cultural Changes." Some items have been completed for you.

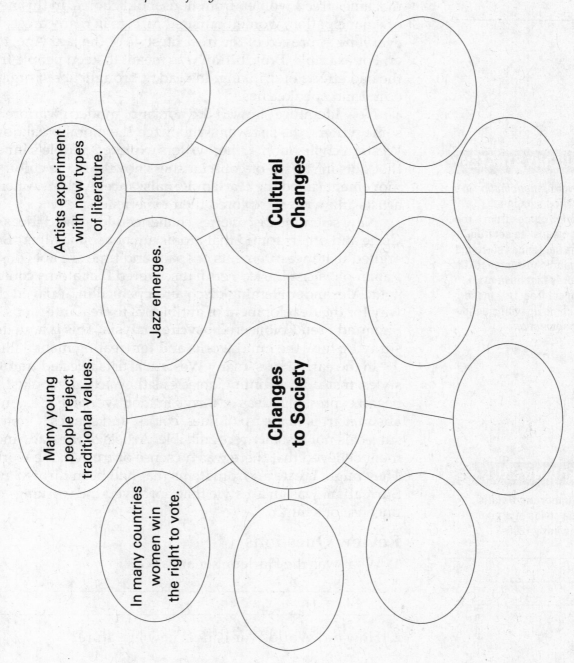

- Artists experiment with new types of literature.
- Jazz emerges.

Cultural Changes

- Many young people reject traditional values.

Changes to Society

- In many countries women win the right to vote.

CHAPTER 16 SECTION 1

Section Summary

POSTWAR SOCIAL CHANGES

After World War I, society and culture changed. During the 1920s, new technologies connected people around the world. So many people listened to jazz that this period is often called the Jazz Age. At this time, young women called **flappers** were a symbol of the new freedom in American culture. Labor-saving machines freed women from household chores. <u>In this new era of emancipation, women pursued careers in many areas.</u> Not everyone approved of the freer lifestyle of the Jazz Age, however. For example, **Prohibition** was meant to keep people from the bad effects of drinking. Instead, it brought about organized crime and **speakeasies.**

New literature showed the horror of modern warfare. To some writers, the last war symbolized the moral breakdown of Western civilization. Other writers explored people's inner thoughts in stream-of-consciousness novels. In the cultural movement called the **Harlem Renaissance,** African American artists and writers explored their experiences.

New scientific discoveries challenged long-held ideas. Marie Curie and others found that atoms are not solid. Albert Einstein argued that measurements of space and time are not constant. Italian physicist Enrico Fermi discovered that atoms could be split. Alexander Fleming discovered penicillin. It paved the way for the development of antibiotics to treat infections. Sigmund Freud pioneered **psychoanalysis.** This is a method of studying how the mind works and for treating mental illness.

In the early 1900s, many Western artists rejected traditional styles. Instead of painting objects as they actually looked, they began expressing ideas or forms in their works. For example, **abstract** art is made up of lines, colors, and shapes. Often the subject is not visually recognizable. Artists of the **dada** movement believed that there was no sense or truth in the world. They might create art from items that had been thrown away. **Surrealism** was an art style that portrayed the workings of the unconscious mind.

Review Questions

1. What was the Harlem Renaissance?

_____

_____

2. How did World War I affect new literature?

_____

_____

Name_____ Class_____ Date_____

Note Taking Study Guide
THE WESTERN DEMOCRACIES STUMBLE

Focus Question: What political and economic challenges did the leading democracies face in the 1920s and 1930s?

A. *As you read "Politics in the Postwar World," "Postwar Foreign Policy," and "Postwar Economics," complete the chart below to identify the main ideas under each heading. Some items have been entered for you.*

Postwar Issues			
Country	**Politics**	**Foreign Policy**	**Economics**
Britain	Conservative party dominated; Irish Free State established in 1922	Sought to soften the treatment of Germany; worked with other nations toward peace	
France		Insisted on enforcement of Versailles treaty; built Maginot Line; worked with other nations for peace	
United States			Became leading economic power

B. *As you read "The Great Depression" and "The Democracies React to the Depression," complete the chart below to identify the main ideas about the causes, effects, and reactions related to the Great Depression. Some items have been entered for you.*

The Great Depression

Causes
- Lower earnings led to falling demand.
-
-
-
-

Effects
- Unemployment
-
-

Reactions
- High tariffs
-
-

CHAPTER 16 SECTION 2

Section Summary
THE WESTERN DEMOCRACIES STUMBLE

After World War I, Britain, France, and the United States appeared strong. However, in the years to come, all three countries faced political and economic problems. Britain had to deal with growing socialism and the "Irish question." In France, political parties competed for power, causing many changes in government. Fear of radicals set off a "Red Scare" in the United States.

The three countries also faced international issues. The French were worried about another German invasion, so they built the **Maginot Line.** The **Kellogg-Briand Pact** was more positive. Nations that signed it promised to "renounce war as an instrument of national policy." In this spirit, the great powers pursued **disarmament.** Unfortunately, the League of Nations could not stop aggression, a weakness noted by some dictators.

The war affected economies all over the world. Both Britain and France owed huge war debts to the United States. In Britain low wages led to unrest. In 1926 over three million workers went on a **general strike.** In contrast, the United States emerged as the world's top economic power. In the 1920s, affluent Americans enjoyed the benefits of capitalism. They bought cars, radios, refrigerators, and other new consumer goods.

However, the good times did not last. Better technologies allowed factories to make more products faster, leading to **overproduction.** This lowered prices. As factories cut back, workers lost their jobs. A crisis in **finance** led the **Federal Reserve** to raise interest rates. Panic set in when stock prices crashed. In 1929, the **Great Depression** began in the United States. Within a short time, it had spread around the world.

In the United States, President **Franklin D. Roosevelt** argued that the government should take an active role in ending the crisis. He introduced programs known as the **New Deal.** Although the New Deal failed to end the Depression, it did ease much suffering. As the Depression wore on, however, many people lost faith in democratic government.

Review Questions
1. Why did the French build the Maginot Line?

_____

_____

2. What caused U.S. workers to lose their jobs?

_____

_____

CHAPTER **16** SECTION 3	# Note Taking Study Guide
	FASCISM IN ITALY

Focus Question: How and why did fascism rise in Italy?

A. *As you read "Mussolini's Rise to Power" and Mussolini's Rule," complete the flowchart below as you identify the main ideas under each heading. Some items have been entered for you.*

Dissatisfaction and Unrest	**Mussolini Takes Power**	**Mussolini Changes Italy**
• Italians dissatisfied with territories at end of World War I. • •	• Mussolini organizes Fascist party. • • • King gives Mussolini control after March on Rome.	• Mussolini becomes dictator. • •

B. *As you read "The Nature of Fascism," use the table below to identify the main ideas for each heading. Some items have been entered for you.*

What Is Fascism?	
Values	No unifying set of beliefs; generally glorifies extreme nationalism, discipline, military, and loyalty to the state
Characteristics	
Differences from Communism	Works for nationalist rather than international goals; supports a society with defined classes
Similarities to Communism	

CHAPTER 16 SECTION 3

Section Summary
FASCISM IN ITALY

READING CHECK

Who were the Black Shirts?

_____

_____

_____

Italy faced many problems after World War I. Italian nationalists were outraged that they did not receive lands that the Allies had promised them. Peasants seized land, workers went on strike, and veterans faced unemployment. Also, trade declined and taxes rose. Into this chaos stepped **Benito Mussolini** to take control. His Fascist party rejected democracy and favored violence to solve problems. Mussolini's special supporters, the **Black Shirts,** used terror to oust elected officials. In the 1922 **March on Rome,** thousands of Fascists swarmed the capital. Fearing civil war, the king asked Mussolini to become prime minister.

Mussolini went on to crush rival parties, muzzle the press, rig elections, and replace elected officials with Fascists. Critics were imprisoned, exiled, or murdered. Secret police and propaganda bolstered Mussolini's rule. He brought the economy under state control, but preserved capitalism. His system favored the upper classes. Workers were not allowed to strike, and their wages were kept low. In Mussolini's new system, loyalty to the state replaced individual goals. Loudspeakers blared and posters proclaimed "Believe! Obey! Fight!" Fascist youth groups chanted slogans. Italians supported Mussolini because he brought order to the country.

VOCABULARY STRATEGY

Find the word *proclaimed* in the underlined sentence. Notice the exclamation points in the phrase "Believe! Obey! Fight!" Think about the tone of that phrase. Ask: What was the purpose of loudspeakers and posters? Use these context clues to help you figure out the meaning of *proclaimed.*

Mussolini built the first modern **totalitarian state.** In this form of government, a one-party dictatorship attempts to control every aspect of citizens' lives. Today, we tend to use the term **fascism** to describe the basic ideas of any centralized dictatorship that is not communist. Fascism is rooted in nationalism. Fascists believe in action, violence, discipline, the military, and blind loyalty to the state. They are anti-democratic. They reject equality and liberty. Fascists disagree with communists on important issues. Communists favor international action and want a classless society. Fascists ally with business leaders, wealthy landowners, and the middle class. Both call for blind devotion to a leader or the state. Both flourish during economic hard times.

READING SKILL

Identify Main Ideas How did the conditions in Italy after World War I help Mussolini come to power?

_____

_____

_____

Review Questions

1. What was the result of the March on Rome?

_____

_____

2. How did Mussolini treat his critics?

_____

_____

Name_____ Class_____ Date_____

Note Taking Study Guide

THE SOVIET UNION UNDER STALIN

Focus Question: How did Stalin transform the Soviet Union into a totalitarian state?

As you read this section in your textbook, complete the chart below by identifying the main ideas about the Soviet Union under Stalin for each heading. Some items have been completed for you.

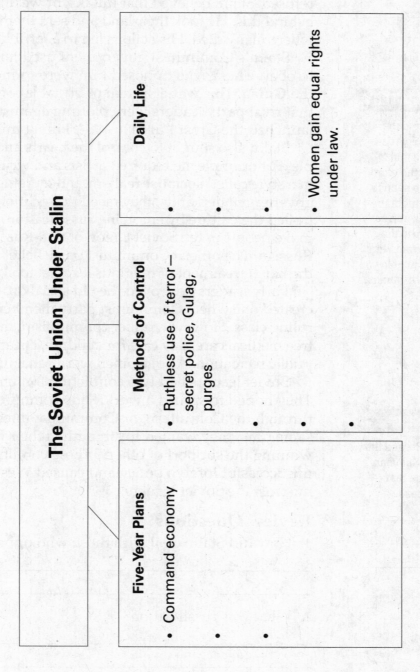

The Soviet Union Under Stalin

Daily Life
-
-
-
- Women gain equal rights under law.

Methods of Control
- Ruthless use of terror—secret police, Gulag, purges
-
-
-

Five-Year Plans
- Command economy
-
-

CHAPTER 16 SECTION 4

Section Summary
THE SOVIET UNION UNDER STALIN

Under Joseph Stalin, the Soviet Union developed into a totalitarian state. It developed a **command economy,** in which the government made most economic decisions. Stalin used five-year plans to try to increase productivity. He wanted all peasants to farm on either state-owned farms or **collectives.** Some peasants refused. Stalin believed that **kulaks,** or wealthy farmers, were behind this. He took their land and sent them to labor camps where many died. His actions led to a terrible famine in 1932.

Stalin's Communist government used terror to force people to obey. Those who opposed him were rounded up and sent to the **Gulag.** This was a system of brutal labor camps. Fearing that rival party leaders were plotting against him, Stalin launched the Great Purge in 1934, killing millions of people.

Stalin also sought to control the hearts and minds of his people. For example, he required artists and writers to create works in a style called **socialist realism.** <u>If they refused to conform to government demands, they faced persecution</u>. Stalin also controlled the culture by enforcing **russification.** His goal was to make people in the Soviet Union of non-Russian cultures more Russian. The official Communist party belief in **atheism** led to the harsh treatment of religious leaders, too.

Party leaders destroyed the old social order. In its place, they created one where Communist party members made up the new ruling class. However, under communism, most people enjoyed free medical care, day care for children, cheaper housing, and public recreation. Also, women were equal under the law.

Soviet leaders had two conflicting foreign policy goals. They hoped to spread a worldwide communist revolution through the **Comintern,** or Communist International. At the same time, they wanted to strengthen their nation's security by winning the support of others. These conflicting goals led to an unsuccessful foreign policy and caused Western powers to mistrust the Soviet leaders.

Review Questions

1. How did Stalin deal with those who opposed him?

_____

_____

2. What was russification?

_____

_____

CHAPTER
16
SECTION 5

Note Taking Study Guide
HITLER AND THE RISE OF NAZI GERMANY

Focus Question: How did Hitler and the Nazi party establish and maintain a totalitarian government in Germany?

As you read this section in your textbook, complete the flowchart below to identify the main ideas about Hitler and the rise of Nazi Germany. Some items have been entered for you.

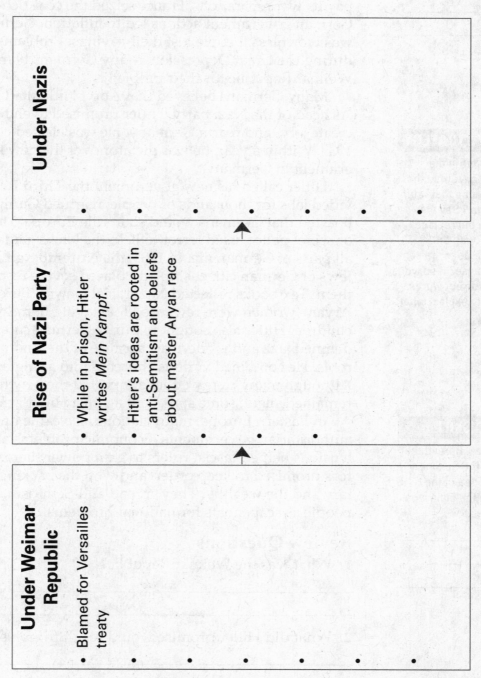

Under Nazis

Rise of Nazi Party
- While in prison, Hitler writes *Mein Kampf.*
- Hitler's ideas are rooted in anti-Semitism and beliefs about master Aryan race

Under Weimar Republic
- Blamed for Versailles treaty

CHAPTER 16 SECTION 5

Section Summary

HITLER AND THE RISE OF NAZI GERMANY

After World War I, German leaders wrote the Weimar constitution. It created the democratic Weimar Republic. This parliamentary government was led by a **chancellor,** gave women the right to vote, and included a bill of rights. However, the new government faced severe problems. When Germany could not pay its war reparations, France seized the coal-rich **Ruhr Valley.** German government actions led to inflation. German money was worthless. People lost their savings. Problems worsened during the Great Depression. Many Germans blamed the Weimar Republic for their problems.

Many Germans believed that Adolf Hitler had the solutions. As head of the Nazi party, Hitler promised to end reparations, create jobs, and rearm Germany. He was elected chancellor in 1933. Within a year, he was dictator over the new fascist government in Germany.

Hitler called his new government the **Third Reich.** He provided jobs for thousands of people, rearmed Germany, and boasted that Germans would soon rule Europe. The **Gestapo,** or secret police, used terror to help the Nazis gain control over all parts of German life. In 1935, the **Nuremberg Laws** deprived Jews of German citizenship and placed severe restrictions on them. Textbooks reflected Nazi racial views. "Pure-blooded Aryan" women were rewarded for staying home and having children. Hitler also sought to purify German culture. He condemned jazz and modern art because of their non-German roots. He combined various churches into a single state church. Although many clergy either supported the new regime or remained silent, some spoke out against Hitler's government.

In Eastern Europe, many nations also came under new authoritarian governments. Economic problems and ethnic tensions helped fascist rulers to gain power there. These dictators promised to keep order, and won the backing of the military and the wealthy. They spread anti-Semitism, using Jewish people as scapegoats for national problems.

Review Questions

1. What was the Weimar Republic?

_____

_____

2. What did Hitler promise would result from his Third Reich?

_____

_____

CHAPTER 17 SECTION 1

Note Taking Study Guide
FROM APPEASEMENT TO WAR

Focus Question: What events unfolded between Chamberlain's declaration of "peace in our time" and the outbreak of a world war?

A. *As you read "Aggression Goes Unchecked" and "Spain Collapses into Civil War," complete the chart below to recognize the sequence of events that led to the outbreak of World War II. Some items have been completed for you.*

Acts of Aggression	
Japan	• Invasion of Manchuria, 1931 • _____
Italy	• _____
Germany	• Buildup of German military • _____
Spain	• _____

B. *As you read "German Aggression Continues" and "Europe Plunges Toward War," complete the timetable below to recognize the sequence of German aggression. One item has been entered for you.*

German Aggression	
March 1938	Anschluss, or union of Austria and Germany, occurs.
September 1938	
March 1939	
September 1939	

CHAPTER 17 SECTION 1

Section Summary

FROM APPEASEMENT TO WAR

VOCABULARY STRATEGY

Find the word *sanctions* in the underlined sentence. Notice that *sanctions* were a response to the Italian invasion of Ethiopia mentioned in the previous sentence. In the same sentence, the phrase "had no power to enforce the punishment" refers to the *sanctions*. Use these context clues to help you figure out the meaning of *sanctions*.

Throughout the 1930s, dictators took aggressive action. However, they were met only by pleas for peace from Western democracies. The dictators became even more aggressive. For example, when the League of Nations condemned Japan's invasion of Manchuria in 1931, Japan just withdrew from the League. Meanwhile, Mussolini invaded Ethiopia. <u>The League of Nations voted sanctions against Italy, but it had no power to enforce the punishment.</u> Hitler, too, defied the Western democracies and the conditions of the Versailles treaty by building up the German military. He also sent troops into the Rhineland. The Western democracies denounced Hitler, but adopted a policy of **appeasement.** Appeasement developed for a number of reasons, including widespread **pacifism.** The United States passed the **Neutrality Acts** at this time. The goal was to avoid war, not prevent it. Germany, Italy, and Japan saw the Western democracies as weak. These three nations formed an alliance known as the **Axis powers.**

In Spain, **Francisco Franco** led a revolt against the new Spanish government. This began a civil war in which Hitler and Mussolini supported Franco, their fellow fascist. The Soviet Union sent troops to support the anti-Fascists, or Loyalists. However, the governments of Britain, France, and the United States remained neutral. By 1939, Franco had triumphed.

German aggression continued. Hitler forced the **Anschluss,** or union with Austria. At the Munich Conference, British and French leaders caved in to Hitler's plans to annex the **Sudentenland,** a part of Czechoslovakia.

In March 1939, Hitler took the rest of Czechoslovakia. A few months later, Hitler and Stalin signed the **Nazi-Soviet Pact.** They agreed not to fight if the other went to war. This paved the way for the German invasion of Poland in September of 1939. Because of this, Britain and France declared war on Germany, starting World War II.

Review Questions

1. How did the League of Nations fail to keep peace?

_____

_____

2. How did Hitler defy conditions of the Treaty of Versailles?

_____

_____

Name_____ Class_____ Date_____

Focus Question: Which regions were attacked and occupied by the Axis powers, and what was life like under their occupation?

A. *As you read "The Axis Attacks," "Germany Invades the Soviet Union," and "Japan Attacks the United States," use the chart below to record the sequence of events. Some items have been entered for you.*

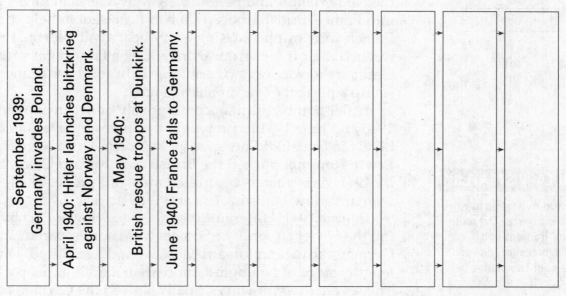

September 1939: Germany invades Poland.

April 1940: Hitler launches blitzkrieg against Norway and Denmark.

May 1940: British rescue troops at Dunkirk.

June 1940: France falls to Germany.

B. *As you read "Life Under Nazi and Japanese Occupation," use the concept web to list supporting details about the occupations. Some items have been entered for you.*

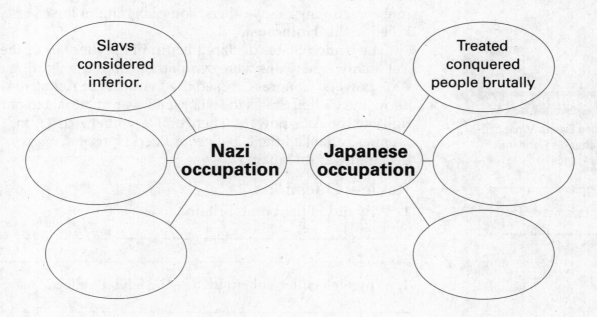

Slavs considered inferior.

Treated conquered people brutally

Nazi occupation

Japanese occupation

CHAPTER 17 SECTION 2

Section Summary
THE AXIS ADVANCES

In September 1939, Nazi forces launched a **blitzkrieg** against Poland. First, the **Luftwaffe** bombed Poland from the air. Then, tanks and troops pushed in. At the same time, Stalin's forces invaded from the east. Poland disappeared.

In early 1940, Hitler's troops conquered Norway, Denmark, the Netherlands, and Belgium. By May, German forces pushed into France. British troops that had been sent to help the French were trapped. Using every boat available, the British rescued their troops from **Dunkirk.** The French gave up, and Germany took over northern France. In southern France, they set up a puppet government in **Vichy.**

Hitler bombed Britain continuously between September 1940 and June 1941 to prepare for an invasion. Despite this blitz, the British did not give in. In North Africa, **General Erwin Rommel** pushed the British back toward Cairo, Egypt. By 1941, Axis powers controlled most of Europe. The Japanese were invading lands in Asia and the Pacific.

VOCABULARY STRATEGY

Find the word *nullified* in the underlined sentence. The root word is *null.* Perhaps you have heard the expression "null and void." Use prior knowledge to help you figure out the meaning of *nullified.*

<u>In June 1941, Hitler nullified the Nazi-Soviet Pact by invading the Soviet Union.</u> The Soviets were not prepared, and the Germans advanced toward Moscow and Leningrad. During a lengthy siege of Leningrad, more than a million people died. The severe Russian winter finally slowed the German advance.

As they marched across Europe, the Nazis sent millions to **concentration camps** to work as slave laborers. Even worse, Hitler established death camps to kill those he judged racially inferior. Among many others, some six million Jews were killed in this **Holocaust.**

The United States declared neutrality at the start of the war. Yet, many Americans were sympathetic to those fighting the Axis powers. Congress passed the **Lend-Lease Act** of 1941 to allow the United States to sell or lend war materials to nations fighting the Axis powers. Then, on December 7, 1941, the Japanese attacked the U.S. fleet at Pearl Harbor. Congress declared war on Japan.

Review Questions

1. Why did Hitler bomb Britain?

_____

_____

2. Why was Hitler able to invade the Soviet Union?

_____

_____

Name_____ Class_____ Date_____

Focus Question: How did the Allies begin to push back the Axis powers?

As you read this section in your textbook, complete the chart below to record the sequence of events that turned the tide of the war in favor of the Allies. Some events have been completed for you.

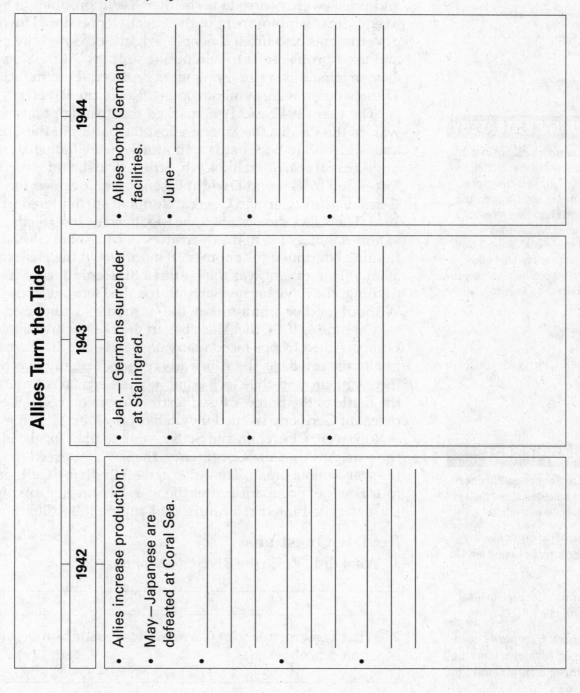

Allies Turn the Tide

1944
- Allies bomb German facilities.
- June—

1943
- Jan.—Germans surrender at Stalingrad.

1942
- Allies increase production.
- May—Japanese are defeated at Coral Sea.

CHAPTER 17 SECTION 3
Section Summary
THE ALLIES TURN THE TIDE

READING CHECK

What happened on June 6, 1944?

_____

_____

_____

VOCABULARY STRATEGY

Find the word *incessant* in the underlined sentence. Notice that the phrase "around-the-clock" follows *incessant.* "Around-the-clock" and *incessant* have similar meanings. What does "around-the-clock" mean? Use this context clue to help you choose the word below that you think means the same as *incessant.*

1. off-and-on

2. nonstop

READING SKILL

Recognize Sequence Number the items below to show the correct sequence of events.

_____ The Allies cross the Mediterranean and land in Sicily.

_____ German General Rommel surrenders.

_____ General Eisenhower, leading Allied forces, traps the German army in North Africa.

To defeat the Axis powers in World War II, the Allies devoted all their resources to the war effort. Governments took a greater role in the economy. For example, auto factories were ordered to make tanks. Consumer goods were rationed. Wages and prices were controlled. The increase in production helped to end the unemployment of the Great Depression. However, governments also limited people's rights, censored the press, and used propaganda to win public support. At the same time, as men joined the military, women replaced them in factories. These women were symbolized by **"Rosie the Riveter."**

The years 1942 and 1943 marked the turning point of the war. In the Pacific, the Japanese lost the battles of the Coral Sea and Midway. In both battles, air attacks were launched from huge **aircraft carriers.** In North Africa, British and American forces, led by General **Dwight Eisenhower,** trapped the German army. German General Rommel surrendered in May 1943. The Allies then crossed the Mediterranean to Sicily. Allied victories in Italy led to the overthrow of Mussolini, although the fighting continued for another 18 months. On the Eastern front, a key turning point was the Battle of **Stalingrad.** After brutal fighting, the Soviet army surrounded the German troops. Without food or ammunition, the Germans surrendered.

On June 6, 1944, the Allies began the **D-Day** invasion of France. Allied troops faced many obstacles, but the Germans finally retreated. As the Allies advanced, Germany was hit with incessant, around-the-clock bombing. A German counterattack, the Battle of the Bulge, caused terrible losses on both sides. The defeat of Germany seemed inevitable, however. The "Big Three" —Roosevelt, Churchill, and Stalin—met to plan for the end of the war. At this **Yalta Conference,** the Soviets agreed to enter the war against Japan. They also agreed to divide Germany into four zones of occupation after the war. However, growing mistrust at Yalta hinted at a future split among the Allies.

Review Questions

1. What did "Rosie the Riveter" symbolize?

_____

_____

2. What agreement about Germany was made at the Yalta Conference?

_____

_____

CHAPTER 17 SECTION 4

Note Taking Study Guide

VICTORY IN EUROPE AND THE PACIFIC

Focus Question: How did the Allies finally defeat the Axis powers?

As you read this section in your textbook, use the timeline below to recognize the sequence of events that led to the defeat of the Axis powers. Some events have been completed for you.

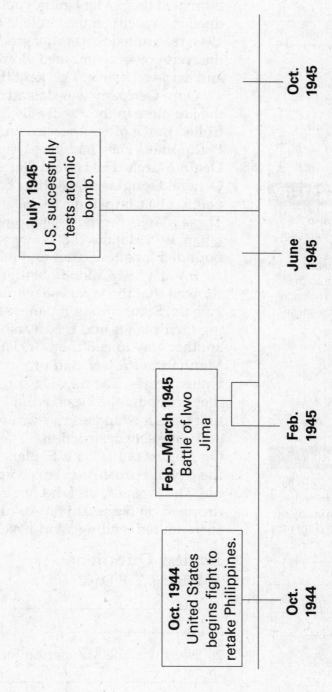

Oct. 1945

July 1945
U.S. successfully tests atomic bomb.

June 1945

Feb.–March 1945
Battle of Iwo Jima

Feb. 1945

Oct. 1944
United States begins fight to retake Philippines.

Oct. 1944

Name_____ Class_____ Date_____

CHAPTER **17** SECTION 4	**Section Summary**
	VICTORY IN EUROPE AND THE PACIFIC

READING CHECK

What was the name for Japanese pilots who went on suicide missions?

_____

_____

_____

VOCABULARY STRATEGY

Find the word *objective* in the underlined sentence. What do you think it means? The sentence says that the islands served as steppingstones to Japan. Use this context clue to help you understand the meaning of *objective.*

READING SKILL

Recognize Sequence Fill in the blanks below to sequence the events that took place in Japan from August 6 to August 10, 1945.

August 6 _____

_____

August 9 _____

_____

August 10 _____

_____

World War II in Europe officially ended on May 8, 1945. This is known as **V-E Day.** The Allies were able to defeat the Germans for many reasons. The Germans had to fight on several fronts at the same time. Hitler also made some poor decisions. He underestimated the Soviet Union's ability to fight. The enormous production capacity of the United States was another factor. By 1944, the United States was producing twice as much as all of the Axis powers combined. Bombing hurt German production and made oil scarce. This kept the Luftwaffe from flying

Once Germany was defeated, the Allies still had to defeat the Japanese in the Pacific. By May 1942, the Japanese controlled much of Southeast Asia, many Pacific islands, and the Philippines. They had killed thousands during the **Bataan Death March.** The United States now took the offensive. General **Douglas MacArthur** began an **"island-hopping"** campaign. The campaign took back islands from the Japanese. These islands served as steppingstones to the next objective— Japan. By 1944, the U.S. Navy was blockading Japan. Bombers pounded Japanese cities and industries.

In early 1945, bloody battles on Iwo Jima and Okinawa showed that the Japanese would fight to the death rather than give up. Some young Japanese became **kamikaze** pilots, crashing their planes into U.S. warships. Scientists now offered another way to end the war. Their research, called the **Manhattan Project,** had produced an atomic bomb for the United States. The new U.S. president, Harry Truman, decided that dropping the bomb would save American lives. The Allies first gave the Japanese a warning to surrender or face "utter and complete destruction." The Japanese ignored the warning. On August 6, 1945, a U.S. plane dropped an atomic bomb on the city of **Hiroshima.** This bomb killed more than 70,000 people. The Japanese still did not give up. Another bomb was dropped on **Nagasaki** on August 9. The next day, Japan finally surrendered, ending World War II.

Review Questions

1. What is V-E Day?

_____

_____

2. What was the Manhattan Project?

_____

_____

CHAPTER
17
SECTION 5

Note Taking Study Guide

THE END OF WORLD WAR II

Focus Question: What issues arose in the aftermath of World War II and how did new tensions develop?

As you read the section in your textbook, recognize the sequence of events following World War II by completing the outline below. Some items have been filled in.

I. The War's Aftermath

   A. Devastation

      1. As many as 50 million are dead.

      2. Horrors of Holocaust are learned.

   B. War Crimes Trials

      1. Axis leaders are tried for crimes against humanity.

      2. Many of those accused are never captured or brought to trial.

      3. Political and military leaders are held accountable for wartime actions.

   C. Occupying Allies

      1. Totalitarian ideologies are discredited.

      2. _____

II. Establishing the United Nations

   A. General Assembly

      1. _____

   B. Security Council

      1. _____

      2. _____

   C. Other UN activities

      1. _____

      2. _____

III. The Alliance Breaks Apart

   A. Differences Grow Between the Allies.

      1. _____

      2. _____

   B. The Cold War Begins.

      1. _____

      2. _____

(Outline continues on the next page.)

CHAPTER
17
SECTION 5

Note Taking Study Guide
THE END OF WORLD WAR II

(Continued from page 187)

        3. _____

IV. New Conflicts Develop

    A. The Truman Doctrine

        1. Results from Soviet incursions into southeastern Europe

        2. _____

        3. _____

    B. The Marshall Plan

        1. United States gives food and economic assistance to European nations.

        2. _____

        3. _____

    C. Germany Stays Divided.

        1. _____

        2. _____

        3. _____

        4. _____

    D. Berlin Airlift

        1. _____

        2. _____

        3. _____

    E. _____

        1. _____

        2. _____

    F. _____

        1. _____

        2. _____

CHAPTER 17 SECTION 5

Section Summary

THE END OF WORLD WAR II

The costs of World War II were great. As many as 50 million people had been killed. At the end of the war, the Allies learned the full extent of the Holocaust. War crimes trials were held in **Nuremberg,** Germany, and in other countries. These trials showed that leaders could be held accountable for their wartime actions. After the war, the Western Allies wanted to ensure peace. As a result, they helped to set up democratic governments in Japan and Germany.

In 1945, delegates from 50 nations convened to form the **United Nations.** Each member nation has one vote in the General Assembly. A smaller Security Council has greater power. It has five permanent members: the United States, the Soviet Union (today Russia), Britain, France, and China. Each has the right to vote down any council decision.

However, distrust and different philosophies soon led to a **Cold War.** This refers to the state of tension between the United States and the Soviet Union between 1946 and 1990. Soviet leader Stalin wanted to spread communism into Eastern Europe. He also wanted to have pro-Soviet countries between the Soviet Union and Germany. By 1948, communist governments were in place throughout Eastern Europe.

Stalin soon began to threaten Greece and Turkey. The United States responded with the **Truman Doctrine.** This policy meant that the United States would resist the spread of communism throughout the world. To strengthen democracies, the United States offered food and economic aid to Europe. This assistance was called the **Marshall Plan.** However, the Soviets now controlled East Germany, which surrounded the city of Berlin. To force the Western Allies out of Berlin, the Soviets blockaded West Berlin. An airlift by the Western Allies forced the Soviets to end the blockade. Tensions continued to grow. In 1949, the United States and nine other nations formed a new alliance called the **North Atlantic Treaty Organization (NATO).** The Soviets then formed the **Warsaw Pact.**

Review Questions

1. What was the basic idea of the Truman Doctrine?

_____

_____

2. What two new alliances were formed after World War II?

_____

_____

READING CHECK

Who are the five permanent members of the UN Security Council?

_____

_____

_____

VOCABULARY STRATEGY

Find the word *convened* in the underlined sentence. What do you think it means? The English word *convene* comes from the Latin *convenire.* In Latin, *con-* means "together" and *venire* means "to come." Using this word-origins clue, which one of the following means the same as *convened*?

1. disperse

2. assemble

3. separate

READING SKILL

Recognize Sequence Number the following events to show the correct sequence.

____ The Soviets blockade West Berlin.

____ The Soviets control East Germany.

____ The blockade ends.

____ The Western Allies mount an airlift.

Name_____ Class_____ Date_____

Focus Question: What were the military and political consequences of the Cold War in the Soviet Union, Europe, and the United States?

As you read this section in your textbook, fill in the chart to summarize the consequences of the Cold War in the Soviet Union, Europe, and the United States. Some items in the chart have been entered for you.

Consequences of the Cold War

Soviet Union
- Created military alliance called the Warsaw Pact
- Developed nuclear weapons in 1949
- •   •   •   •   •

Europe
- The Cold War divided Europe—communists ruled in the East and democracies were in the West.
- Berlin divided between East Germany and West Germany
- •   •   •   •

United States
- Formed military alliance called North Atlantic Treaty Organization (NATO)
- Entered disarmament talks with Soviet Union
- •   •   •   •   •   •

Section Summary
THE COLD WAR UNFOLDS

After World War II, the United States and the Soviet Union emerged as **superpowers.** They formed military alliances with nations they protected or occupied. The United States helped form the North Atlantic Treaty Organization (NATO). <u>This comprised its Western European allies.</u> The Soviet Union formed the Warsaw Pact with Eastern European countries.

The superpowers also took part in a nuclear weapons race. Throughout the Cold War, the leaders met in disarmament talks. One agreement limited the use of **anti-ballistic missiles (ABMs).** These weapons were designed to shoot down incoming missiles. ABMs were a threat because they could give one side more protection. Some believed that more protection might encourage a nation to attack. In the 1980s, U.S. President **Ronald Reagan** supported a missile defense program known as "Star Wars." However, international agreements to limit the number of nuclear weapons eased Cold War tensions. This period, called the era of **détente,** ended with the Soviet invasion of Afghanistan in 1979.

The Cold War was a global conflict. During the 1950s, **Fidel Castro** led a revolution in Cuba and became its leader. To bring down Castro's communist regime, U.S. President **John F. Kennedy** supported an invasion of Cuba, but it failed. One year later, the Soviets sent nuclear missiles to Cuba. Many feared a nuclear war. After U.S. protests and a naval blockade, Soviet leader **Nikita Khrushchev** agreed to remove the missiles.

The Soviets wanted to spread communist **ideology** around the globe. Although Khrushchev halted some of Stalin's cruel policies, repression returned under **Leonid Brezhnev.** U.S. leaders followed a policy of **containment** to keep communism from spreading to other nations. In the United States a "red scare" developed. During this time, Senator Joseph McCarthy led a hunt for communists he thought were in the U.S. government and military.

Review Questions

1. What military alliances did the United States and the Soviet Union form after World War II?

_____

_____

2. What were ABMs and why were they considered a threat?

_____

_____

READING CHECK

What is containment?

_____

_____

_____

VOCABULARY STRATEGY

Find the word *comprised* in the underlined sentence. What clues can you find in the surrounding text that could help you better understand what *comprised* means? Circle the words that could help you figure out what *comprised* means.

READING SKILL

Summarize What events led to the era of détente?

_____

_____

_____

CHAPTER
18
SECTION 2

Note Taking Study Guide
THE INDUSTRIALIZED DEMOCRACIES

Focus Question: How did the United States, Western Europe, and Japan achieve economic prosperity and strengthen democracy during the Cold War years?

As you read this section in your textbook, use the chart below to categorize economic and political changes in the industrialized democracies. Some items have been entered for you.

Economic and Political Changes in the Industrialized Democracies

Japan
- Emperor's power ends; Japan becomes a democracy.
- Occupation forces introduced social reforms, including education systems opened to all people and equality for women.
- •   •   •

Western Europe
- Division of Germany in 1949 and reunification in 1990
- Marshall Plan helped rebuild Western Europe.
- •   •   •   •   •   •   •

United States
- The United States became the world's wealthiest economy.
- Exports of goods and services helped build U.S. foreign trade.
- •   •   •   •   •   •   •   •   •

CHAPTER 18 SECTION 2

Section Summary

THE INDUSTRIALIZED DEMOCRACIES

Postwar economic strength changed life in the United States. During the 1950s and 1960s, **recessions** were brief and mild. <u>As Americans prospered, they had more money to spend on goods.</u> Many people left the cities for homes in the suburbs. This movement is called **suburbanization.** By the early 1970s, however, higher oil and gas prices left Americans with less money to buy other goods. This caused a serious recession in 1974.

Despite the prosperity, ethnic minorities faced **segregation** in housing and education. Also, minorities suffered **discrimination** in jobs and voting. **Dr. Martin Luther King, Jr.,** became an important civil rights leader in the 1960s. He helped end segregation for African Americans. Other minority groups were inspired by successes like these. For example, the women's rights movement helped end much gender-based discrimination. Also, Congress created programs to help the poor. However, in the 1980s, the government reduced many of these programs.

Western Europeans rebuilt after World War II. The American Marshall Plan helped European countries restore their economies. Under Chancellor **Konrad Adenauer,** Germany built modern cities and factories. European governments also developed programs for the poor and middle class, such as national healthcare and old-age pensions. These **welfare states** required high taxes to pay for their programs.

Not long after the war, European nations began working together to improve trade and increase their economic power. This cooperation led to the start of the **European Community.** It made it possible for members to trade freely with each other.

Much of Japan was destroyed during the World War II. Afterward, occupation forces introduced social changes, such as land reform and equal rights for women. Like Germany, Japan also built new factories. Its **gross domestic product (GDP)** soared. Japan succeeded by making goods for export.

Review Questions

1. List two results of the strong, postwar U. S. economy.

_____

_____

2. What was the purpose of the European Community?

_____

_____

READING CHECK

Who helped end discrimination for African Americans in the United States?

_____

_____

_____

VOCABULARY STRATEGY

Find the word *prospered* in the underlined sentence. The word *decline* is an antonym of the word *prosper*. The word *decline* means "to fade" or "to sink." Use context clues and the meanings of *decline* to figure out the meaning of *prospered*.

READING SKILL

Categorize Was the European Community founded as an economic organization or a social organization?

_____

_____

CHAPTER
18
SECTION 3

Note Taking Study Guide
COMMUNISM SPREADS IN EAST ASIA

Focus Question: What did the Communist victory mean for China and the rest of East Asia?

As you read this section in your textbook, complete the flowchart below to help you summarize the effects of the Communist Revolution on China and the impact of the Cold War on China and Korea. Some items have been filled in for you.

Impact of Communism and the Cold War in East Asia

Korea in the Cold War

- Korean Peninsula split at 38th parallel after World War II.
- Kim II Sung ruled North Korea; Syngman Rhee controlled South Korea.
- • • • • • • • •

China in the Cold War

- China allied with Soviet Union in 1950s.
- Border clashes and disputes over ideologies resulted in the Soviets withdrawing aid and advisors by 1960.
- • • • •

Chinese Communist Revolution

- Mao Zedong's Communists defeated Jiang Jieshi's Nationalists.
- Communists ended oppression by landlords and distributed land to peasants.
- • • • • •

CHAPTER 18 SECTION 3

Section Summary

COMMUNISM SPREADS IN EAST ASIA

After World War II, Mao Zedong led communist forces to victory over the Nationalists, who fled to Taiwan. Mao then began to reshape China's economy. He gave land to the peasants. Then he called for **collectivization,** or the pooling of land and labor. <u>As part of the **Great Leap Forward,** people moved from small villages and individual farms into communes of thousands of people on thousand of acres.</u> Communes were supposed to grow more food and produce more goods. Instead, the system produced useless or low-quality goods and less food. To remove "bourgeois" tendencies, Mao also began the **Cultural Revolution.** Skilled workers and managers were forced to work on farms or in labor camps. This resulted in a slowed economy and a threat of civil war.

At first, the United States supported the Nationalist government that had formed on Taiwan. The West was concerned that the Soviet Union and China would become allies. As the Cold War continued, however, the Soviets withdrew their aid and advisors from China. U.S. leaders thought that by "playing the China card," or improving relations with the Chinese, they would isolate the Soviets even more. In 1979, the United States established diplomatic relations with China.

After World War II, American and Soviet forces had agreed to divide Korea at the **38th parallel.** Communist **Kim Il Sung** ruled the North and U.S. ally **Syngman Rhee** ruled the South. In 1950, North Korean troops attacked South Korea. The United Nations forces stopped them along a line known as the **Pusan Perimeter,** then began advancing north. Mao sent Chinese troops to help the North Koreans. The UN forces were pushed back south of the 38th parallel. In 1953, both sides agreed to end the fighting, but troops remained on either side of the **demilitarized zone (DMZ).** Over time, South Korea enjoyed an economic boom, while communist North Korea's economy declined.

Review Questions

1. What was the purpose of the Great Leap Forward?

_____

_____

2. What was the 38th parallel?

_____

_____

READING CHECK

Who was Kim Il Sung?

_____

_____

_____

VOCABULARY STRATEGY

Find the word *commune* in the underlined sentence. The terms *group home*, *community*, and *collective farm* are all synonyms of *commune*. They are words with similar meanings. Use the synonyms to help you figure out the meaning of *commune*.

READING SKILL

Summarize Reread the first paragraph. Then summarize Mao Zedong's attempts to reshape China's economy and society.

_____

_____

_____

Name_____ Class_____ Date_____

Focus Question: What were the causes and effects of war in Southeast Asia, and what was the American role in this region?

As you read this section in your textbook, complete the flowchart below to summarize the events in Southeast Asia after World War II. Some items have been filled in for you.

War in Southeast Asia

Aftereffects of War

- Cambodia and Laos were dominated by communists.
- The Khmer Rouge, a force of communist guerrillas, came to power in Cambodia.
- • • • •

Vietnam War

- Domino theory
- Viet Cong, with North Vietnamese support, tried to overthrow South Vietnam.
- • • • • • • • •

Indochina After World War II

- Local guerrillas led by Ho Chi Minh opposed European colonialists.
- French tried to regain power, but were defeated at Dienbienphu in 1954.
- • • • •

CHAPTER 18 SECTION 4

Section Summary
WAR IN SOUTHEAST ASIA

In the 1800s, the French ruled the area in Southeast Asia called French Indochina. During World War II, Japan tried to take over, but faced resistance from **guerrillas.** After the war, the French tried to regain control, but the Vietnamese, led by **Ho Chi Minh,** fought them. The French were defeated at the battle of **Dienbienphu.** After that, Ho controlled the northern part of Vietnam while the United States supported the noncommunist government in the south. Ho supported communist guerrillas in the south, called **Viet Cong.**

U.S. leaders saw Vietnam as an extension of the Cold War. They developed the **domino theory.** This was the view that if communists won in South Vietnam, communism would spread throughout Southeast Asia. In 1964, the North Vietnamese attacked a U.S. naval ship. Congress granted the president the power to take military action to stop further communist aggression in the region. Eventually, more than 500,000 American troops fought in what became known as the Vietnam War.

Despite U.S. support for South Vietnam, the Viet Cong continued to attack. During the **Tet Offensive,** Viet Cong and their North Vietnamese allies attacked cities all over the south. Even though the communists were not able to hold any cities, the attack was a turning point in U.S. public opinion. Upset by civilian and military deaths, many Americans began to oppose the war. President Nixon came under increasing pressure to terminate the conflict. He signed the Paris Peace Accord in 1973, and U.S. troops soon withdrew. Two years later, North Vietnam conquered South Vietnam. Thousands of Vietnamese tried to leave the country.

Communism did spread to neighboring countries. In Cambodia, communist guerrillas called the **Khmer Rouge** came to power. Their ruler, **Pol Pot,** oversaw forced work camps and the genocide of more than a million Cambodians. Laos also ended up with a communist government. However, communism did not spread any farther in Southeast Asia.

Review Questions
1. What did Congress do in 1964?

_____

_____

2. Who were the Khmer Rouge?

_____

_____

READING CHECK

Which Southeast Asian countries ended up with communist governments?

_____

_____

_____

VOCABULARY STRATEGY

Find the word *terminate* in the underlined sentence. Note that the word is a verb, which means it describes an action. Ask yourself what action President Nixon was pressured to take. Use this strategy to help you figure out what *terminate* means.

READING SKILL

Summarize What was the domino theory?

_____

_____

_____

Note Taking Study Guide

CHAPTER 18 SECTION 5

THE END OF THE COLD WAR

Focus Question: What were the causes and the effects of the end of the Cold War?

As you read this section in your textbook, complete this flowchart to help you categorize events connected to the end of the Cold War. Some items have been completed for you.

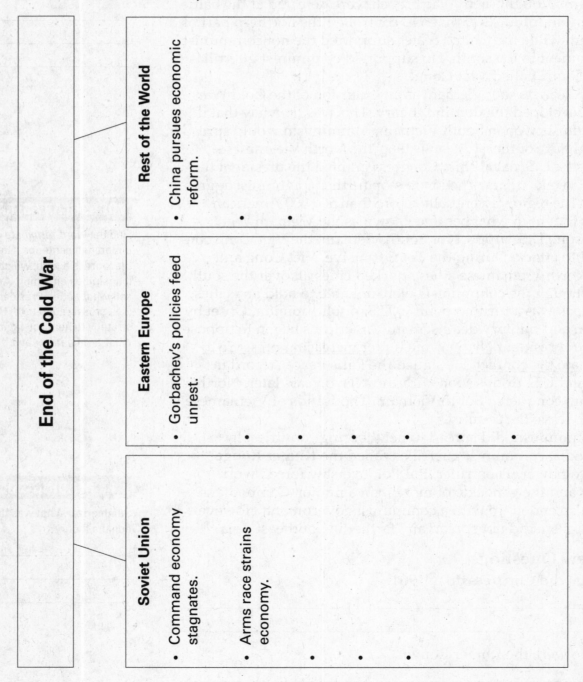

End of the Cold War

Rest of the World
- China pursues economic reform.
-
-

Eastern Europe
- Gorbachev's policies feed unrest.
-
-
-
-
-
-

Soviet Union
- Command economy stagnates.
- Arms race strains economy.
-
-
-

CHAPTER 18
SECTION 5

Section Summary
THE END OF THE COLD WAR

The Soviet Union emerged from World War II as a superpower with control over many Eastern European countries. When challenged, the Soviet Union used its military to subdue unrest. However, the Soviet command economy could not produce enough food to feed its people. Consumer products were poorly made and workers were poorly paid. Lifetime job security, however, meant that they did not have to worry about losing their jobs. Therefore, workers had little incentive to produce higher-quality goods. Further economic strain came when Soviet forces invaded Afghanistan in 1979. They had few successes battling the **mujahedin,** or Muslim religious warriors.

Soviet leader **Mikhail Gorbachev** urged reforms. He called for **glasnost,** or openness. He ended censorship and encouraged people to discuss the country's problems. Gorbachev also called for **perestroika,** or a restructuring of the government and economy. His policies, however, fed unrest across the Soviet empire. Eastern Europeans began to demand an end to Soviet rule. By the end of the 1980s, a powerful democracy movement was sweeping the region. In Poland, **Lech Walesa** led **Solidarity,** an independent labor union demanding economic and political changes.

Meanwhile, East German leaders resisted reform, and thousands of East Germans fled to the West. In Czechoslovakia, **Václav Havel**, a writer who fought for independence, was elected president. One by one, communist governments fell. Most changes happened peacefully, but when Romanian dictator **Nicolae Ceausescu** refused to step down, he was executed. The Baltic States regained independence. By the end of 1991, the remaining Soviet republics had all formed independent nations. The Soviet Union ceased to exist.

In 1992, Czechoslovakia was divided into Slovakia and the Czech Republic. Additionally, some communist governments in Asia, such as China, instituted economic reforms.

Review Questions

1. What were some problems with the Soviet economy?

_____

_____

2. What kinds of reforms did Gorbachev make?

_____

_____

READING CHECK

What was Solidarity?

_____

_____

_____

VOCABULARY STRATEGY

Find the word *incentive* in the underlined sentence. The words *motivation* and *reason* are synonyms of *incentive*. They have similar meanings. Use these synonyms to help you figure out the meaning of *incentive*.

READING SKILL

Categorize Which leaders mentioned in this summary supported reform and which leaders opposed reform?

_____

_____

_____

Name _____ Class _____ Date _____

Focus Question: What were the consequences of independence in South Asia for the region and for the world?

As you read this section in your textbook, fill in the concept web below to record causes and effects of events in South Asia. Some of the items have been completed for you.

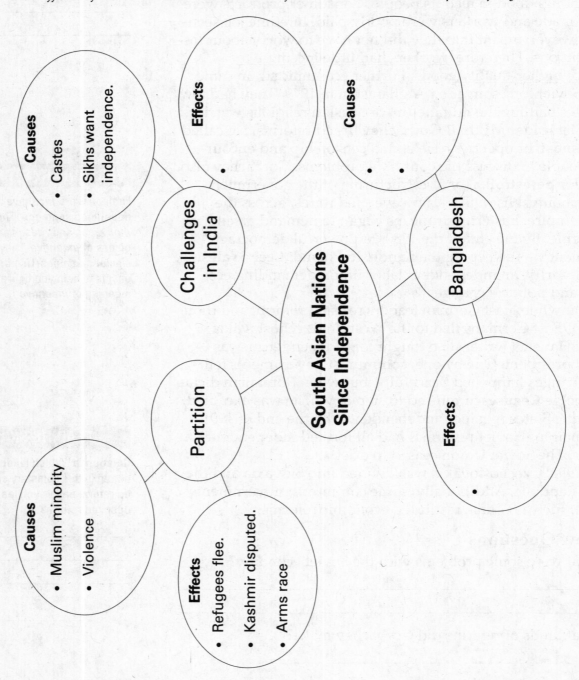

Causes
- Castes
- Sikhs want independence.

Effects
- •

Causes
- • •

Challenges in India

Bangladesh

South Asian Nations Since Independence

Partition

Effects
- •

Causes
- Muslim minority
- Violence

Effects
- Refugees flee.
- Kashmir disputed.
- Arms race

CHAPTER **19** SECTION 1	**Section Summary**
	INDEPENDENT NATIONS OF SOUTH ASIA

In the 1940s, tensions between Hindus and Muslims in India led to violence. The ruling British decided that the only solution was to **partition** India into two countries. India would have a Hindu majority. Pakistan would have a Muslim majority. After independence, Muslims fled to Pakistan. Hindus fled to India. As they moved, Muslims, Hindus, and **Sikhs,** members of another religious group, attacked and killed one another.

Tensions have continued in the region. India and Pakistan have fought wars over **Kashmir,** a state in the north. Both countries have developed nuclear weapons. In Sri Lanka, Tamil rebels have fought for a separate Tamil nation for many years.

In 1947 **Jawaharlal Nehru,** India's first prime minister, tried to improve the economy and the treatment of outcastes, or **dalits.** His daughter, **Indira Gandhi,** became prime minister in 1966. In 1984, Sikhs occupied the **Golden Temple.** They wanted independence for their state of **Punjab.** Gandhi sent troops to the temple, and thousands of Sikhs were killed. Gandhi's Sikh bodyguards killed her.

In 1947, Pakistan was a divided country. A thousand miles separated West Pakistan from East Pakistan. West Pakistan tended to control the nation's government. Most people in East Pakistan were Bengalis. They felt that the government neglected their region. In 1971, Bengalis declared that East Pakistan was an independent nation called **Bangladesh.** Pakistan tried to crush the rebels, but India supported the rebels by defeating the Pakistani army in Bangladesh. Eventually Pakistan was compelled to recognize the independence of Bangladesh.

Pakistan has often been politically unstable. There have been disagreements between Islamic fundamentalists and those who want a separation between religion and government. Over the years, fundamentalists have gained power.

Despite their differences, India and Pakistan helped organize a conference of newly independent states in 1955. This was the start of **nonalignment**—political and diplomatic independence from the United States or the Soviet Union.

Review Questions

1. How has Kashmir contributed to tension?

_____

_____

2. What present-day country was formerly East Pakistan?

_____

READING CHECK

What is the term for political and diplomatic independence from the United States or the Soviet Union?

_____

_____

_____

VOCABULARY STRATEGY

Find the word *compelled* in the second underlined sentence. Note that Pakistan first tried to crush the rebels. How might the presence of India's army force Pakistan to do something? Use these clues to help you figure out what *compelled* means.

READING SKILL

Identify Causes and Effects
What caused the British to partition, or divide, India into two countries? What effects did this division have on Muslims and Hindus?

_____

_____

Name_____ Class_____ Date_____

Focus Question: What challenges did Southeast Asian nations face after winning independence?

As you read this section in your textbook, fill in the concept web below to keep track of the effects of recent historical processes in Southeast Asia. Some of the items have been completed for you.

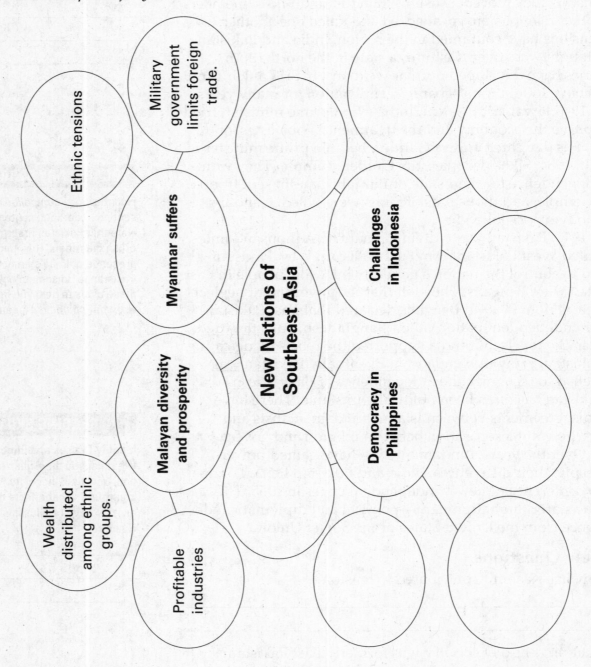

CHAPTER 19 SECTION 2 — Section Summary

NEW NATIONS OF SOUTHEAST ASIA

Mainland Southeast Asia is a region of contrasts. Thailand and Malaysia have prospered as market economies. By contrast, Myanmar has suffered under an **autocratic** government, with unlimited power. The government has limited foreign trade. Living standards remain low. In 1990, elections were held in Myanmar. A party led by **Aung San Suu Kyi** won. However, the military rejected the election results, and Suu Kyi was put under house arrest.

After World War II, Indonesia gained its independence. There have been many obstacles to its unity. Indonesia consists of over 13,000 islands. There are hundreds of ethnic groups. About 90 percent of Indonesians are Muslims. The population also includes Christians, Buddhists, and Hindus. After independence, Indonesia formed a democratic parliamentary government. It was led by Indonesia's first president, **Sukarno.** In 1966, an army general, **Suharto,** took control. He ruled as a dictator until 1998. Religious and ethnic tensions have caused violence in parts of Indonesia. In 1975, Indonesia seized **East Timor,** which is mostly Catholic. The East Timorese fought until they gained their independence in 2002.

In the Philippines, Catholics are the predominant religious group, with a Muslim minority in the south. In 1946, the Philippines gained freedom from United States control. The Filipino constitution set up a democratic government. However, a wealthy elite controlled politics and the economy. **Ferdinand Marcos** was elected president in 1965. He became a dictator and cracked down on basic freedoms. He even had a rival, **Benigno Aquino,** murdered. When Benigno's wife, **Corazon Aquino,** was elected in 1986, Marcos tried to deny the results. The people of Manila held demonstrations that forced him to resign. Since then, the democracy has struggled to survive. However, Communist and Muslim rebels continue to fight across the country.

Review Questions

1. What happened after 1990 elections in Myanmar?

_____

_____

2. About 90 percent of Indonesians belong to what religious group?

_____

_____

READING CHECK

From what country did the Philippines gain independence in 1946?

_____

_____

_____

VOCABULARY STRATEGY

Find the word *predominant* in the underlined sentence. What do you think it means? Note that the sentence also mentions another group, which is a minority. A minority is a smaller group. Use this context clue to decide which word below is closest in meaning to *predominant*. Circle the word you chose.

1. heaviest

2. largest

READING SKILL

Understand Effects When Corazon Aquino was elected in 1986, Ferdinand Marcos tried to deny the results. What was the effect of his action?

_____

_____

Name_____ Class_____ Date_____

Focus Question: What challenges did new African nations face?

As you read this section in your textbook, fill in the concept web below to identify causes and effects of independence in Africa. Some of the items have been completed for you.

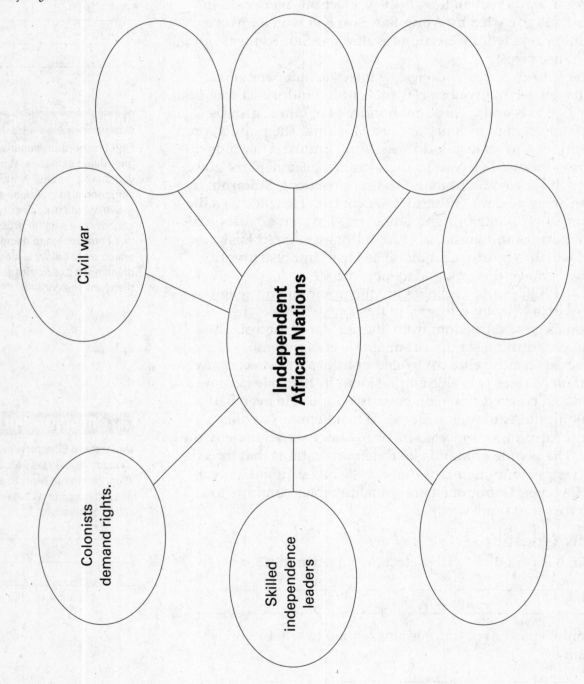

CHAPTER 19 SECTION 3 — Section Summary

AFRICAN NATIONS GAIN INDEPENDENCE

Africa is a diverse continent. Rain forests, deserts, and vast **savannas,** or tree-dotted grasslands, cover much of Africa.

After World War II, many Africans demanded independence. After gaining it, a few nations had peace and democracy. Most faced civil wars, military rule, or corrupt dictators. European powers had divided Africa into colonies with no regard for ethnic groups. This led to ethnic conflict in many new nations.

Kwame Nkrumah led Gold Coast, now renamed Ghana, to independence in 1957. His corrupt government was overthrown in a military coup d'etat. A **coup d'etat** is the overthrow of a government. Today Ghana is a democracy.

In Kenya, white settlers had passed laws to ensure their control of the country. In the 1950s, rebels turned to guerrilla warfare. The British crushed the rebels, but Kenya finally became independent in 1963. **Jomo Kenyatta,** one of Kenya's independence leaders, became the country's first president. However, it wasn't until 2002 that Kenya held its first fair election.

In Algeria, independence from France was finally achieved in 1962. A coup in 1965 began a long period of military rule. Free elections finally occurred in 1992. An **Islamist** party won, but the military rejected the results. Seven years of civil war followed. Fighting stopped, yet the country remains tense.

After Congo became independent from Belgium, the province of **Katanga** rebelled. The United Nations ended the rebellion in 1963. **Joseph Mobutu** ruled as a harsh military dictator from 1965 to 1997. Civil war then raged. Rivals fought to control mineral riches. In 2006, Congo had its first free elections in 41 years, but faced deep scars from years of conflict.

Nigeria won its independence in 1960. However, Nigeria faced ethnic, religious, and regional conflict, including a war to end a rebellion in **Biafra,** the homeland of the Ibo people in the oil-rich southeast. A series of military dictators then ruled the country, but Nigeria returned to democracy in 1999. However, ethnic conflict continued, including attacks by rebels seeking a share of oil wealth in the southeast.

Review Questions

1. Name two leaders of independence movements in Africa.

_____

_____

2. Summarize events in Algeria after independence.

_____

_____

READING CHECK

What is another name for the tree-dotted grasslands in Africa?

_____

VOCABULARY STRATEGY

Find the word *ensure* in the underlined sentence. What do you think it means? The prefix *en-* means "to make" or "cause to be." For example, the word *endanger* means "to cause something to be in danger." What does the root word, *sure,* mean? Use this clue to help you figure out the meaning of *ensure.*

READING SKILL

Identify Causes and Effects
European powers divided Africa into colonies without regard for the territories of Africa's ethnic groups. What effect did this have in many African nations?

_____

_____

_____

Name_____ Class_____ Date_____

Focus Question: What are the main similarities and differences among Middle Eastern nations?

As you read the section, fill in the concept web below to record causes and effects of events in the Middle East since 1945. Some items have been completed for you.

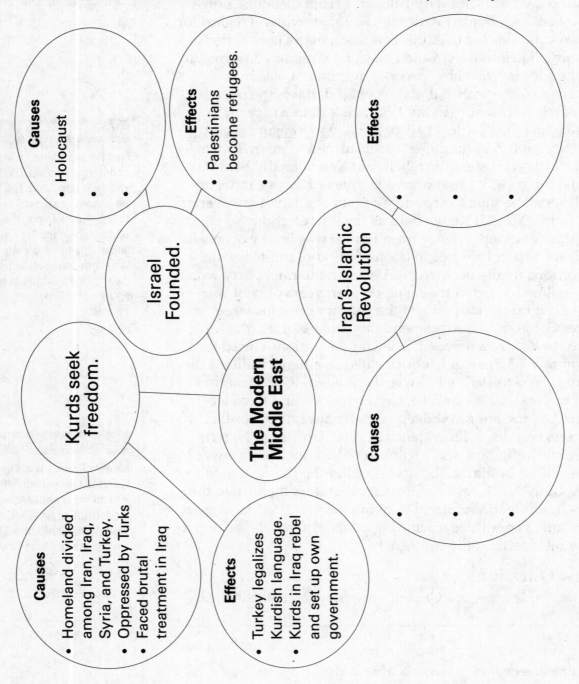

Causes
- Holocaust
- •
- •

Effects
- Palestinians become refugees.
- •

Effects
- •
- •
- •

Israel Founded.

Iran's Islamic Revolution

Kurds seek freedom.

The Modern Middle East

Causes
- •
- •
- •

Causes
- Homeland divided among Iran, Iraq, Syria, and Turkey.
- Oppressed by Turks
- Faced brutal treatment in Iraq

Effects
- Turkey legalizes Kurdish language.
- Kurds in Iraq rebel and set up own government.

CHAPTER 19 SECTION 4

Section Summary

THE MODERN MIDDLE EAST

In the Middle East, most people are Muslims. There are also many Christians, and Israel is largely Jewish. Most countries also have large minorities, such as the Kurds.

The Holocaust created support for a Jewish homeland after World War II. The UN drew up a plan to divide Palestine into an Arab and a Jewish state. In 1948, Israel became an independent state, and 700,000 Arab Palestinians were forced from their homes. In spite of these conflicts, Israel has developed rapidly. It has a skilled workforce. Kibbutzim work on what is called a **kibbutz,** or collective farm. The Middle East has also had conflicts over resources and religion. It has the world's largest oil and gas reserves. As a result, the region has strategic importance.

Some Middle Eastern countries have **secular,** or nonreligious, governments and laws. However, many Muslim leaders argue that a renewed commitment to Islamic doctrine is needed. In Iran and Saudi Arabia, women are required to wear the **hejab.** This is the traditional Muslim garment for women.

Egypt is important because it controls the **Suez Canal.** Under **Gamal Abdel Nasser,** Egypt fought two unsuccessful wars against Israel. His successor, **Anwar Sadat,** made peace with Israel. However, Islamists were upset that the government did not end corruption and poverty. In 1981, Muslim fundamentalists killed Sadat.

In Iran, Shah Mohammad Reza Pahlavi ruled with U.S. support. The United States helped remove one of the shah's opponents, **Mohammad Mosaddeq.** In the 1970s, the shah's enemies supported the Ayatollah **Ruhollah Khomeini.** Protests forced the shah into exile. Khomeini then set up an Islamic **theocracy.** This is a government ruled by religious leaders.

Saudi Arabia has the world's largest oil reserves and Islam's holy sites are there. Kings from the Sa'ud family have ruled since the 1920s, and their close ties to the West have been criticized by Islamic fundamentalists.

Review Questions

1. What religion do most people in the Middle East practice?

_____

_____

2. The Suez Canal is controlled by what country?

_____

_____

READING CHECK

What is the name of the traditional Muslim garment for women?

_____

_____

_____

VOCABULARY STRATEGY

Find the word *doctrine* in the underlined sentence. What do you think it means? Each religion has its own *doctrine*. The word *doctor* is related to *doctrine*. It originally meant "teacher." Use these word-family clues to help you figure out what *doctrine* means.

READING SKILL

Identify Causes and Effects
What effect did the creation of Israel have on the Arab Palestinians who lived there?

_____

_____

Name_____ Class_____ Date_____

20 Note Taking Study Guide

SECTION 1 **CONFLICTS DIVIDE NATIONS**

Focus Question: Why have ethnic and religious conflicts divided some nations?

As you read this section in your textbook, fill in the flowchart below to help you recognize the sequence of events that took place in Northern Ireland, Chechnya, and Yugoslavia.

Sequence of Conflicts

Yugoslavia

- **Before 1991:** Yugoslavia is multiethnic.
- **1991:** _____
- **1992:** _____

Chechnya

- **Mid–1990s:** Russia crushes Chechen revolt.
- **1997:** _____

Northern Ireland

- **1922:** Six Irish counties vote to remain in United Kingdom.
- **After 1922:** Minority Catholics demand civil rights and unification with the south.
- **1960s:** _____
- **1960s–1990s:** _____

© Pearson Education, Inc., publishing as Pearson Prentice Hall. All rights reserved.

208

Name_____ Class_____ Date_____

<table>
<tr><td>CHAPTER
20
SECTION 1</td><td>**Section Summary**
CONFLICTS DIVIDE NATIONS</td></tr>
</table>

In recent decades, there have been many conflicts around the world. Often they have been based on ethnic or religious differences. For example, ethnic differences between Sinhalese Buddhists and Tamils led to a civil war in Sri Lanka.

Northern Ireland also had problems. In 1922 Ireland became independent from Britain. However, six counties in the North remained part of Britain. Catholics in those counties wanted to unite with the rest of Ireland, where there was a Catholic majority. Extremists on both sides used violence. Peace talks dragged on for years. In 1998, both sides finally agreed to peace in the **Good Friday Agreement.**

Ethnic and religious minorities in several former Soviet republics also fought for independence. Probably the worst fighting was in **Chechnya.** There, Chechens fought for independence from Russia. In the mid-1990s, Russia crushed a Chechen revolt and many civilians were killed. Later, some Chechens turned to terrorism. In Nagorno-Karabakh, ethnic Armenians fought against Azerbaijanis.

Yugoslavia, too, was divided by ethnic tensions. Before 1991, it was a **multiethnic,** communist country. <u>The Serbs dominated Yugoslavia, which was controlled by the Communist Party.</u> The end of communism stirred up nationalism in the small states that made up Yugoslavia. Fighting broke out between Serbs and Croats in Croatia. The fighting soon spread to Bosnia. During the war, all sides committed terrible acts. In Bosnia, the Serbs conducted a terrible campaign of **ethnic cleansing.** Finally, the war in Bosnia ended in 1995. At the same time, new fighting broke out when Serbian president **Slobodan Milosevic** began oppressing Albanians in **Kosovo.** However, UN and NATO forces eventually restored peace. In 2008, Kosovo declared independence from Serbia.

In some countries, conflicts have been solved peacefully. For example, in Canada the democratic government helped prevent conflict between French and English speakers.

Review Questions

1. What is often the basis of conflicts around the world?

_____

_____

2. Who is Slobodan Milosevic?

_____

_____

READING CHECK

Which country found a peaceful solution to a conflict?

_____

_____

_____

VOCABULARY STRATEGY

Find the word *dominated* in the underlined sentence. Look for context clues to help you figure out what it means. For example, there is a synonym for *dominated* in the same sentence. It is the word *controlled.* If you know what *controlled* means, you can use that knowledge to help you figure out what *dominated* means.

READING SKILL

Recognize Sequence What event set off the conflict in Northern Ireland, and when did it happen?

_____

_____

_____

Name_____ Class_____ Date_____

Focus Question: Why have conflicts plagued some African countries?

A. *As you read "South Africa Struggles for Freedom," "South Africa's Neighbors Face Long Conflicts," and "Ethnic Conflicts Kill Millions," record the sequence of events in the conflicts in South Africa and its neighbors.*

1910: White minority controls government of independent South Africa.
1948: South African government expands racial segregation, creating apartheid.
1960:
1975:
1994:
2000:
2004:

B. *As you read "Ethnic Conflicts Kill Millions," identify the causes and effects of the conflicts in Rwanda, Sudan, Burundi, and Darfur.*

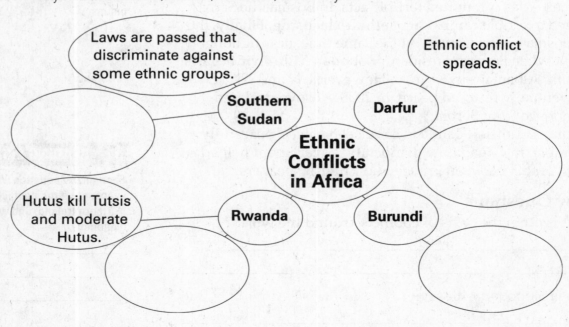

CHAPTER 20 SECTION 2

Section Summary
STRUGGLES IN AFRICA

In the 1950s and 1960s, many nations won independence in Africa. However, several nations still faced fighting and civil wars. In 1910, South Africa became independent from Britain. Despite this, civil rights were limited to whites. The black majority could not vote. In 1948, the government created a legal system of racial prejudice. It was called **apartheid.** Under apartheid, nonwhites faced many restrictions. <u>For example, it stipulated that restaurants, beaches, and schools must be segregated.</u> The **African National Congress (ANC)** fought against apartheid. The group led the fight for majority rule. In 1960 police shot 69 people during a peaceful protest in **Sharpeville,** a black township. The government then outlawed the ANC. ANC leader **Nelson Mandela** was sent to prison for life.

In the 1980s, many called for an end to apartheid. During this time, Bishop **Desmond Tutu** was awarded the Nobel Peace Prize for his fight against apartheid. In addition, leaders all over the world called for Nelson Mandela's release. Finally, in 1990 South African president **F.W. de Klerk** freed Mandela. Four years later Mandela was elected president of South Africa.

South Africa's neighbors also faced conflict. Portugal had colonies in Angola and Mozambique. Nationalists fought for many years. Portugal then agreed to withdraw from Africa, but the United States and South Africa supported rebel groups within Angola and Mozambique. Fighting did not end in Mozambique until 1992 and in Angola until 2002.

After independence, ethnic conflicts flared up in many nations. In Rwanda a deadly war began between the majority **Hutus** and the minority **Tutsis.** In 1994, extremist Hutus killed about 800,000 Tutsis and moderate Hutus.

In Sudan, non-Muslim peoples in the south fought Arab Muslims from the north. This, along with drought and famine, killed millions. By 2005 there was peace in the south, but by then, ethnic conflict had spread to Darfur in western Sudan. Signs of war crimes and genocide brought calls for UN peacekeepers.

Review Questions

1. What was apartheid?

_____

_____

2. What happened in the Rwanda conflict?

_____

_____

READING CHECK

Where is Darfur?

_____

_____

_____

VOCABULARY STRATEGY

Find the word *stipulated* in the underlined sentence. What do you think it means? Note that here the word refers to laws. The previous sentence mentions the restrictions non-whites faced. Use these context clues to help you figure out the meaning of the word *stipulated.*

READING SKILL

Recognize Sequence When was Nelson Mandela elected president of South Africa?

_____.

_____

CHAPTER 20 SECTION 3

Note Taking Study Guide

CONFLICTS IN THE MIDDLE EAST

Focus Question: What are the causes of conflict in the Middle East?

As you read this section in your textbook, use the flowchart to record the sequence of events in the conflicts in the Middle East.

Middle Eastern Conflicts

Iraq
- **1970s:** Kurds fight for power in northern Iraq.
- **1979:** Saddam Hussein comes to power.

Lebanon
- **1975:** Civil war begins.

Arab-Israeli Conflict
- **1948:** Israel is founded.
- **1956:** Arab-Israeli war is fought.
- **1960s:** PLO leads struggle against Israel.

Name_____ Class_____ Date_____

CHAPTER **20** SECTION 3	**Section Summary**
	CONFLICTS IN THE MIDDLE EAST

The Middle East has seen many conflicts. Modern Israel was created in 1948. Palestinian Arabs claimed the same land. After Arab countries attacked Israel in 1967, Israel took control of lands that came to be called the **occupied territories.**

The Palestine Liberation Organization, led by **Yasir Arafat,** fought against the Israelis. In the occupied territories, some Palestinians took part in revolts called **intifadas,** and suicide bombers attacked Israel. Israel responded with armed force. Palestinian bitterness increased. Israeli Prime Minister **Yitzhak Rabin** signed a peace accord. The city of **Jerusalem,** however, was an obstacle to peace. The city is sacred to Jews, Muslims, and Christians. In recent years, new conflicts flared between Israel and the Palestinians that set back hopes for peace.

Lebanon is another country in the region with diverse ethnic and religious groups. Arab Christians, Sunni Muslims, Shiite Muslims, and Druze all live there. Christian and Muslim **militias** fought in a long civil war that ended in 1990. In 2006, attacks by the radical group Hezbollah brought a brief but destructive war with Israel.

Conflicts also plagued Iraq. Iraq's Sunni Arab minority had long dominated the Kurdish minority and Shiite Arab majority. In 1979 **Saddam Hussein** took power as a dictator. He fought a long war against neighboring Iran in the 1980s. In 1990, Iraq invaded Kuwait. In response, the United States led a coalition that liberated Kuwait and crushed Iraqi forces. However, Saddam Hussein continued his brutal rule. The U.N. set up **no-fly zones** to protect the Kurds and Shiites. It worked to keep Saddam Hussein from building biological, nuclear, or chemical weapons, called **weapons of mass destruction (WMDs).**

In 2003, the United States led a coalition that invaded Iraq and overthrew Saddam Hussein. In 2005, national elections were held for the first time. **Insurgents** and ethnic conflict were still problems. Nevertheless, leaders hoped for peace.

Review Questions
1. What is the main reason for the conflict in Israel?

_____

_____

2. What are WMDs?

_____

_____

READING CHECK

Against whom did Iraq fight a war in the 1980s?

_____

_____

_____

VOCABULARY STRATEGY

Find the word *diverse* in the underlined sentence. Notice that in the next sentence four groups are mentioned. How does this help describe the population of Lebanon? Use this context clue to help you understand the meaning of *diverse.*

READING SKILL

Recognize Sequence What event led to the Gulf War?

_____

_____

_____

Name_____ Class_____ Date_____

Focus Question: How have the nations of the developing world tried to build better lives for their people?

As you read this section in your textbook, complete the chart below with details from the text about economic development and developing countries. Some items have been completed for you.

Development

Changes in Patterns of Life
- New opportunities for women emerge.
-
-

Obstacles
- Rapid population growth burdens governments.
-
-
-
-
-

Economic Change
- Railroads, highways, and dams are built.
- New schools are built.
-
-
-
-

Name_____ Class_____ Date_____

After World War II, development became a central goal in Africa, Asia, and Latin America. **Development** is the process of creating a more advanced economy and higher living standards. Nations that are trying to develop economically are, all together, known as the **developing world.** They are also called the global South, because most are south of the Tropic of Cancer. Most industrialized nations are north of the Tropic of Cancer, so they are sometimes called the global North.

To pay for development, many of these nations procured large loans from the global North. Developing nations have tried to improve their agriculture and industry. They have also built schools to increase **literacy.** For centuries, most countries in the global South had **traditional economies.** Some changed to command economies after gaining independence from European colonists. However, when these countries had trouble paying their loans, lenders from the global North made them change to market economies. Now many of these countries depend on the global North for investment and exports.

Beginning in the 1950s, better seeds, pesticides, and farm equipment led to a **Green Revolution** in many parts of the global South. This helped to feed more people. However, many small farmers could not afford the new tools and better seeds. They were forced to sell their land and move to cities.

The global South still faces many challenges. Some countries have only one export product. If prices for that product drop, their economies suffer. Also, population has grown rapidly, and many people are caught in a cycle of poverty. More and more people are moving to cities, but they often have trouble finding jobs. Many people in the cities are forced to live in crowded and dangerous **shantytowns.**

Economic development has brought other changes to the developing world. Women often have more opportunities. However, religious **fundamentalists** in some developing countries oppose changes that undermine religious traditions.

Review Questions
1. Why did many developing nations need loans?

_____

_____

2. How did the Green Revolution help the global South?

_____

_____

READING CHECK

What is another term for the developing world?

_____

_____

_____

VOCABULARY STRATEGY

Find the word *procured* in the first underlined sentence. What do you think it means? Notice that *procured* refers to loans. Find the second underlined sentence, which also mentions loans. Which of the following do you think means the same as *procured?*

1. obtained

2. paid off

READING SKILL

Identify Supporting Details
Record details that support this statement: "The global South faces many challenges."

_____

_____

_____

Name_____ Class_____ Date_____

Focus Question: What challenges have African nations faced in their effort to develop their economies?

As you read this section in your textbook, complete the concept web below to record the main ideas about challenges faced by African nations, and details that support those main ideas.

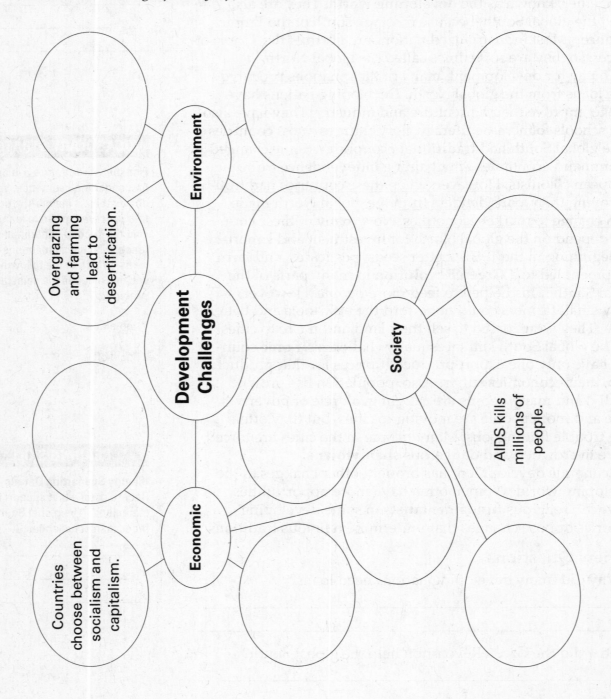

CHAPTER 21 SECTION 2

Section Summary

AFRICA SEEKS A BETTER FUTURE

After World War II, African nations had little capital to invest. This meant that they had to make difficult economic choices. Some nations chose **socialism.** This is a system in which the government controls parts of the economy. These nations hoped to end foreign influence in their countries. They also wanted to close the gap between the rich and the poor. Yet socialist governments often led to large bureaucracies.

Other nations relied on capitalism, or market economies. These economies were often more efficient. However, foreign owners of local businesses often took profits out of these countries. Some governments tried to pay for development by growing crops for export. This left less land for food to be grown on, so food had to be imported. Governments then had to subsidize part of the cost of importing food.

African nations have faced many other problems. Droughts led to famine in parts of Africa, especially in the Sahel. There, overgrazing and farming led to **desertification.** AIDS has killed millions of people in Africa. Another problem in African nations is **urbanization.** This is the shift from rural areas to cities. It has weakened traditional cultures. It has also increased economic opportunities for women in West Africa. Another concern is environmental threats. Many of Africa's animal habitats have been destroyed. As a result, many animals have become **endangered species.** One environmental activist, **Wangari Maathai,** has tried to make a difference. She started the Green Belt Movement. This organization helps women with projects of **sustainable development,** such as replanting trees and selling them.

Tanzania has experienced the problems that are common in many African countries. In the early 1960s, the Tanzanian government tried "African socialism." This failed to increase farm output. In 1985, new leaders began economic reforms. Yet Tanzania is still poor and relies on foreign aid.

Review Questions

1. Why did some governments decide to grow crops for export?

_____

_____

2. What disease has killed millions of people in Africa?

_____

_____

READING CHECK

What is socialism?

_____

_____

_____

VOCABULARY STRATEGY

Find the word *subsidize* in the underlined sentence. *Subsidize* comes from a Latin word that means "aid" or "support." What kind of aid or support did the governments provide? Use the information about the orgin of *subsidize* to help you figure out its meaning.

READING SKILL

Identify Main Ideas What is the main idea of this Summary?

_____

_____

_____

Name_____ Class_____ Date_____

CHAPTER 21 SECTION 3

Note Taking Study Guide

CHINA AND INDIA: TWO GIANTS OF ASIA

Focus Question: How do China and India compare in building strong economies and democratic governments?

As you read this section in your textbook, complete the table below to record the main ideas about reform and change in China and India. Some items have been completed for you.

Reform and Change in China and India

Type	China	India
Economic	• Free market • Communes dismantled • • • • •	• Elements of command economy adopted. • • Nehru promotion of Green Revolution; crop output improves. • •
Political	• Mao succeeded by moderates, such as Deng Xiaoping. • •	• Democratic government • •

CHAPTER 21 SECTION 3

Section Summary

CHINA AND INDIA: TWO GIANTS OF ASIA

By 1981, the new leader of China, **Deng Xiaoping,** allowed features of a free-market economy. He called his program the Four Modernizations. Some citizens were allowed to own property or businesses. Farmers could sell crops and keep the profits. Foreign investment was also welcomed. China's economic output is now four times what it was 30 years ago. But a gap exists between poor farmers and rich city dwellers.

Ruling Communist Party leaders allowed economic reforms but refused to allow more political freedom. Demonstrators gathered in **Tiananmen Square** in Beijing in May 1989. They wanted democratic reforms. <u>When the demonstrators refused to disperse, the government sent in troops and tanks to force them away.</u> Thousands were killed or wounded.

China still faces many challenges. Its population is the largest in the world, hurting economic development. However, after the government started the **one-child policy,** population growth slowed. Millions of rural workers have moved to cities, but they often live in poverty. Pollution and HIV/AIDS are also problems. Human rights abuses continue.

By contrast, India has a democratic government. After gaining independence, India tried a socialist model. Yet development was uneven. The Green Revolution improved crop output, but most farmers still used traditional methods. Since the 1980s, India has shifted to a free-market system. It has developed more industry and technology.

India's population growth has made it difficult to improve living conditions, however. The government has encouraged family planning, but it has had limited success. More than one-third of Indians live below the poverty line. Millions of families have moved to cities like **Kolkata** and **Mumbai.** This rapid urbanization has stressed city services. **Mother Teresa** started the Missionaries of Charity in India to help the urban poor.

Education and economic growth have helped India's lowest social castes and women. The constitution bans discrimination against **dalits,** the lowest caste. It gives women equal rights.

Review Questions

1. What happened to the demonstrators in Tiananmen Square?

_____

_____

2. How are the governments in China and India different?

_____

_____

READING CHECK

Who are dalits?

_____

_____

_____

VOCABULARY STRATEGY

Find the word *disperse* in the underlined sentence. What do you think it means? Read the paragraph and notice that demonstrators gathered in Tiananmen Square and then refused to *disperse.* Which of the following words or phrases do you think has the closest meaning to the word *disperse?*

1. stay

2. go away

READING SKILL

Identify Main Ideas Write a sentence that describes the state of India and China today.

_____

_____

_____

CHAPTER
21
SECTION 4

Note Taking Study Guide

LATIN AMERICA BUILDS DEMOCRACY

Focus Question: What challenges have Latin American nations faced in recent decades in their struggle for democracy and prosperity?

As you read this section in your textbook, identify the main ideas and supporting details about challenges faced by Latin American nations to complete the outline. Some items have been completed for you.

I. Economic and Social Forces

    A. Society

        1. Uneven distribution of wealth

        2. Population explosion

        3. _____

        4. _____

    B. Economy

        1. Reliance on single cash crop or commodity

        2. _____

        3. _____

        4. _____

II. The Difficult Road to Democracy

    A. Social unrest leads to rise of military dictators.

        1. Harsh, autocratic regimes result.

        2. _____

        3. _____

    B. Revolutionary unrest continues.

        1. _____

        2. _____

    C. Role of United States

        1. Dominates OAS

        2. Seeks to defend democracy and human rights

        3. _____

        4. _____

        5. _____

        6. _____

        7. _____

(Outline continues on the next page.)

CHAPTER 21 SECTION 4

Note Taking Study Guide

LATIN AMERICA BUILDS DEMOCRACY

(Continued from page 220)

> **D.** Civil wars shake Central America.
>   1. _____
>   2. _____
> **E.** _____
>   1. _____
>   2. _____
> **III.** _____
> **A.** Stability in early 1900s
>   1. Robust economy based on exports of beef and grain
>   2. _____
> **B.** _____
>   1. _____
>   2. _____
>   3. _____
>   4. _____
>   5. _____

CHAPTER 21 SECTION 4

Section Summary
LATIN AMERICA BUILDS DEMOCRACY

Who was Argentina's president from 1946 to 1955?

_____

_____

_____

VOCABULARY STRATEGY

Find the word *alleged* in the underlined sentence. The noun form of this word is *allegation.* It means "something said without proof," or "a charge made without proof." Use these clues to help you understand the meaning of *alleged.*

READING SKILL

Identify Main Ideas and Supporting Details Outline the last paragraph in the Summary.

I. The Example of Argentina

  A._____

    1._____

    2._____

    3._____

  B._____

After World War II, many governments in Latin America encouraged industries to manufacture goods that had previously been imported. This is called **import substitution.** More recently, governments have encouraged the production of goods for export. More land has been opened to farming, but much of the best land belongs to large **agribusinesses.** In many countries, a few people control the land and businesses. Population growth has made poverty worse. However, many religious leaders in Latin America have worked to end poverty and injustice. This movement is known as **liberation theology.**

Democracy has been difficult to achieve in Latin America because of poverty and inequality. Between the 1950s and 1970s, military leaders seized power in some countries. Civil wars shook parts of Central America. In Guatemala, the military killed thousands of the **indigenous,** or native, people.

The United States has had a powerful influence in Latin America. It has dominated the **Organization of American States (OAS).** During the Cold War, the United States supported dictators who were anti-communist. When rebels called **Sandinistas** came to power in Nicaragua, the United States supported the **contras.** These were guerrillas who fought the Sandinistas. The United States also urged Latin American governments to help stop the drug trade. Yet many Latin Americans alleged that the problem was not in Latin America; it was based on the demand for drugs in the United States.

By the 1990s, free elections had been held in several countries, including Argentina. For example, since the 1930s, Argentina has experienced political turmoil. From 1946 to 1955, President **Juan Perón** had strong support from workers. But he was overthrown in a military coup. The military seized control again in 1976. Thousands were murdered or kidnapped. Mothers of missing people marched in protest. They became known as the **Mothers of the Plaza de Mayo.** By 1983, the military was forced to allow elections.

Review Questions
1. Name two obstacles to democracy in Latin America.

_____

_____

2. What country dominates the OAS?

_____

_____

CHAPTER
22
SECTION 1

Note Taking Study Guide
INDUSTRIALIZED NATIONS AFTER THE COLD WAR

Focus Question: How did the end of the Cold War affect industrialized nations and regions around the world?

As you read this section in your textbook, complete the chart below to compare developments in industrialized nations after the Cold War. Some of the items have been completed for you.

Asia
• After World War II, Japan dominated Pacific Rim.
•
•
•
•
•

Russia/United States
Russia
• Russia changed to a market economy.
•
•
United States
• United States emerged as the world's only superpower.
•
•
•

Europe
• 1991—Germany is reunified.
•
•
•
•
•

CHAPTER **22** SECTION 1	Section Summary
	INDUSTRIALIZED NATIONS AFTER THE COLD WAR

After the end of the Cold War, what country became the only superpower?

_____

_____

_____

Find the word *inflation* in the underlined sentence. What do you think it means? The word *inflate* is related to *inflation*. Picture what happens when you *inflate* a balloon. Does it get larger or smaller? *Inflation* is an economic term that has to do with prices. If prices are *inflated*, would you expect them to be higher or lower? Use these clues to help you figure out the meaning of *inflation*.

Compare and Contrast How was the U.S. economy in the 1990s the same as—and different from—its economy in the early 2000s?

_____

_____

_____

A global economy developed after the Cold War. With Eastern and Western Europe no longer divided, business and travel became easier. However, unemployment rose. More people immigrated to Europe from the developing world. One exciting change, however, was the reunification of Germany in 1991.

In the 1990s, the European Economic Community became the **European Union** (EU). Later, the **euro** became the currency of most of the EU member countries. Some Eastern European nations have joined the EU, too. However, older members of the EU were concerned about these new members' weaker economies. Most Eastern European nations also wanted to join NATO, and some did.

After the breakup of the Soviet Union, Russia became a market economy. This was not easy. Prices soared, and crime increased. In 1998, Russia **defaulted** on much of its foreign debt. High inflation and the collapse of the Russian currency forced banks and businesses to close. In 2000, **Vladimir Putin** became president. He promised to end corruption and make Russia's economy stronger. Yet, he also increased government control and cut back on people's freedom.

After the Cold War, the United States became the world's only superpower. Among other things, it was involved in Middle East peace talks and war in Iraq. In the 1990s, there was an economic boom in the United States. This produced a budget **surplus**. However, slow economic growth and high military spending led to budget **deficits** by the early 2000s.

The **Pacific Rim** nations have become important to the global economy. Following World War II, Japan grew into an economic powerhouse. However, by the 1990s, Japan's economy weakened, while China's economy boomed. Other powerhouses include the "Asian tigers"—Taiwan, Hong Kong, Singapore, and South Korea. They are known for their electronics exports. However, the global recession that began in 2008 hurt these economies.

Review Questions

1. When did the new global economy begin?

_____

_____

2. Which Pacific Rim country became an economic powerhouse following World War II?

_____

_____

CHAPTER
22
SECTION 2

Note Taking Study Guide
GLOBALIZATION

Focus Question: How is globalization affecting economies and societies around the world?

As you read this section in your textbook, use the Venn diagram to compare the effects of globalization on developed nations with its effects on developing nations. Some of the items have been completed for you.

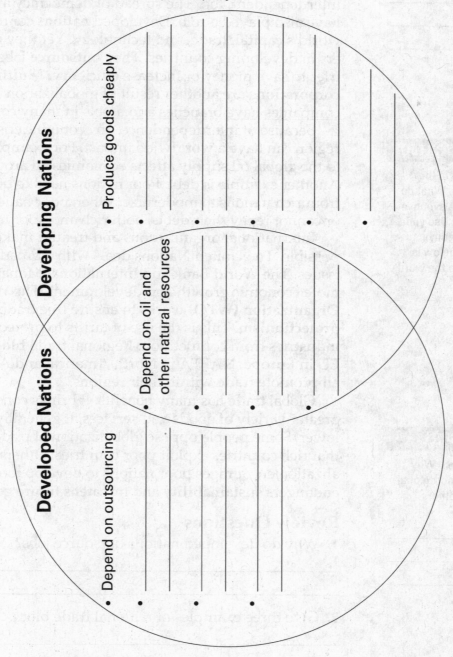

CHAPTER **22** SECTION 2	**Section Summary**
	GLOBALIZATION

Globalization links nations around the world economically, politically, and culturally. It leads to economic **interdependence**—countries depend on one another for goods, resources, knowledge, and labor. Improvements in transportation and communication have made the world more interdependent, too. The spread of democracy and free trade have also played a role. Developed nations control much of the world's capital, trade, and technology. Yet they rely on workers in developing countries. They **outsource** jobs to these countries to save money or increase efficiency. **Multinational corporations** are another result of globalization. These global companies have branches and assets in many countries.

Because of interdependence, an economic crisis in one region can have a worldwide impact. For example, any change to the global oil supply affects economies all around the world. Another example is debt. Poor nations need to borrow money from rich nations to modernize. When poor nations struggle to or cannot repay their debts, both rich and poor nations are hurt.

International organizations and treaties make global trade possible. The United Nations deals with a broad range of issues. The World Bank and International Monetary Fund promote economic growth and development. The **World Trade Organization (WTO)** works to ensure free trade. It opposes **protectionism.** This is the use of tariffs to protect a country's industries from competition. Regional trade **blocs,** such as the EU in Europe, NAFTA in North America, and APEC in Asia all promote trade within their regions.

Global trade has many benefits. It brings consumers a greater variety of goods and services. It generally keeps prices lower. Some people oppose globalization of trade. They claim that rich countries exploit poor countries. Others say that globalization encourages poor nations to develop too rapidly. This endangers **sustainability** and threatens future generations.

VOCABULARY STRATEGY

Find the word *assets* in the underlined sentence. What do you think it means? A synonym for *asset* is *property*. Use your knowledge of the synonym to decide which word below is closest in meaning to the word *assets?*

1. possessions

2. debts

READING SKILL

Compare and Contrast Why do some people support globalization of trade and others oppose it?

_____

_____

_____

Review Questions

1. Why do developed nations outsource jobs?

_____

_____

2. Give three examples of regional trade blocs.

_____

_____

CHAPTER 22
SECTION 3

Note Taking Study Guide
SOCIAL AND ENVIRONMENTAL CHALLENGES

Focus Question: How do poverty, disease, and environmental challenges affect people around the world today?

As you read this section in your textbook, complete the chart below to compare aspects of globalization. Some of the items have been completed for you.

Aspects of Globalization

Environmental Issues
- Industrialization
  -
  -
  -
  -

Human Rights
- Universal Declaration of Human Rights
  -
  -
  -
  -
  -
  -

Poverty/Disease
- Natural disasters
- May earn less than $2 a day.
  -
  -
  -
  -
  -
  -
  -

CHAPTER 22 SECTION 3

Section Summary

SOCIAL AND ENVIRONMENTAL CHALLENGES

When a disease spreads rapidly, what is it called?

_____

_____

_____

Find the word *inhibit* in the underlined sentence. What does it mean? The word *assist* is an antonym of *inhibit*. That means it has the opposite meaning. Use what you know about the antonym *assist* to help you understand the meaning of *inhibit*. Which of the following words do you think is closest in meaning to *inhibit*?

1. prevent

2. aid

Compare What do the Universal Declaration of Human Rights and the Helsinki Accords have in common?

_____

_____

_____

Poverty, disaster, and disease are still challenges today. The gap between rich and poor nations is growing. Half of the people in the world earn less than $2 a day. However, ending poverty is difficult. Many poor nations owe billions in debt. As a result, they have little money to improve living conditions. Many other factors inhibit efforts to reduce poverty. These include political upheavals, civil war, corruption, poor planning, and rapid population growth.

Natural disasters cause death and destruction around the world. One example is the **tsunami** in the Indian Ocean in 2004. Natural disasters can cause unsanitary conditions. This leads to disease. Diseases can spread quickly around the world. When a disease spreads rapidly, it is called an **epidemic.** HIV/AIDS is an epidemic that has killed millions of people. Natural disasters can also cause **famine.** Wars and problems distributing food contribute to famine, too. Poverty, disasters, and wars have forced many people to become **refugees.**

International agreements have tried to guarantee basic human rights around the world. The Universal Declaration of Human Rights and the Helsinki Accords are two examples. Still, human rights abuses continue. Women in many parts of the world lack equal rights. Worldwide, children suffer terrible abuses. Indigenous people also face mistreatment.

Industrialization and the world population explosion have hurt the environment. Strip mining, chemical pesticides, and oil spills are all threats to the environment. Gases from power plants and factories produce **acid rain.** Pollution from nuclear power plants is another threat. Desertification and **deforestation** are major problems in certain parts of the world. Deforestation can lead to **erosion.** It is also a threat to the rain forests. One hotly debated issue is **global warming.** Many scientists believe that it is caused by humans burning fossil fuels. Others argue that it is caused by natural changes in Earth's climate.

Review Questions

1. Why have many people become refugees?

_____

_____

2. Name two international agreements that have tried to guarantee human rights.

_____

_____

Name_____ Class_____ Date_____

Focus Question: What kinds of threats to national and global security do nations face today?

As you read this section in your textbook, complete the chart below to compare threats to global security. Some items have been completed for you.

Threats to Security					
Nuclear Weapons	Nuclear weapons are unsecured in Soviet Union.				
Nuclear Proliferation	Four nations have not signed treaty; others are suspected of violating treaty.				

CHAPTER 22
SECTION 4

Section Summary
SECURITY IN A DANGEROUS WORLD

READING CHECK

What group was responsible for the attacks on the United States on September 11, 2001?

_____

_____

_____

VOCABULARY STRATEGY

Find the word *priority* in the underlined sentence. What do you think it means? Notice the sentences that follow it. What did the United States do to make fighting terrorism a *priority?* Use this context clue to help you figure out the meaning of the word *priority*. Which of the following phrases best explains the meaning of *priority?*

1. something of the greatest importance
2. something of little importance

READING SKILL

Compare and Contrast Compare and contrast information about nuclear weapons before and after the Nuclear Nonproliferation Treaty was signed.

_____

_____

_____

During the Cold War, the United States and Russia produced many nuclear weapons. Nations soon became afraid that nuclear weapons would **proliferate,** or spread rapidly. As a result, many nations signed the Nuclear Nonproliferation Treaty in 1968. However, some nations have not signed the treaty. Others are suspected of violating it. Nuclear weapons in the former Soviet Union are a special concern. Russia lacks the money to protect those weapons from smugglers.

Many people fear that terrorist groups will acquire and use WMDs. **Terrorism** is the use of violence, often aimed at civilians, to achieve political goals. Terrorists' actions include bombings, shootings, and kidnappings. Regional terrorist groups in places like Northern Ireland have operated for many years. More recently, the Middle East has become a training ground for terrorists. Many belong to Islamic fundamentalist groups such as **al Qaeda.** Led by Osama bin Laden, al Qaeda terrorists were responsible for attacks on the United States on September 11, 2001.

In response to these attacks, the United States and other nations made fighting terrorism a priority. In 2001, Osama bin Laden and other al Qaeda leaders were living in **Afghanistan.** Afghanistan's government was controlled by the **Taliban,** an Islamic fundamentalist group. When the Taliban would not hand over the terrorists, the United States attacked Afghanistan. Because President Bush claimed that Iraq had WMDs, the United States later declared war on Iraq.

During the early 2000s, concerns grew that North Korea was developing nuclear weapons. In 2006, North Korea actually tested such a weapon. Meanwhile, Iran announced plans to develop nuclear power plants. The United States and other nations, however, believed that Iran aimed to build nuclear weapons, too. The United States and other countries worked to stop this nuclear proliferation.

Review Questions

1. What are terrorists' aims?

_____

_____

2. What Islamic fundamentalist group controlled the government of Afghanistan until the United States invaded?

_____

_____

CHAPTER 22 SECTION 5	Note Taking Study Guide
	ADVANCES IN SCIENCE AND TECHNOLOGY

Focus Question: How have advances in science and technology shaped the modern world?

As you read this section in your textbook, complete the chart below to compare the impacts of modern science and technology. Some items have been completed for you.

Important Science and Technology

Medicine and Biotechnology
- Vaccines prevent the spread of diseases.
-
-
-
-
-
- Cloning raises ethical issues.

Computers
- Computers lead to Information Age.
-
-
-
-

Space Science
- Soviet Union and United States compete in space race.
-
-
-
-

CHAPTER 22 SECTION 5

Section Summary
ADVANCES IN SCIENCE AND TECHNOLOGY

Since 1945, scientific research and technological developments have transformed human life. During the Cold War, the United States and the Soviet Union competed in the "space race." This began in 1957 when the Soviet Union launched *Sputnik*, the first **artificial satellite.** In 1969, the United States landed the first human on the moon. The United States and the Soviet Union both explored military uses of space. They also put spy satellites in Earth's orbit. Since the Cold War ended, nations have worked together in space. Several countries are involved in the **International Space Station (ISS).** There are now thousands of artificial satellites orbiting Earth, launched by many nations.

Another important new technology is the computer. **Personal computers,** or **PCs,** have replaced typewriters and account books in homes and offices. Many factories now use computerized robots instead of people. Computers also control satellites and probes in space. The **Internet** links computer systems worldwide. It allows people to communicate instantly around the globe and access vast amounts of information in new ways.

There have also been important developments in medicine and **biotechnology.** Biotechnology applies biological knowledge to industry, engineering, and technology. Vaccines have been developed that help prevent the spread of disease. In the 1970s, surgeons learned to transplant human organs. **Lasers** have made many types of surgery safer and more controlled. Computers have helped doctors diagnose and treat disease. There have been dramatic developments in genetics and genetic engineering. **Genetics** is the study of genes and heredity. **Genetic engineering** <u>is the manipulation, or changing, of genetic material to produce specific results.</u> Genetic research has produced new drugs to fight disease. It has also created new, hardier strains of fruits and vegetables. Genetic cloning has practical uses, but it raises ethical issues about how science should be used to change or create life.

Review Questions

1. What does the Internet allow people to do?

_____

_____

2. Name two important developments in surgery.

_____

_____

Concept Connector Journal

Belief Systems

 Essential Question: How do religions and belief systems help shape society?

I. WARM-UP

Throughout history, religions and belief systems have influenced how people act and what they value. A national survey conducted among 2,003 adults had the following findings about how Americans felt about the influence of religion in the United States.

Influence of Religion

	On American Life (%)	On American Government (%)
Increasing	34	42
Good thing	21	15
Bad thing	11	24
Decreasing	59	45
Good thing	6	8
Bad thing	50	36
No change	2	2
Don't know	5	7
NET: Want more*	71	51
NET: Want less**	17	32

* Increasing is good or decreasing is bad
** Increasing is bad or decreasing is good
Source: Pew Research Center for the People & the Press and the Pew Forum on Religion & Public Life, 2006

1. What generalization can you make about people's feelings about the influence of religion in the United States?

_____

_____

Concept Connector Journal

Belief Systems (continued)

2. According to the U.S. Constitution, Congress cannot make laws establishing a religion or prohibiting the exercise of religion. List three ways this law affects you.

a. _____

_____

b. _____

_____

c. _____

_____

3. Indicate on the scale below whether you think religion or belief systems have had a major impact on American life and government.

Strongly ←————————————————————————→ **Strongly**
Agree   **Disagree**

II. EXPLORATION

Whether or not you have been aware of it, religion and belief systems have influenced traditions and laws in the United States. As you complete the following journal entries, you will see that religion and belief systems have shaped societies throughout history.

1. Animism: How did ancient people's belief that gods inhabited nature affect rituals and the structure of ancient society?

Early drawings made in caves may have been part of religious ritual. People appealed

to many gods, such as river gods and sun gods. They built temples to gods. Ceremonies

required the full-time attention of priests, who had special training and knowledge.

_____

2. Early religions: Match the civilization in Column A with an impact of religion in Column B.

Column A

_D___ 1. Sumer

_A___ 2. Persians

_C___ 3. Egypt

_B___ 4. Israelites

Column B

A. Belief in teachings of Zoroaster helped unite the empire.

B. Prophets taught a strong code of ethics.

C. Belief in afterlife led to elaborate burial procedures.

D. Ziggurats were dedicated to the chief god or goddess.

Concept Connector Journal

3. WebQuest: Religion and Belief Systems How has what you have learned about religion in current societies affected your ideas about the impact of belief systems?

> **Transfer Your Knowledge**
> **For:** WebQuest **Web Code:** nbh-0308

_____

_____

_____

4. Egyptian and Indian Religions: Ancient Egyptians believed that the god Osiris would judge them after death. The evil would be condemned and the good would live forever in bliss. How did Hinduism and Buddhism shape expectations of right behavior?

Both religions stressed nonviolence and believed in karma (the actions of a person's

life that affect his or her fate in the next life), dharma (the religious and moral duties

of an individual), and a cycle of rebirth. Buddhists rejected the caste system and

offered the hope of nirvana (or union with the universe) regardless of birth.

5. Christianity: How did Christianity become influential in Western Civilization?

• In the first century A.D., Jesus begins teaching.

• After the death of Jesus, followers spread message to Jews of Judea.

• Paul spreads message to Greece and Asia Minor.

• Unity of Roman empire provides protection for missionaries.

• Edict of Milan in A.D. 313 ends persecution of Christians.

• In the 400s, Rome falls and Christianity becomes a central institution of Western civilization for 1000 years.

6. Byzantine Empire: How did religion influence the Byzantine Empire?

a. Great Schism: Eastern Orthodox Church separated from the Roman Catholic Church.

b. Crusades: Venetians gained control of Byzantine trade, draining the wealth from the empire.

c. Heritage: Byzantines blended Christian religious beliefs with Greek science, philosophy, arts, and literature.

Concept Connector Journal

7. Islam: How did the teachings of Islam appeal to conquered peoples?

Early Umayyad caliphates did not attempt to convert Jews, Christians, and Zoroastrians.

Some people were attracted because Islam emphasized equality of all believers, regardless

or race, gender, class, or wealth.

8. China: Confucianism is a belief system that supports the following values.

* Harmony results when people accept their place in society.

* Respect for one's parents is above all other duties.

* A ruler should rule by example, not by harsh laws.

* The superior man understands righteousness; the inferior man understands profit.

How did Confucianism affect China's response to the West and Western influence? How
did China's choices affect its history? *(Chapter 12, Section 5)*

_____

_____

_____

_____

_____

III. ESSAY

Bring together what you have read in your textbook with the information you have
gathered online about this concept. **On a separate sheet of paper, answer the essential
question: How do religions and belief systems affect society?**

Concept Connector Journal

Conflict

 Essential Question: When, if ever, should people go to war?

I. WARM-UP

Conflict is a part of everyone's life. Usually, conflicts are resolved in a way acceptable to all parties; sometimes conflicts escalate into serious problems.

1. Think of a conflict that you have recently had with someone—a friend, sibling, parent, or even an organization. Write what the conflict was about on the line below, and then fill in the speech balloons to show the opposing points of view.

_____

_____

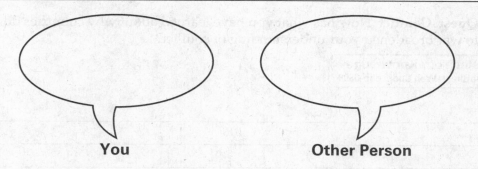

You   **Other Person**

2. What does it take to resolve a conflict?

_____

_____

_____

II. EXPLORATION

Too often throughout history, conflict has led to violence or war. As you complete the following journal entries, you will see how conflict has resulted in turning points for people and nations.

1. The Persian War: Why did Alexander want to conquer Persia?

He was ambitious and he wanted to extend his empire. He dreamed of conquering all of

Asia.

_____

Concept Connector Journal

2. Roman Imperialism: How did imperialism lead to conflict in the Roman Republic?

a. Incredible riches from trade routes poured into Rome and created <u>a new class of people</u> who bought up <u>huge farming estates</u>.

b. As Romans captured more and more land, they forced <u>war prisoners to work as slaves on the latifunda</u>.

c. Landless farmers flocked to Rome where they joined unemployed workers and began to <u>riot</u>.

d. Two tribunes who favored reform angered the senate and were <u>killed in street violence instigated by senators</u>.

e. Popular political leaders and senators disagreed over reform measure for the poor because the senators saw the reforms as a threat to their <u>political power</u>.

3. WebQuest: Conflict How has what you have learned about why countries do or do not go to war broadened your understanding of conflict?

> **Transfer Your Knowledge**
> **For:** WebQuest **Web Code:** nbh-0808

_____

_____

_____

_____

_____

4. Crusades: In the late 1000s, the Byzantine emperor asked Pope Urban II for Christian knights to help him fight the Seljuk Turks, who were Muslims. The pope called for a crusade to free the Holy Land from the Seljuk Turks.

a. Pilgrims were prevented from going to the Holy Land. _____

b. The Seljuk Turks had overrun Byzantium, threatening the Byzantine Empire. _____

c. Urban hoped to increase his power in Europe and to heal the schism between the

Roman and Byzantine churches. _____

Concept Connector Journal

5. European Exploration: Complete the web to identify factors that would lead to conflict between two European nations in the 1600s and 1700s. *(Chapter 2, Section 3)*

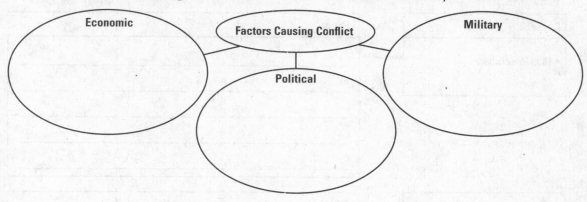

6. Enlightenment Ideas: Read the Enlightenment ideas below. Then explain why these ideas might cause conflict between colonists and their rulers. *(Chapter 5, Section 1)*

• Government's power comes from the people.

• People have natural rights to life, liberty, and property.

_____

_____

_____

_____

_____

7. Opposing Ideologies: Fill in the chart to show what Europeans with different ideologies wanted in the early 1800s. *(Chapter 8, Section 1)*

Conservatives	Liberals	Metternich
•	•	•
•	•	•
•	•	•

Concept Connector Journal

8. European Revolutionaries: Complete the cause-and-effect charts to show the immediate results of the revolutions of 1830 and 1848 in France. *(Chapter 8, Section 2)*

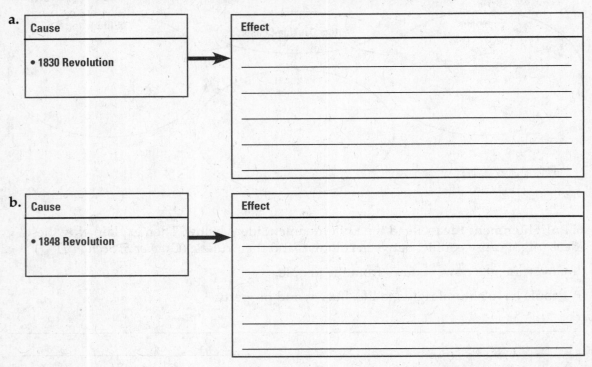

a.

Cause	Effect
• 1830 Revolution	

b.

Cause	Effect
• 1848 Revolution	

9. Nationalism: Why was nationalism a factor in Austria's declaration of war on Serbia in 1914? *(Chapter 14, Section 1)*

_____

_____

_____

10. World War II: The end of World War II was followed by the establishment of the United Nations as a peacekeeping organization. However, new conflicts soon arose among the former allies of the war. Why were the United States and the Soviet Union on opposing sides during the Cold War? *(Chapter 17, Section 5)*

_____

_____

_____

Name _____ Class _____ Date _____

Concept Connector Journal

Conflict (continued)

11. Religious Conflict: Complete the chart below to show examples of places in the world where religious differences have caused conflict. *(Chapter 20, Sections 1, 2, and 3)*

Country or Region	Religions Involved

III. ESSAY

Bring together what you have read in your textbook with the information you have gathered online about this concept. **On a separate sheet of paper, answer the essential question: When, if ever, should people go to war?**

Concept Connector Journal

Cooperation

Essential Question: With whom should we cooperate and why?

I. WARM-UP

Cooperation is working together for a common benefit. You have the opportunity to cooperate with others in many aspects of your life. Consider how you do or don't do this and the outcome.

1. Complete the table below.

Place	Action	Cost/Benefits
Home		
School		
Team/community		

2. Suppose that you are a highly skilled ball player who knows that a college scout is in the stands. Should you make every effort to be the star of the game, scoring as many points as you can, or should you make every effort to be a "team player" and set up shots for others to execute? Which approach would you take, and why?

_____

_____

_____

_____

II. EXPLORATION

Cooperation can yield great benefits or, at times, exact great costs. As you complete the following journal entries you will see how cooperation has played a role in the outcome of world events.

1. Iroquois League: Why did competing Iroquois groups create the Iroquois League?

In order to keep peace among themselves, five Iroquois nations met together in

councils to deal with common issues.

_____

Concept Connector Journal

Cooperation (continued)

2. Defeat of the Aztecs: What were the short-term and long-term effects of the cooperation of Aztec enemies with the Spanish conquistador, Cortes? Complete the cause and effect chart below. *(Chapter 3, Section 1)*

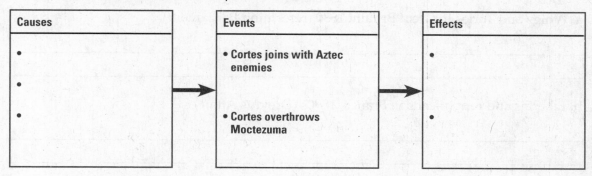

Causes	Events	Effects
•	• Cortes joins with Aztec enemies	•
•		
•	• Cortes overthrows Moctezuma	•

3. American Revolution, 1776: How did cooperation influence the outcome of the American Revolution? *(Chapter 5, Section 3)*

_____

_____

_____

4. Coalition Against Napoleon: Sometimes a state becomes powerful and tries to impose its way on others. At some point, other states join together in opposition. Fill in the blanks to show how Napoleon lost power. *(Chapter 6, Section 4)*

In ancient times, the Athenians sought to dominate their world: Athens creates Delian League ⟶ Establishes Athenian Empire by force ⟶ Sparta creates Peloponnesian League ⟶ Athenians defeated in Peloponnesian War ⟶ Athens declines.

In the early 1800s, Napoleon tried to dominate the world: Napoleon gains

control of France ⟶ _____

_____ ⟶ _____

_____ ⟶ Napoleon is exiled.

5. The Opening of Japan: Was the Japanese decision to open its ports to the United States in 1854 a wise decision? Why or why not? *(Chapter 13, Section 1)*

_____

_____

_____

Name _____ Class _____ Date _____

Concept Connector Journal

6. Political Alliances: Sometimes groups of people, or factions, form coalitions to achieve their goals. Describe what each of the following did and the outcome. *(Chapter 11)*

a. Whigs and Tories in Great Britain, 1830 (reforming Parliament)

_____

_____

b. Liberals and republicans in France, 1890s (Dreyfus Affair)

_____

_____

c. Confederate states, United States, 1861 (slavery)

_____

_____

d. Farmers and city workers, United States, 1890s (reform)

_____

_____

7. Competing Alliances: Complete the web of alliances to show how Europe was enmeshed in entangling alliances. *(Chapter 13, Section 1)*

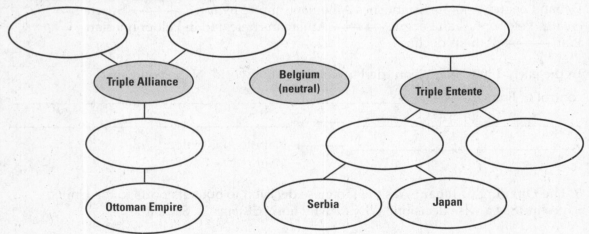

Concept Connector Journal

8. Munich Pact: How would you judge Neville Chamberlain's decision to cooperate with Adolph Hitler at the Munich Conference? Why? *(Chapter 17, Section 1)*

_____

_____

_____

9. United Nations: With the failure of the League of Nations to prevent war, nations looked for a better way to work together. Fill in the chart below. *(Chapter 17, Section 5)*

Organization/Membership	Terms of Agreement
League of Nations—40 nations, but not including the United States	• Negotiate disputes • Take common action against aggressors • No power over nonmembers
United Nations, including the United States	• •

10. European Community: In 1993, the European Union was established. In 2002, twelve European Union nations replaced their individual currencies with the euro? How did the European Community set the stage for this increased economic cooperation? *(Chapter 18, Section 2)*

_____

_____

_____

11. WebQuest: Cooperation How did the WebQuest affect your ideas about when and when not to cooperate? *(Chapter 18, Section 1)*

> **Transfer Your Knowledge**
> **For:** WebQuest **Web Code:** nbh-3008

_____

_____

_____

Concept Connector Journal

12. NGOs: Why is assistance from nongovernment agencies important for providing help around the world? *(Chapter 22, Section 2)*

_____

_____

_____

III. ESSAY

Bring together what you have read in your textbook with the information you have gathered online about this concept. **On a separate sheet of paper, answer the essential question: With whom should we cooperate and why?**

Concept Connector Journal

Cultural Diffusion

 Essential Question: How does cultural diffusion occur?

I. WARM-UP

Today, thanks to immigrants from all over the world, Americans enjoy foods from many cultures. This is just one example of cultural diffusion in the United States.

1. What are some other ways that cultural diffusion affects Americans? Write an example for each category on the web below.

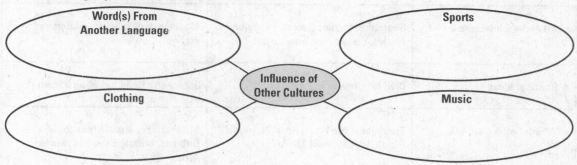

2. How has cultural diffusion enriched your life?

_____

_____

II. EXPLORATION

Cultural diffusion began in ancient times when people first began trading and migrating. As you complete the following journal entries, you will see how various aspects of cultures have spread.

1. Alphabet: What role did trade play in the Greek alphabet?

Traders from Greece returned to their homeland from Phoenicia with new ideas such as

the Phoenician alphabet. As the Greeks expanded overseas, Greek settlers and traders

carried their ideas and their culture.

2. Spread of Roman Culture: The graphic organizer below shows the traditions that produced the Greco-Roman civilization.

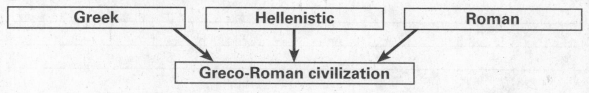

Name _____ Class _____ Date _____

Concept Connector Journal

Cultural Diffusion (continued)

3. Byzantine Empire: See the chart below to compare how the Byzantines spread their culture with how the Romans spread theirs.

	Roman Culture	Byzantine Culture
a. Language and Learning	Used Latin in literature	Preserved Roman learning, developed own, used Greek language
b. Religion	Diverse religions, then rise of Christianity with pope as head	Byzantine Church with emperor as patriarch or head
c. Art and Architecture	Sculpture, frescoes, mosaics, columns, arches, domed roof, aqueducts	Mosaics, icons, improved Roman arches
d. Political Ideas	Civil law, law of the nations	Justinian's Code based on Roman law
e. Where Culture Spread	Throughout Mediterranean, Northern Africa, Europe, Asia Minor	Mediterranean and Black Seas, Balkans, Middle East, and Northern Africa
f. How Culture Spread	Conquest, trade	Trade routes, migration

4. Spread of Islam: List at least four reasons that help explain how Islam spread.

a. A shared faith that united many formerly competing Arab tribes

b. Conquests of weakened empires like the Persians and Byzantines

c. Conversions of people drawn to the message of Islam and its emphasis, in principle, on equality

d. Tolerance of other beliefs, such as those of Jews, Christians, and Zoroastrians

5. WebQuest: Cultural Diffusion How has what you have learned about the movement of goods and ideas expanded your understanding of cultural diffusion?

> **Transfer Your Knowledge**
> **For:** WebQuest **Web Code:** nbh-1108

_____

_____

_____

Concept Connector Journal

Cultural Diffusion (continued)

6. Mongols: In what ways did Kublai Khan try to maintain Mongol identity after he defeated China?

In addition to keeping the Chinese from serving in the military, Kublai Khan reserved the highest government positions for Mongols and had Arab architects design his palace.

7. a. What ideas of the Abbasid dynasty (750–850) and the Renaissance helped make these periods golden ages? *(Chapter 1, Section 1)*

_____

_____

_____

b. How were these ideas spread?

_____

_____

_____

8. Roots of Democracy: Complete the graphic organizer to show four ideas of the Enlightenment that were the roots of the United States Constitution. *(Chapter 5, Sections 1 and 3)*

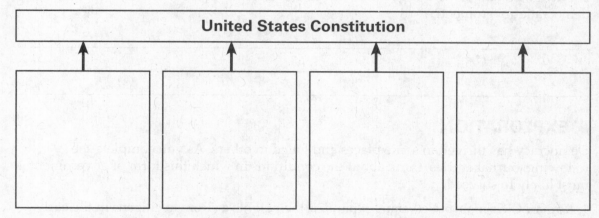

III. ESSAY

Bring together what you have read in your textbook with the information you have gathered online about this concept. **On a separate sheet of paper, answer the essential question: How does cultural diffusion occur?**

Concept Connector Journal

Democracy

 Essential Question: Under what conditions is democracy most likely to succeed?

I. WARM-UP

As you know, nations have different forms of government. The government of the United States is a democracy. The government gets its power from the people.

1. What does living in a democracy mean to you? Write your ideas on the web below.

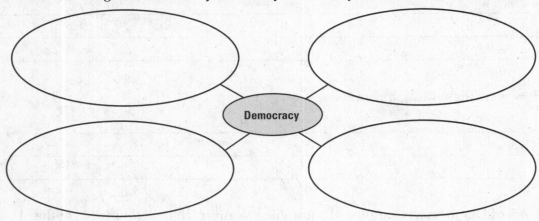

Democracy

2. Why do you think the U.S. government has served as a model for nations seeking a democratic government?

_____

_____

_____

II. EXPLORATION

Democracy has thrived in some places and failed in others. As you complete the following journal entries, think about the conditions in which this form of government is most likely to succeed.

1. Roman Citizenship: Plebeians expanded their rights as Roman citizens in the early days of the Roman Republic.

a. They gained the right to elect their own officials. _____

b. They forced the senate to choose plebeians as consuls. _____

c. They got Roman laws written down, making it possible for plebeians to appeal judgments of patrician judges. _____

Concept Connector Journal

2. Edward I: How did King Edward I give the common people of England a voice in government, and how did that affect the monarchy?

In 1295, King Edward called for inclusion of representatives of the common people in Parliament. Since Parliament had to approve his spending, this step limited the power of the monarchy. Later, this Parliament became known as the Model Parliament because it set up the framework of England's legislature.

3. English Bill of Rights: List two ways that the English Bill of Rights, laws passed by Parliament in 1629, increased the rights of English subjects. List two ways that this document lessened the power of the monarch. *(Chapter 4, Section 3)*

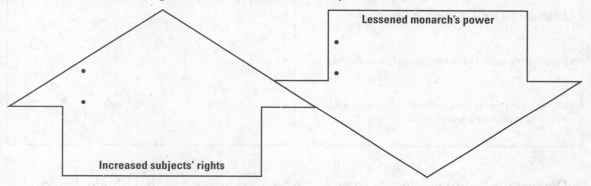

Lessened monarch's power

Increased subjects' rights

4. American Declaration of Independence: During the 1600s, government changed in England through inheritance, civil war, and the Glorious Revolution. By the end of the century, Britain had a constitutional government, but it was still an oligarchy, ruled by the few. The government established by the Americans went beyond its British roots. On what principles expressed in the Declaration of Independence was American constitutional government based? *(Chapter 5, Section 3)*

_____

_____

_____

_____

5. Napoleon: At the end of the French Revolution, Napoleon Bonaparte moved from victorious general to powerful political leader. *(Chapter 6, Section 4)*

a. How did he weaken democratic gains in France?

_____

_____

_____

Concept Connector Journal

b. How did he strengthen democracy in France?

_____

_____

_____

6. Simón Bolivar: Complete the chart to compare the outcome of the American Revolution with those in Latin America. Use these points of comparison: social classes, constitutions, and cooperation between colonies. *(Chapter 8, Section 3)*

American Revolution	Latin American Revolutions
• Embraced the ideas of liberty and equality	•
• Constitution called for a democratic government.	•
• Worked together to form federal government made up of states with own governments	•

7. Democratic Reforms: Identify some of the democratic reforms that Britain, France, and the United States achieved during the 1800s. *(Chapter 11, Sections 1–4)*

Britain	France	United States
•	•	•
•	•	•
•	•	•

Name _____ Class _____ Date _____

Concept Connector Journal

8. Democracy in India: Complete the sentences in the flowchart to show how Gandhi's protests led to a democratic movement in India. *(Chapter 15, Section 3)*

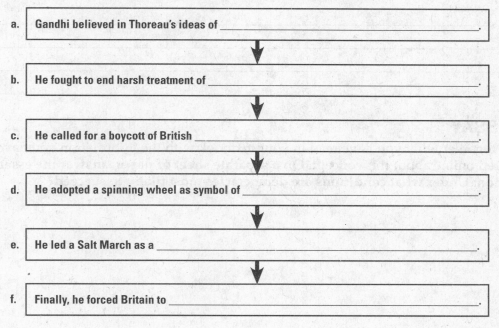

a. | Gandhi believed in Thoreau's ideas of _____.

b. | He fought to end harsh treatment of _____.

c. | He called for a boycott of British _____.

d. | He adopted a spinning wheel as symbol of _____.

e. | He led a Salt March as a _____.

f. | Finally, he forced Britain to _____.

9. Internment of Japanese Americans: Are actions by a democratic government that limit the individual rights of citizens ever justified? Show where you stand on this issue by checking a box on the continuum. Then explain your reasons. *(Chapter 17, Section 3).*

Always Justified ☐ ☐ ☐ ☐ ☐ Never Justified

_____

_____

_____

10. WebQuest: Democracy How has what you have learned about democratic countries expanded your understanding of why democracy succeeds or fails?

> **Transfer Your Knowledge**
> **For:** WebQuest **Web Code:** nbh-3308

_____

_____

_____

Concept Connector Journal

Democracy (continued)

11. Communications and Democracy: Make a prediction about how advances in communication might increase democracy throughout the world. *(Chapter 24)*

_____

_____

_____

_____

III. ESSAY

Bring together what you have read in your textbook with the information you have gathered online about this concept. **On a separate sheet of paper, answer the essential question: Under what conditions are democracies most likely to succeed?**

Concept Connector Journal

Dictatorship

 Essential Question: Why do people sometimes support dictators?

I. WARM-UP

How do governments remain in power? President Ronald Reagan offered his view.

> *"Someone once said that every form of government has one characteristic peculiar to it and if that characteristic is lost, the government will fall. In a monarchy, it is affection and respect for the royal family. If that is lost the monarch is lost. In a dictatorship, it is fear. If the people stop fearing the dictator he'll lose power. In a representative government such as ours, it is virtue. If virtue goes, the government fails."* —Ronald Reagan

How would you define *dictatorship*? Why might fear be a key part of the success of a dictatorship?

_____

_____

_____

II. EXPLORATION

During times of turmoil and great change, people often turn to powerful leaders to solve problems. As you complete the following journal entries, you will see how dictators have risen and why people sometimes support dictatorships.

1. Reasons for Dictatorships: What circumstances gave rise to dictators in Europe after World War I? Complete the web below. *(Chapter 16, Section 2)*

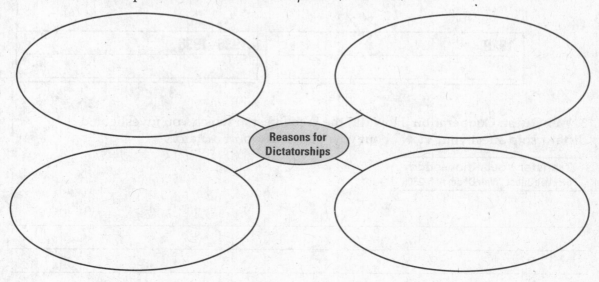

Concept Connector Journal

2. Italy and Russia: A totalitarian state is a form of government in which a one-party dictatorship tries to regulate all aspects of the lives of its citizens.

a. Complete this timeline to show the steps in the rise to power of Benito Mussolini.

Rise of Mussolini

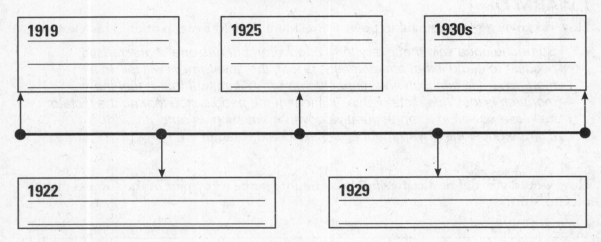

b. Complete this timeline to show the steps in the rise to power of Joseph Stalin.

Rise of Stalin

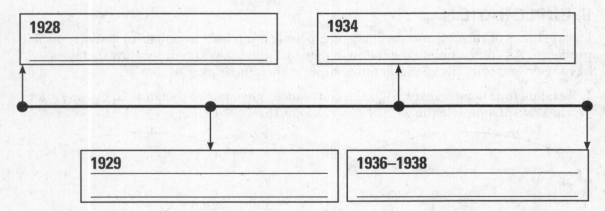

3. WebQuest: Cooperation How did the WebQuest in which you investigated dictatorship affect your view about why people support dictators?

Transfer Your Knowledge
For: WebQuest **Web Code:** nbh-2808

_____

_____

_____

Concept Connector Journal

4. Cultural Revolution: Complete the chart below to show the impact of aspects of Mao Zedong's Cultural Revolution on Chinese society. *(Chapter 18, Section 3)*

Impact of Cultural Revolution on Chinese Society	
Red Guards	
Propaganda	
Forced labor camps	
Civil war	

Did Mao's Cultural Revolution strengthen or weaken his control over China? Explain.

_____

_____

_____

5. Africa: a. Make generalizations about how one-party rule affected each of the following elements after African nations gained independence. *(Chapter 19, Section 3)*

- Political systems _____

_____

- Economies _____

_____

- Civil wars _____

_____

- Regional conflict _____

_____

b. Despite conflicts and divisions, why do you think people in the new African nations often supported dictators?

_____

_____

Concept Connector Journal

6. Iraq: a. Describe the outcome of these events in Iraq during the rule of Saddam Hussein. *(Chapter 20, Section 3)*

• Saddam Hussein begins war with Iran. _____

_____

• Iraq invades neighboring Kuwait. _____

_____

• Saddam Hussein crushes revolts by minorities. _____

_____

• UN imposes economic sanctions on Iraq. _____

_____

• UN coalition forces invade Iraq. _____

_____

b. Given the outcome of events under Saddam Hussein's rule, why did he keep power so long?

_____

_____

7. Latin America: Why would the following issues lead the United States to support dictatorships or repressive governments in Latin America? Fill in the chart. *(Chapter 21, Section 4)*

Issues	Reasons for U.S. Support
Cold war	
Containment policy	
Economy	

III. ESSAY

Bring together what you have read in your textbook with the information you have gathered online about this concept. **On a separate sheet of paper, answer the essential question: Why do people sometimes support dictatorships?**

Name _____ Class _____ Date _____

Concept Connector Journal

Economic Systems

Essential Question: How should resources and wealth be distributed?

I. WARM-UP

An economic system is the method used by a society to produce and distribute goods and services. As trade and industrialization become more complex, societies develop economic systems to meet their needs.

1. Suppose you and your classmates are holding a bake sale in the school lobby to raise money for a class trip. In a market economy, you need to consider certain elements when you price the goods you have made. On the chart below, write a question you might ask to help you decide on a price.

Economic Element	My Question
Supply and Demand	a.
Competition	b.
Self-Interest	c.

2. Suppose you have unsold items at the end of the sale. Would you lower the price or give away the leftover goods? Why?

_____

_____

_____

II. EXPLORATION

An economic system reflects how a society chooses to use its resources to meet the needs and wants of its people. As you complete the following journal entries, you will see how economic systems are linked to history.

1. Mercantilism and Manorialism: In the Middle Ages, under the feudal system, wealth was based on how much land a noble owned and how many peasants provided labor to work the land. Who gained in wealth after the rise of mercantilism? What was the source of this wealth? *(Chapter 3, Section 5)*

_____

_____

_____

Name _____ Class _____ Date _____

Concept Connector Journal

2. Middle Ages and Industrial Revolution: Complete the web to show how labor unions that arose during the Industrial Revolution played a similar role to the guilds that arose during the Middle Ages trade revival. *(Chapter 9, Section 2)*

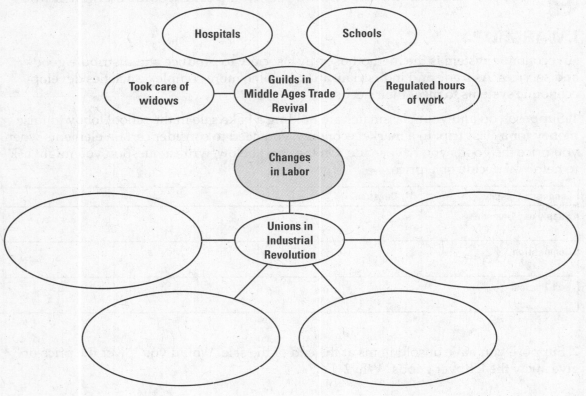

3. WebQuest: Economic Systems How has what you have learned as you completed your WebQuest affected your view about how economic systems differ?

> **Transfer Your Knowledge**
> **For:** WebQuest **Web Code:** nbh-1908

_____

_____

_____

_____

4. Market Economy: List three key elements of a market economy. *(Chapter 7, Section 4)*

a. _____

b. _____

c. _____

Concept Connector Journal

Economic Systems (continued)

5. Centrally Planned Economy: Who makes the key economic decisions in a centrally planned economy? What are some drawbacks to this kind of economy? *(Chapter 7, Section 4)*

_____

_____

_____

6. Mixed Economy: What is the goal of a mixed economy? *(Chapter 7, Section 4)*

_____

_____

7. Capitalism and Socialism: Write a statement in the chart to compare how wealth is attained and distributed in capitalism and socialism. *(Chapter 7, Section 4)*

Capitalism	Socialism

8. Globalization: Give an example of how globalization links the rich and poor nations of the world. *(Chapter 22, Section 2)*

_____

_____

III. ESSAY

Bring together what you have read in your textbook with the information you have gathered online about this concept. **On a separate sheet of paper, answer the essential question: How should resources and wealth be distributed?**

Concept Connector Journal

Empire

 Essential Question: How does a state gain or lose power over others?

I. WARM-UP

1. Power can be defined as the possession of control, authority, or influence over others. In the first web below, indicate whom you have power over. In the second web, indicate who has power over you.

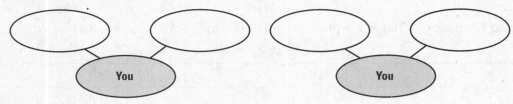

2. How did you get power over others? How have others gained power over you?

_____

_____

II. EXPLORATION

Throughout history, empires have played a critical role. As you complete the following journal entries, you will see how these empires have gained and lost power.

1. Darius I: How did the Persian emperor Darius I unite his vast empire through his policies in the following areas?

a. established a bureaucracy that followed set rules, divided empire into provinces ruled

by a governor, set up a single code of laws _____

b. respected customs of diverse people in the empire, new empire-wide religious belief

_____

c. built hundreds of roads for transportation and communication

_____

d. common weights and measures, use of single Persian coinage

_____

e. Greeks rebelled against Persian rule and united to throw off Persian control. Persians

defeated in several naval battles with the Greeks. _____

Concept Connector Journal

Empire (continued)

2. Roman Empire: How did the expansion of the Roman Empire contribute to its ultimate decline?

Through conquest and trade, wealthy Romans lived lives of luxury, which fostered greed and corruption, while ordinary Romans remained poor. Heavy taxes were needed to support the military and the bureaucracy. The upper classes devoted themselves to luxury. "Bread and circuses" were costly and may have undermined the self-reliance of the masses.

3. Aztecs and Incas: Compare the time span, location, and reason for decline of the Aztec and Incan empires.

Empire	Time Span	Place	Reason for Decline
Aztec	1300–1400s	Mexico	Defeated by the Spanish conquistador, Hernan Cortes
Inca	1438–1525	Coastal area of South America west of the Andes	Defeated by the Spanish conquistador, Francisco Pizarro

4. In 768, Charlemagne became king of the Franks. He briefly united Western Europe—France, Germany and part of Italy. How did the following policies of Charlemagne enable him to keep control of his vast empire?

• Close relations with the Church spread Christianity and created a unified empire.

• Use of *missi dominici* made sure that provincial rulers were governing justly. They also checked on roads and listened to grievances.

• Promotion of scholarship spread learning across the empire, encouraged schools.

5. Byzantine Empire: (a) Complete the following chart about the Byzantine Empire.

Empire	Time Span	Geographic Limits	Reason for Decline
Byzantine	300s–1400s	At its height, the Balkans, Middle East, North Africa	Struggles over succession, court intrigues, constant wars, plunder by Crusaders, loss of trade routes to Venice, defeat by Ottoman Turks

(b) How did the influence of the Byzantine Empire continue after its political decline?

Byzantine accomplishments in religious art and architecture influence Western styles to the present time. The Byzantines preserved and spread ancient Greek literature and produced works on history. Their knowledge of Greek and Byzantine culture contributed to the European Renaissance.

Concept Connector Journal

6. Abbasid, Mughal, and Ottoman Empires: Compare the time span, location, and reason for decline of the Abbasid, Mughal, and Ottoman empires.

Empire	Time Span	Place	Reason for Decline
Abbasid	750–1258	Northern Africa, Arabian peninsula, Persian Empire	Control fragmented, independent dynasties arose, Shiite rulers came to power, a series of invasions led to chaos
Mughal	1526–1857	Northern India	Persecution of Hindus, economic hardships and discontent sparked rebellions, Europeans got a foothold because of discontent
Ottoman	1400s–early 1900s	At its height, Eastern Europe and Balkans to Middle East	Corrupt government, weak commerce and military technology, local rulers broke away; later, provinces revolt and establish independent nations and autonomous regions, territory divided up by European powers

7. Tang Empire: Describe how the following contributed to the economy and strength of the Tang Empire.

- tributary states <u>forced to pay tribute and taxes on land to central government</u>

- land reform <u>redistribution of land to peasants strengthened the economy through more tax revenues and weakened power of large land owners</u>

- central government <u>bureaucracy rebuilt, new flexible law code developed</u>

8. Qing Empire: Explain how these Qing dynasty policies contributed to the expansion of its empire. *(Chapter 2, Section 4)*

- adopted Confucian system of government _____

_____

- able military leaders _____

_____

- imported new crops _____

_____

- encouraged silk, cotton, porcelain industries _____

_____

Concept Connector Journal

Empire (continued)

9. Spanish and British Empires: Complete the chart to compare the establishment of the Spanish and British empires in the Americas as you study Chapter 3 and Chapter 5. *(Chapter 3, Sections 1, 2, 3, 5; Chapter 5, Section 3)*

	Spanish Empire	British Empire
Political systems		
Economic systems		
Religion		

10. Second Reich: (a) Fill in the timeline below to show actions Chancellor Otto von Bismarck took that resulted in the formation of the Second Reich. *(Chapter 10, Section 1)*

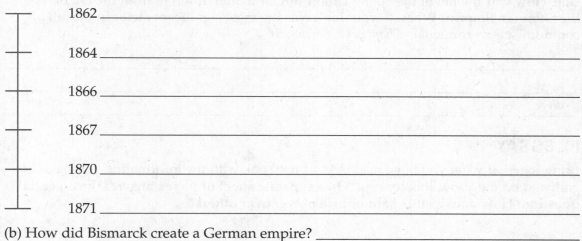

1862 _____

1864 _____

1866 _____

1867 _____

1870 _____

1871 _____

(b) How did Bismarck create a German empire? _____

_____

_____

11. Imperialism: How did European strategies of indirect rule, exploitation, trade, and treaties enable these powers to control their colonies? *(Chapter 12, Sections 1–5)*

_____

_____

_____

_____

Concept Connector Journal

12. WebQuest: Empire How has what you have learned about specific empires broadened your understanding of how a state gains or loses its power over others?

> **Transfer Your Knowledge**
> **For:** WebQuest **Web Code:** nbh-0808

_____

_____

_____

_____

_____

13. Decline of the Soviet Union: By the late 1800s, the Ottoman Empire was in a state of decline. Among the causes of the decline of the Ottoman Empire were nationalist revolts, economic problems, corruption, competition among European nations to expand their influence, and the efforts of some officials to reject reform and try to rebuild autocratic rule. How was the fall of the Soviet Union similar to and different from the fall of the Ottoman Empire? What do you think was the most significant factor in the fall of communist governments? *(Chapter 18, Section 5)*

_____

_____

_____

III. ESSAY

Bring together what you have read in your textbook with the information you have gathered online about this concept. **On a separate sheet of paper, answer the essential question: How does a state gain or lose power over others?**

Concept Connector Journal

Genocide

 Essential Question: Why do people sometimes commit the crime of genocide?

I. WARM-UP

Crimes against humanity are committed by governments as well as by individuals. The most horrific of these crimes is called genocide.

1. You are most likely familiar with the word *homicide*. This word comes from two Latin words: *homo*, meaning "man," and *cide*, meaning "killing." So a homicide is the killing of a person. The word *genocide* comes from the Greek word *geno*, meaning "race or tribe," and the Latin word *cide*. Based on this information, write a definition on the chart below for the word *genocide*.

English Word	Word Parts	Greek or Latin Meanings	English Meaning
homicide	homo + cide	man + killing	killing of a person
genocide	geno + cide	race or tribe + killing	

2. How much of the meaning of *genocide* does your definition capture? What else would you say to explain what genocide is?

_____

_____

_____

II. EXPLORATION

The word *genocide* was not used before 1944, but such killings of entire populations had occurred at earlier times in history. During the Third Punic War between the Romans and the Carthaginians, the Romans killed or sold into slavery the entire population of Carthage in North Africa and poured salt on the land so that nothing could grow. As you complete the following journal entries, you will learn more about times in history when a stronger group has committed the crime of genocide against a weaker foe.

Concept Connector Journal

1. Native Americans: How did genocide occur among Native Americans after the arrival of the Europeans? *(Chapter 15, Section 1)*

_____

_____

_____

_____

2. Armenians: In the 1890s, tensions arose between Turkish nationalists in the Ottoman Empire and minority groups, like the Armenians, who sought their own states.

a. What political reason did Muslim Turks offer for killing Christian Armenians? *(Chapter 24, Section 3)*

_____

_____

_____

b. How might the theory of Social Darwinism explain how Muslim Turks could justify the Armenian massacre? *(Chapter 21, Section 3)*

_____

_____

_____

3. WebQuest: Genocide How has what you have learned as you completed your WebQuest affected your view about why some people commit genocide?

> **Transfer Your Knowledge**
> **For:** WebQuest **Web Code:** nbh-2908

_____

_____

_____

_____

Concept Connector Journal

Genocide (continued)

4. Holocaust: Complete the cause-and-effect chart to show some of the reasons that ordinary Germans and other Europeans failed to stand up to Hitler's Final Solution policies. *(Chapter 28, Sections 1 and 5; Chapter 29, Section 3)*

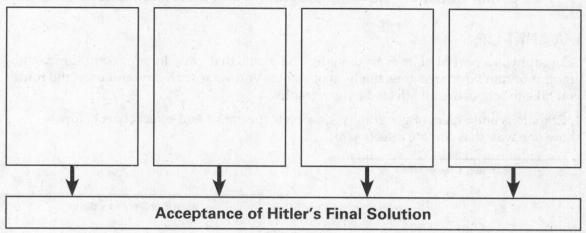

Acceptance of Hitler's Final Solution

5. Bosnia Civil War: What advantage did the dominant ethnic group in Bosnia hope to gain by ethnic cleansing? *(Chapter 32, Section 1)*

_____

_____

_____

_____

III. ESSAY

Bring together what you have read in your textbook with the information you have gathered online about this concept. **On a separate sheet of paper, answer the essential question: Why do people sometimes commit the crime of genocide?**

Name _____ Class _____ Date _____

Geography's Impact

 Essential Question: How do geography and people affect one another?

I. WARM-UP

Geography is a part of your everyday life. The plants that grow in your community, the amount of rain your area gets, the type of clothes you wear each day, and even the route you take to school are all affected by geography.

1. Climate is one aspect of geography. Complete the cause-and-effect chart below to show one way that climate affects you.

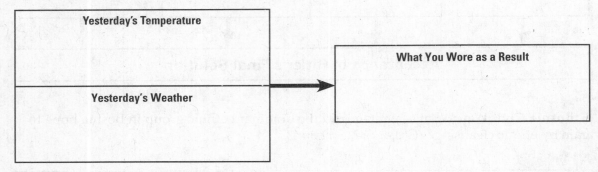

2. How else does the climate in your region affect your life? How does it affect your community?

_____

_____

_____

_____

II. EXPLORATION

Geography has always played a role in history. As you complete the following journal entries, you will see how geography has influenced people's lives throughout time.

1. Early People: What was the most important difference between the way Old Stone Age people and New Stone Age people used their environment to get food?

Old Stone Age	New Stone Age
Hunted and gathered	Stayed in one place and farmed

Name _____ Class _____ Date _____

Concept Connector Journal

2. First Civilizations: Early civilizations arose in river valleys for a number of reasons.

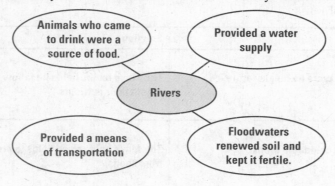

3. Tigris and Euphrates: a. Describe the location of the Tigris and Euphrates rivers.

The Tigris and Euphrates rivers arise in Asia Minor and flow southeast into the Persian Gulf. They flow through the region named Mesepotamia, or "land between the rivers" by the ancient Greeks.

b. How did the Tigris and Euphrates rivers affect the development of Mesopotamia?

The floodwaters of the rivers created rich soil for farming; the rivers provided a means of transportation for traders. The region became a crossroads for people and ideas.

4. Aegean and Mediterranean Seas: a. Describe the location of the Aegean and Mediterranean seas.

The Aegean Sea lies between Greece and Asia Minor, north of the Mediterranean Sea. The Mediterranean Sea lies between Europe and Africa.

b. What was the impact of the Aegean and Mediterranean seas on Greek trade and cultural diffusion?

The Greeks became skilled sailors and traded throughout the eastern Mediterranean. In addition to cargo, they returned with ideas such as the Phoenician alphabet.

Name _____ Class _____ Date _____

Concept Connector Journal

5. Farming in Mesoamerica: Complete the chart to show how the Maya and Aztecs solved farming problems.

Problem	Solution
After a few years, fields were no longer fertile.	The Maya let the fields lie fallow every few years to regain their nutrients.
Floodwaters from rivers could ruin crops.	The Maya built raised fields to protect their crops from floods.
There was limited land for crops in a lake environment.	The Aztecs made artificial islands on which to grow crops.

6. The Vikings: How did the Vikings' use of the seas affect trade and cultural diffusion?

They opened trade routes that connected northern Europe to lands in the Mediterranean. They also settled in different parts of Europe and Russia and mixed with the people there.

7. Impact of Rivers: Complete the chart with examples to compare how rivers affected the development of Russia with how they affected the development of Sumer in Mesopotamia.

How Rivers Affected Development	
Sumer in Mesopotamia	Russia
• trade: traded with Egypt and India	• trade: Kiev on the Dnieper River was at the heart of trade with Constantinople.
• migration: Akkadians and Babylonians arrive.	• migration: The Vikings or Varangians migrated south along the rivers.
• cultural diffusion: Akkadians, Babylonians, Assyrians adapt cuneiform to use with their own languages.	• cultural diffusion: They adopted the Cyrillic alphabet.

Name _____ Class _____ Date _____

Concept Connector Journal

8. Africa's Geography: Compare and contrast the impact of geography on East Africa and West Africa. See the Venn diagram below.

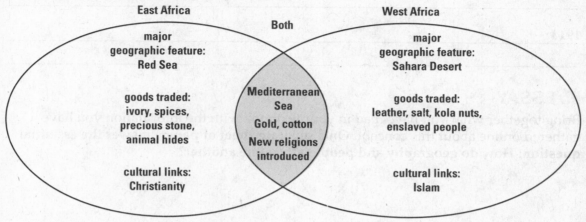

9. WebQuest: Geography's Impact How has what you have learned about the impact of geography broadened your understanding of the relationship between people and geography?

> **Transfer Your Knowledge**
> **For:** WebQuest **Web Code:** nbh-0608

_____
_____
_____

10. Latin America: Complete the timeline by listing an event and its significance for each date that linked the U.S. and Latin America between 1800 and 1914. (*Chapter 25, Section 4*)

1800s Ideas from American Revolution influence Latin American revolutionaries

1823 _____

1848 _____

1898 _____

(Continued)

Concept Connector Journal

1904 _____

_____

1914 _____

_____

III. ESSAY

Bring together what you have read in your textbook with the information you have gathered online about this concept. **On a separate sheet of paper, answer the essential question: How do geography and people affect one another?**

Concept Connector Journal

Human Rights

 Essential Question: How are human rights won or lost?

I. WARM-UP

Human rights are a basic set of freedoms and protections that all people are entitled to. Protecting human rights begins with showing respect for others who are different from you. Suppose you are with some friends and one of them tells a joke that makes fun of someone of a different ethnic group. Check off what you would do.

_____ Repeat the joke to others.

_____ Join in the laughter, but not repeat the joke yourself.

_____ Not join in the laughter.

_____ Not join in the laughter and explain privately to your friend why you do not think he or she should tell that kind of joke.

_____ Not join in the laughter and tell your friend in front of others why you don't think he or she should tell that kind of joke.

How can refusing to listen to ethnic jokes be a step toward strengthening human rights?

_____

_____

II. EXPLORATION

Throughout history, people have struggled to gain human rights, a basic set of freedoms and protections to which all humans are entitled. As you complete the following journal entries, you will see how people have sometimes won their rights or sometimes lost them.

1. Spain: In the 1400s, under Muslim rule in Spain, Jews, Christians, and Muslims were allowed freedom of worship. In 1492, the Spanish monarchs Ferdinand and Isabella united Spain under Christian rule and forced religious conformity on everyone. Complete the chart below about the effects of Ferdinand and Isabella's denial of religious freedom to Jews and Muslims.

Cause
Ferdinand and Isabella decide to enforce Christianity as the only religion in Spain.

Effect	Effect	Effect
Church courts tried those accused of heresy and set punishments.	Hundreds of thousands of Jews and Muslims fled Spain or risked execution.	Spain lost many of its skilled people who had contributed to its economy and culture.

Concept Connector Journal

Human Rights (continued)

2. Totalitarian Rulers: a. How were culture, education, and propaganda used by Mussolini, Stalin, and Hitler to deprive their citizens of their human rights? List at least three ways. *(Chapter 16, Sections 3, 4, 5)*

Dictators	Culture	Education	Propaganda
Mussolini	• • •	• • •	• • •
Stalin	• • •	• • •	• • •
Hitler	• • •	• • •	• • •

b. How might these steps above be effective in depriving people of their human rights?

_____

_____

_____

3. Civil Rights Movement: As a result of the Atlantic slave trade that began in the 1600s and lasted to the 1800s, millions of enslaved Africans were transported to the Americas against their will. Even after they gained their freedom as a result of the Civil War and the 14th Amendment to the U.S. Constitution, former slaves and their descendents still were denied their human rights. How did the government and the people bring about changes in human rights following World War II? *(Chapter 18, Section 2)*

_____

_____

_____

Concept Connector Journal

4. South Africa: When South Africa won its independence from Britain in 1910, the white minority government passed laws severely limiting the rights of the black majority. How did black South Africans finally win their human rights? *(Chapter 32, Section 2)*

a. Restrictions on black South Africans: _____

_____

b. African National Congress (ANC) response: _____

_____

c. Steps to ending apartheid: _____

_____

5. WebQuest: Human Rights How has what you have learned while completing your WebQuest influenced your understanding about the ways human rights are won and lost?

Transfer Your Knowledge
For: WebQuest **Web Code:** nbh-3408

_____

_____

_____

III. ESSAY

Bring together what you have read in your textbook with the information you have gathered online about this concept. **On a separate sheet of paper, answer the essential question: How are human rights won or lost?**

Name _____ Class _____ Date _____

Concept Connector Journal

Impact of the Individual

 Essential Question: How can an individual change the world?

I. WARM-UP

Many changes across the globe have been the result of one individual's actions. The chart shows five individuals whose actions changed the world.

Individual	Actions	Changes
Indian leader Mahatma Gandhi	Led a long, nonviolent struggle against British rule of India; set an example to gain support	Freed India from British rule; led to weakening and eventual collapse of the British Empire
Ecologist/writer Rachel Carson	Wrote of dangers of chemicals to the environment; founded the environmental movement	Made people aware of effects of pollution; spurred worldwide efforts to eliminate it
Medical scientist Jonas Salk	Developed the first successful vaccine against polio	Greatly reduced or wiped out polio around the world; furthered medical research
Computer engineer Tim Berners-Lee	Developed software systems; invented the World Wide Web; worked with others to promote its use	Revolution in communications that spread ideas and information across a global network
Theologian Martin Luther	Protested actions and teachings of the Catholic Church; urged others to reject Church authority	Caused the Protestant Reformation that split the Christian world; led to reforms in the Catholic Church

1. Choose one of the individuals and explain how their actions affect you.

_____

_____

2. Think of a situation in your school or community in which you would like to see some change. How could you go about helping to make that change?

_____

_____

Concept Connector Journal

II. EXPLORATION

In the course of history, actions by many individuals have had a significant impact on the lives of people around the world. As you complete the following journal entries, you will see how an individual's efforts can bring about change.

1. Hammurabi and Confucius: Two individuals who have gained fame for their influence are Hammurabi and Confucius. About 1790 B.C. Hammurabi brought much of Mesopotamia under his control. He established Hammarabi's Code, the first major known attempt of a ruler to codify the laws of his state. He had the laws carved on pillars where everyone could see them. How did Confucius influence Chinese society?

Confucius was concerned with ensuring social order and good government. He taught

that everyone had duties and responsibilities. Superiors should care for inferiors and

lead by example. The best rulers consider the advice of educated men.

2. Muslim Leaders: Muslim leaders, such as Muhammad and Akbar the Great had a lasting impact on history.

Muslim Leader	Actions	Influence
Muhammad	Devoted his life to spreading Islam	Thousands of Arabs adopted Islam, which has spread around the world.
Akbar the Great	Was tolerant of Hindus, hired effective officials, modernized the army, introduced land reforms	Recognized India's diversity and strengthened its government

3. John Locke: What ideas of John Locke influenced Thomas Jefferson? *(Chapter 5, Section 1)*

_____

_____

_____

4. Leaders of the American Revolution: Of the leaders of the American Revolution, which individual's actions do you think had the greatest influence on the outcome of the war? *(Chapter 5, Section 3)*

Leader and actions _____

_____

Influence on outcome of the war _____

_____

Concept Connector Journal

Impact of the Individual (continued)

5. WebQuest: Impact of the Individual How has what you have learned as you completed your WebQuest affected your view about the impact of any one individual?

> Transfer Your Knowledge
> **For:** WebQuest **Web Code:** nbh-1808

_____

_____

_____

6. Jiang Jeishi and Mao Zedong: a. Fill in the Venn Diagram below to show the goals of Jiang Jeishi and Mao Zedong.

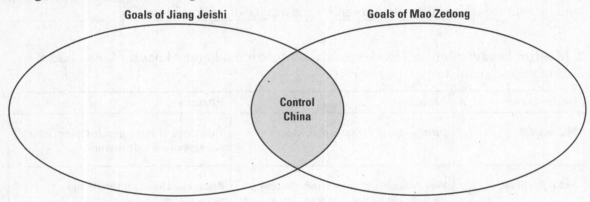

b. How did Mao Zedong's success change the course of the history of China? *(Chapter 15, Section 4)*

_____

7. Nelson Mandela: How did Nelson Mandela help change the course of history in South Africa? *(Chapter 17, Section 2)*

_____

_____

_____

III. ESSAY

Bring together what you have read in your textbook with the information you have gathered online about this concept. **On a separate sheet of paper, answer the essential question: How can an individual change the world?**

Concept Connector Journal

Migration

 Essential Question: Under what circumstances do people migrate?

I. WARM-UP

People have been moving from place to place on Earth since early times. Migration still goes on today.

1. Have you or members of your family ever moved? If so, what were the main reasons for moving?

_____

_____

_____

2. How does moving affect someone's life? Fill in the web below to show some of the ways.

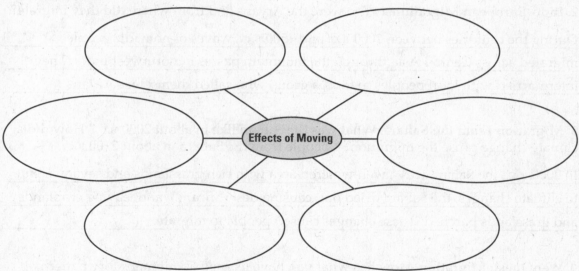

Effects of Moving

II. EXPLORATION

Migration occurs when large groups of people move from one place to another. As you complete the following journal entries, you will see how migration has played a role in world events.

Concept Connector Journal

1. Early People: Look at the chart below to see how different factors contributed to the migration of early people.

Contributing Factors	Examples
Food sources	Migration of animals led people to follow them.
Climate changes	Drought
Environmental events	Earthquake or flood
Competition with other groups	For land, resources, food

2. Indo-European Migrations: Who were the Aryans and from where did they migrate?

During the centuries between 2000 B.C. and 1500 B.C., waves of nomadic people

migrated across Central Asia through the mountain passes in northwest India. They

intermarried with local peoples to form a group who called themselves Aryans.

3. Migration From the Sahara: What was the Sahara like in about 2000 B.C.? How did a climate change cause the migration of people from the Sahara in about 2500 B.C.?

In 2000 B.C., the Sahara was a well-watered area with rich grasslands and savanna. Due

to climate changes, the Sahara dried out, causing desertification and leaving croplands

and grasslands parched. These changes caused people to migrate.

4. WebQuest: Migration How has what you have learned about migratory patterns broadened your understanding of why people migrate?

Transfer Your Knowledge
For: WebQuest **Web Code:** nbh-2308

_____

_____

_____

Concept Connector Journal

5. Irish and American Migration: Just as thousands of people in the past migrated in search of a better life, large numbers of people were on the move in the nineteenth century. Millions of Irish migrated to the United States, starting in the mid 1800s. At the same time, Americans began migrating westward across their continent. Complete the cause-and-effect charts to show why these migrations occurred and what happened to Native Americans as a result of the westward push. *(Chapter 11, Sections 2 and 4)*

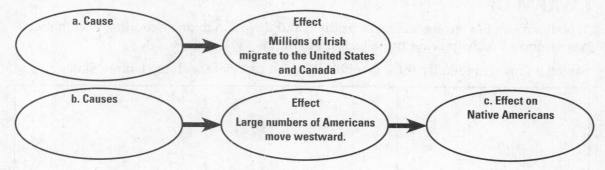

a. Cause

Effect

Millions of Irish migrate to the United States and Canada

b. Causes

Effect

Large numbers of Americans move westward.

c. Effect on Native Americans

6. Westward Movement: How did the concept of Manifest Destiny affect the nation's boundaries? *(Chapter 11, Section 4)*

_____

_____

_____

III. ESSAY

Bring together what you have read in your textbook with the information you have gathered online about this concept. **On a separate sheet of paper, answer the essential question: Under what circumstances do people migrate?**

Concept Connector Journal

Nationalism

Essential Question: How can nationalism be a unifying and a divisive force?

I. WARM-UP

1. Nationalism is a strong feeling of pride in and devotion to one's country. Each nation has symbols that help bring those feelings to mind.

Sketch below and identify three symbols that you associate with the United States.

How do these symbols help foster a feeling of unity in the nation?

_____

_____

_____

II. EXPLORATION

Nationalism can be an ideology, a feeling, or a social or political movement that focuses on the nation. As you complete the following journal entries, you will see how nationalism has been a unifying and divisive force in shaping the modern world.

1. French Revolution: Review the songs, symbols, and slogans associated with the French Revolution.

Songs	Symbols	Slogans
Marseillaise: "Forward children of the homeland / The day of glory has arrived / Against us, tyranny's bloody standard / Has been raised."	Tricolor flag Red cap of liberty Everyone called "citizen" Elaborate clothes abolished	"Liberty, Equality, Brotherhood, or Death" "Tremble, enemies of France"
La Carmagnole: "Let's dance the Carmagnole / Long live the canon's roar."		

Concept Connector Journal

How did these songs, symbols, and slogans foster nationalism? *(Chapter 6, Section 3)*

_____

_____

_____

_____

2. Balkan Nationalism: The breakup of the Ottoman Empire in the nineteenth century planted the seeds of further conflict in the region that stretched from Eastern Europe and the Balkans to North Africa and the Middle East. The unresolved problems of the late nineteenth century eventually spilled over into the late twentieth and early twenty-first centuries. Complete the chart of the effects of Balkan nationalism on the Empire and Europe in the late 1800s and early 1900s. *(Chapter 10, Section 4)*

Cause	Effects
Independence movements helped weaken the multinational Ottoman Empire, leaving it subject to attack by European powers.	• _____ • _____ • _____ • _____

3. WebQuest: Nationalism How has what you have learned as you completed your WebQuest affected your view about whether nationalism is a unifying or divisive force?

> **Transfer Your Knowledge**
> **For:** WebQuest **Web Code:** nbh-2208

_____

_____

_____

4. Imperialism: How did British imperialism spark nationalism in India and China? *(Chapter 12, Sections 4 and 5)*

_____

_____

_____

Concept Connector Journal

Nationalism (continued)

5. Latin America: During the 1920s and 1930s, Latin American nationalism was influenced by events around the world. How did these events unify or divide the nations of Latin America? *(Chapter 15, Section 1)*

a. World economy _____

_____

b. United States influence _____

_____

c. Types of governments that developed in Latin America _____

_____

6. India: In India, religion and the state are separate, but the Bharatiya Janata Party (BJP) has called for a government based on the principles of Hinduism. Would this be a unifying or a divisive force in India? Why? *(Chapter 19, Section 1)*

_____

_____

_____

III. ESSAY

Bring together what you have read in your textbook with the information you have gathered online about this concept. **On a separate sheet of paper, answer the essential question: How can nationalism be a unifying and divisive force?**

Name _____ Class _____ Date _____

Concept Connector Journal

Political Systems

 Essential Question: How do political systems rise, develop, and decline?

I. WARM-UP

A political system, or government, is set up to make decisions for a society, and when necessary, defend it from attack. The Greeks identified three main kinds of political systems: rule by one, rule by a few, and rule by many.

1. Create an organization chart of your school government. An organization chart is a visual representation of levels of responsibility and relationships.

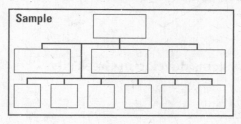

2. What responsibilities does your student government have? In what ways is it like and unlike a true political system?

_____

_____

_____

II. EXPLORATION

Throughout history, political systems have taken many forms, depending on circumstances. As you complete the following journal entries, you will see how political systems have affected the way civilizations have developed.

Name _____ Class _____ Date _____

Concept Connector Journal

1. Zhou Dynasty: The rise and fall of the Zhou Dynasty was an example of the dynastic cycle. The Zhou overthrew the Shang and in turn were replaced by the Qing. How did feudal lords under the Zhou help China's economic growth? How did feudalism contribute to the end of the Zhou dynasty? Write your answers in the arrows below.

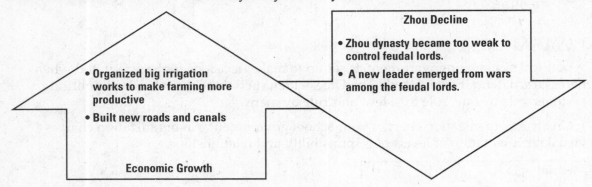

• Organized big irrigation works to make farming more productive

• Built new roads and canals

Economic Growth

Zhou Decline

• Zhou dynasty became too weak to control feudal lords.

• A new leader emerged from wars among the feudal lords.

2. Political systems: How did each of these political systems develop in Greek city-states?

a. monarchy At first, the ruler of the polis was a king. _____

_____

b. aristocracy Power shifted from the king to the aristocracy who were the only ones who could afford weapons. At first the aristocrats defended the king, then they won power for themselves.

c. oligarchy Wealthy middle class merchants, farmers, and artisans challenged the landowning nobles for power and began to dominate some city-states in an oligarchy.

3. Republic: List three ways plebeians made the Roman senate more democratic.

a. They gained the right to elect their own tribunes.

b. The tribunes could veto any laws that were unfavorable to plebeians.

c. They got the Laws of the Twelve Tables set up in the Forum so everyone could know what the laws were.

Concept Connector Journal

4. Aztecs and Incas: Well before Europeans reached the America, powerful civilizations developed in the Americas. Two of the longest lasting were the Aztecs in Mexico and the Incas in Peru. Identify the source of power and role of each of these civilizations' emperors.

a. Aztec Emperor: Elected by a council of nobles, priests, and military leaders; carried on continual warfare; had prisoners of war sacrificed to the gods.

b. Incan Emperor: Proclaimed himself emperor, claimed to be divine, laid claim to all the land, herds, mines, and people of his empire; demanded that everyone in the empire adopt the Incan language and religion; quickly put down any rebellions; passed his position on to his son.

5. End of Feudal System: The chart below shows how the Agricultural Revolution and the revival of trade and travel led to the decline of feudalism.

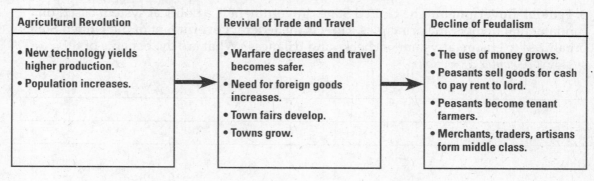

Agricultural Revolution	Revival of Trade and Travel	Decline of Feudalism
• New technology yields higher production. • Population increases.	• Warfare decreases and travel becomes safer. • Need for foreign goods increases. • Town fairs develop. • Towns grow.	• The use of money grows. • Peasants sell goods for cash to pay rent to lord. • Peasants become tenant farmers. • Merchants, traders, artisans form middle class.

6. WebQuest: Political Systems How has what you have learned while completing your WebQuest expanded your understanding of how political systems rise, develop, and decline?

Transfer Your Knowledge
For: WebQuest **Web Code:** nbh-1508

_____

_____

_____

Concept Connector Journal

7. Absolute Monarchs: Write a brief description of how each of the following rulers weakened his empire by using absolute power. *(Chapter 4, Sections 1, 2, 3, and 5)*

a. Philip II _____

_____

b. Louis XIV _____

_____

c. Charles I _____

_____

d. Peter the Great _____

_____

8. Federal Government: The United States government is a political system based on fundamental democratic principles. How is the federal government of the United States organized to ensure a system of checks and balances? What are the benefits of this system? *(Chapter 5, Section 3)*

_____

_____

_____

III. ESSAY

Bring together what you have read in your textbook with the information you have gathered online about this concept. **On a separate sheet of paper, answer the essential question: How do political systems rise, develop, and decline?**

Name _____ Class _____ Date _____

Concept Connector Journal

Revolution

 Essential Question: Why do political revolutions occur?

I. WARM-UP

A revolution is associated with change. Often, advertisers or salespeople use the word "revolutionary" to draw consumer attention to a new and different product.

1. What do you think about when you hear that something is "revolutionary"? Write your ideas on the web below.

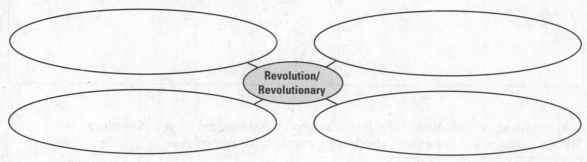

Revolution/
Revolutionary

2. Do you think a revolution always improves a society? Why or why not?

_____
_____
_____
_____

II. EXPLORATION

Numerous political revolutions have occurred over time in all parts of the world. As you complete the following journal entries, you will see how revolutions have changed the course of history in different ways.

1. Glorious Revolution: List three reasons that support the idea that the Glorious Revolution was a true revolution. *(Chapter 4, Section 3)*

a. _____
_____

b. _____
_____

c. _____
_____

Name _____ Class _____ Date _____

Concept Connector Journal

Revolution (continued)

2. French Revolution and Peasants' Revolt in Germany: Both the Peasants' Revolt in Germany in 1542 and the French Revolution in the late 1700s were started by suppressed people hoping to improve their living conditions and gain civil rights. Complete the chart to show how the outcome of the French Revolution differed from that of the Peasants' Revolt. *(Chapter 1, Section 3 and Chapter 6, Sections 2 and 3)*

Outcome of Peasants' Revolt	Outcome of French Revolution
• Peasants fail to get support of Martin Luther. • Nobles suppress revolt, killing tens of thousands.	• •

3. WebQuest: Revolution: How has what you have learned as you completed your WebQuest affected your view about why revolutions occur?

> **Transfer Your Knowledge**
> **For:** WebQuest **Web Code:** nbh-2008

_____

_____

_____

4. Latin American Revolutions: Why did the social structure of Latin America lead to revolt there? *(Chapter 8, Section 3)*

_____

_____

_____

Concept Connector Journal

5. Revolution of 1905: Complete the cause-and-effect chain to show how one concession of the tsars was impacted by industrialization in the years leading up to the Revolution of 1905. *(Chapter 10, Section 5)*

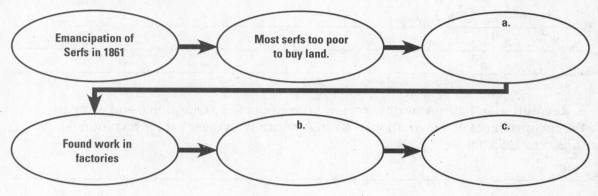

6. French and Russian Revolutions: Complete the chart to compare the Russian Revolution with the French Revolution. *(Chapter 14, Section 5)*

	French Revolution	Russian Revolution
Causes	Influenced by American Revolution; financial woes; class system; lack of social reform	
Duration/Phases	10 years; Commune, Reign of Terror, Directory	
Leaders	Lafayette; Robespierre	
World Reaction	Some countries threatened to intervene to protect monarchy	
Results	Overthrow of king; church under state control; social reform; nationalism; Declaration of the Rights of Man and the Citizen	

Concept Connector Journal

7. Independence movements: Compare the emergence of a new nation after World War II with the American Revolution, including how independence was achieved and the challenges facing the new nation. *(Chapter 19)*

_____

_____

_____

8. Revolution in Latin America: Review your response to Question 6 and compare the circumstances of a revolution in Latin America with these earlier revolutions. *(Chapter 21, Section 4)*

_____

_____

_____

III. ESSAY

Bring together what you have read in your textbook with the information you have gathered online about this concept. **On a separate sheet of paper, answer the essential question: Why do political revolutions occur?**

Concept Connector Journal

Science and Technology

 Essential Question: What are the benefits and costs of science and technology?

I. WARM-UP

Science and technology have propelled civilizations forward throughout history. Even today, they play a very significant role in creating economic and social benefits. However, technological advances also have costs.

1. Complete the web below to show three ways you communicate with others.

2. What are the benefits and costs of these types of communication?

_____

_____

_____

II. EXPLORATION

Science and technology are responsible for enormous changes in the lives of humans and the development of civilizations. As you complete the following journal entries, you will see how science and technology have affected history.

Concept Connector Journal

Science and Technology (continued)

1. Egypt and Mesopotamia: Name three technological advances made by Egyptians or the people of Mesopotamia and explain how those advances affected their civilization.

a. Cuneiform developed by Sumerians enabled people to record economic exchanges. As it improved, they could also record prayers, myth, laws and business contracts.

b. Extracting iron from ore enabled Hittites to make stronger tools and weapons, which gave them an advantage over other civilizations.

c. Mummification enabled Egyptians to learn more about the human body and disease. It enabled later historians to learn more about how Egyptians lived and died.

2. China and Greece: The Chinese and the Greeks both made advances in knowledge about astronomy and medicine. Imagine two people from these ancient civilizations bragging about their accomplishments. Complete the dialogue.

China

We measured the movement of stars and planets and improved calendars. Our doctors developed anesthetics, herbal remedies, and acupuncture.

Greece

We determined that the Earth was round, rotated on its axis, and orbited the sun. Hippocrates studied the cause of illnesses and looked for cures. He set ethical standards for doctors.

3. Movable Type: How did the development of movable type help spread Chinese learning and culture?

It's faster to print text with movable type; it meant Chinese text could be printed in greater quantities.

_____

Concept Connector Journal

4. Gunpowder: What was the benefit of gunpowder to the Chinese? What was a possible cost?

Gunpowder provided the Chinese with a weapon that was more effective than hand combat. The cost was the possibility of a greater loss of human life.

_____

5. Scientific Revolution: How did the scientific method differ from earlier approaches to science? How did it pave the way for scientific thinking today? *(Chapter 1, Section 5)*

_____

_____

_____

6. WebQuest: Science and Technology How has what you have learned while completing your WebQuest influenced your view about the benefits and costs of scientific and technological advances?

> **Transfer Your Knowledge**
> **For:** WebQuest **Web Code:** nbh-1308

_____

_____

_____

_____

7. Compass: How did an improvement to the compass help lead the way to a global age? *(Chapter 2, Section 1)*

_____

_____

_____

Concept Connector Journal

8. Steam Engine: Just as the printing press changed how people shared information, the steam engine became key to the Industrial Revolution. Complete the chart to compare the impact of the two developments. *(Chapter 7, Section 2)*

	Printing Press	Steam Engine
a. Who benefited		
b. How same jobs were done before		
c. Why it was important		

9. Changing Lives: a. Choose a scientific discovery or advance from the Scientific Revolution and the Industrial Revolution. Explain how each discovery changed people's lives. *(Chapter 1, Section 5 and Chapter 9, Section 1)*

Scientific Revolution

Industrial Revolution

b. Choose one current scientific or technological development and describe how it is changing people's lives.

_____

_____

_____

_____

Concept Connector Journal

10. Technological Changes: One chart below shows the impact of a technological change in the High Middle Ages. Choose a technological advance in the Industrial Revolution and complete the second chart to show what effects it had on the economy and peoples' lives. *(Chapter 9, Sections 1 and 2)*

High Middle Ages

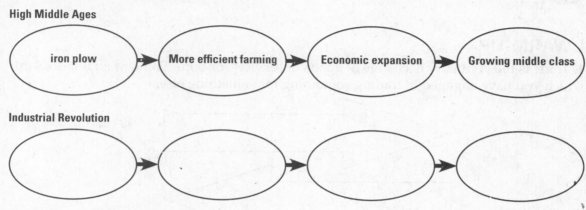

Industrial Revolution

11. Atomic Research: Describe a benefit and a cost resulting from the atomic research of Marie Curie and Albert Einstein. *(Chapter 16, Section 1)*

_____

_____

_____

III. ESSAY

Bring together what you have read in your textbook with the information you have gathered online about this concept. **On a separate sheet of paper, answer the essential question: What are the benefits and costs of science and technology?**

Concept Connector Journal

Trade

 Essential Question: What are the intended and unintended effects of trade?

I. WARM-UP

1. Trade is the voluntary exchange of goods or services, or both. Think of an occasion in which you have engaged in trading something for something else.

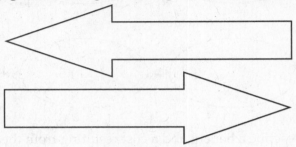

a. What did you trade? _____

b. What did you get in exchange? _____

c. Were you satisfied with the trade? Why or why not? _____

_____

d. What conditions have to be fulfilled for you to engage in trade? _____

_____

2. Why do nations trade?

_____

_____

II. EXPLORATION

From ancient times, individuals and groups have engaged in trade. It has had a major impact on economics and culture. As you complete the following journal entries, you will see the intended and unintended effects of that trade.

1. Phoenician Sea Traders: How did Phoenicians earn the title "carriers of civilization"?

The Phoenicians, who emerged as an independent people after the decline of the Egyptians, occupied land in the eastern Mediterranean region, now Lebanon and Syria. By trading with people and setting up colonies all around the Mediterranean Sea, they spread Middle Eastern civilization beyond its original borders.

Concept Connector Journal

2. Trade Networks: See the chart below for a comparison of China's Silk Road to the Phoenician trade network.

	PHOENICIAN TRADE	CHINA'S SILK ROAD
WHERE	From North Africa westward through the Mediterranean to the Atlantic Ocean	Silk Road stretched 4,000 miles from Western Asia to the Middle East
WITH WHOM	North Africa, Sicily, Spain, Britain	India, Rome, Persia, civilizations in Central Asia
WHAT GOODS	Glass, purple dye, tin	Fruits, furs, muslin cloth, glass, silk.
WHAT ELSE	Greeks adapted Phoenician alphabet	Chinese inventions, science, medicine spread to West

3. Trade in the Middle Ages: How was trade in the 1100s affected by each of the following factors?

a. population growth Traders began to crisscross Europe to meet the growing demand for goods that were caused by growing populations and demand by the wealthy for new goods.

b. decrease in foreign invasions Less turmoil allowed people to travel more extensively and trade more goods with local merchants.

c. merchant caravans Merchants banded together for protection and, as a result, revived old trade routes.

d. Hanseatic League This association of German towns protected traders interests and dominated trade in Northern Europe for more than 150 years.

e. banks As trade revived and the use of money increased, banks met the need for money for investment and provided a source of credit.

4. Russian Trade: Phoenicia was an early trading center along the coast of the Mediterranean Sea. In early Russia, the city of Kiev was established by Vikings and became a hub of trade.

a. Phoenicians sailed their ships around the Mediterranean to trade. Vikings traveled by longboats south from Scandinavia along rivers between the Baltic and Black seas and mixed their culture with that of the Slavs. Phoenicians established colonies throughout the Mediterranean. Vikings collected tribute from the Slavs and carried on a thriving trade with Constantinople.

Concept Connector Journal

b. How were Vikings affected by their trade with Constantinople?

Vikings founded Kiev and gave their name to Russia. Through trade with Byzantium, Kiev
rulers eventually adopted much of Byzantine art and culture. Constantinople sent Christian
missionaries to convert the Slavs. The missionaries adapted the Greek alphabet so they
could translate the Bible into the Slavic tongue. This Cyrillic alphabet is still used in Russia.

5. Asia and East Africa: By the 600s, a flourishing trade existed between East Africa and
Asia. The following diagram shows the exchange of goods and ideas.

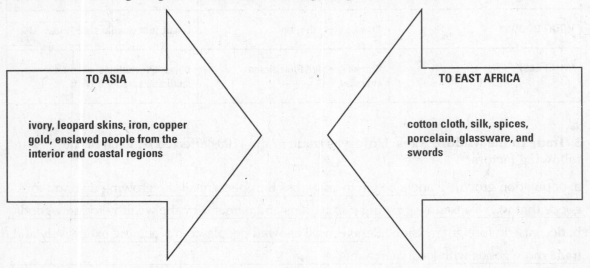

TO ASIA

ivory, leopard skins, iron, copper
gold, enslaved people from the
interior and coastal regions

TO EAST AFRICA

cotton cloth, silk, spices,
porcelain, glassware, and
swords

What was a major unintended consequence of this contact?

The development of the Swahili language and culture, which intermingled elements of
African and Arab cultures

6. WebQuest: Trade How has what you have learned about free trade increased your
understanding of the intended and unintended consequences of trade?

> **Transfer Your Knowledge**
> **For:** WebQuest **Web Code:** nbh-1208

_____

_____

_____

Name _____ Class _____ Date _____

Concept Connector Journal

7. Dutch Trading Empire: How did the Dutch affect trade in Southeast Asia?
(Chapter 2, Section 3)

_____

_____

_____

8. Indian Trade in Southeast Asia: What was the result of French and English influence on the Mughal Empire? *(Chapter 2, Section 3)*

_____

_____

_____

9. A Global Age: The 1400s through the 1700s can be considered a global age. Curiosity and the desire for wealth drove Europeans to venture across the seas to the Americas, Africa, South Asia, and East Asia. For each region, write a brief description of the role trade played in this expanded contact. Think in terms of economics, politics, and society. *(Chapter 2)*

• Americas _____

_____

• Africa _____

_____

• South Asia _____

_____

• East Asia _____

_____

• Europe _____

_____

Concept Connector Journal

10. Slave Trade: a. Who benefited most from the transatlantic slave trade? Why?
(Chapter 3, Section 4)

_____

_____

_____

b. What were some unintended consequences of the slave trade for African states and societies?

_____

_____

_____

11. Japan: In 1853, the United States demanded that Japan open its doors to trade. Unable to defend itself from American threats to use military force, Japan agreed to give trading and other rights to the United States. How did Japan benefit? What were the costs? Use the graphic below to list three benefits and three costs. *(Chapter 13, Section 1)*

Opening of Japan	
Benefits	**Costs**
1. _____	1. _____
2. _____	2. _____
3. _____	3. _____

III. ESSAY

Bring together what you have read in your textbook with the information you have gathered online about this concept. **On a separate sheet of paper, answer the essential question: What are the intended and unintended effects of trade?**